Design
and Analysis

Bernard Leupen

Christoph Grafe

Nicola Körnig

Marc Lampe

Peter de Zeeuw

VAN NOSTRAND REINHOLD

I(T)P® A Division of International Thomson Publishing Inc.

New York • Albany • Bonn • Boston • Detroit • London • Madrid • Melbourne
Mexico City • Paris • San Francisco • Singapore • Tokyo • Toronto

I⟨T⟩P® A Division of International Thomson
Publishing Inc. The ITP logo is a registered
trademark used herein under license.

Design and Analysis is first published in the English
language in The United States of America, and
Canada in 1997 by Van Nostrand Reinhold,
115 Fifth Avenue, New York, NY 10003, USA

Design and Analysis is first published in all other
countries by 010 Publishers, Watertorenweg 180,
3063 HA Rotterdam, The Netherlands

Printed in The Netherlands
1 2 3 4 5 6 7 8 9 10 101 03 02 01 00 99 98 97

Library of Congress Cataloging-in-Publication Data

Ontwerp en analyse. English
Design and analysis / Bernard Leupen... [et al.].
p.   cm.
Includes bibliographical references and index.
ISBN 0 442 02580 7
1. Architectural design. 2. Architecture —
Environmental aspects. 3. Architecture —
Composition, proportion, etc.
1 Leupen, Bernard. II Title.
NA2750.05813 1997 97-3505
720'.47 — dc21 CIP

www.vnr.com
product discounts · free email newsletters
software demos · online resources
email: info@vnr.com
A service of ITP®

Foreword

Ever since the Renaissance Western culture has been plagued by a conflict—that between the idea of the *homo universalis* and the sheer variety of design disciplines. It was only a matter of time before calls to draw the two domains together arose. However, what is general and what specific in the designing of such diverse objects as buildings, cities and landscapes?

If architectural thinking is the "mater et magistra" of space design, then this role can be fulfilled only if the validity of its rules of composition are examined. By methodically examining the way designs fit together, diverging design tasks and ideas can be placed in meaningful confrontation. The issue really becomes interesting once the designs are abstracted—architectural types, formal means and rules of composition can then be reintroduced in another context. Such experimental activity enables us to transgress the limitations of both subject and scale, bringing to light unexpected relationships between architectural, urban and landscape designs.

Is this a cry to abolish these autonomous disciplines? Far from it. It is not our wish to undo history, but to open the way to developing the design disciplines further. Boundary-hopping can be done at any time; first, though, we should have an accurate picture of where those boundaries lie. Merely clarifying the architectural grammar is not enough; it is equally important to determine the range and dynamics of each design discipline. We need to balance their autonomy against their potential relationship.

This book evolved during the daily practice of teaching design at the Faculty of Architecture at Delft. Presenting design analysis as a link between design education and research, it offers countless new points of contact between the two. In that sense this study has burgeoned into a broadly applicable handbook for space design.

It is our pleasure to present the knowledge brought together within these pages for colleagues, students and others with an interest in the subject to digest and develop.

Jan Heeling, Professor of Urban Design
Arie Hogeslag, Professor of Structural Design
Clemens Steenbergen, Professor of Landscape Architecture
Carel Weeber, Professor of Architectural Design

Contents

Introduction

Design and Analysis is about the history and practice of architectural, urban and landscape design. It examines the diversity of ideas on design and places the evolution of design instruments in a historical perspective. Providing material for a methodical study of these design fields, it unfolds an ordered system which enables the reader to define factors influencing designers' decisions and to relate these to the result. It thereby introduces the analytical drawing as a way to obtain insight into the process of designing.

Directed at students, teachers and colleagues throughout the field, *Design and Analysis* takes its examples from architecture, urban design and landscape architecture. Though primarily intended for use in colleges, its broad approach makes it accessible to others outside of educational institutions.

Since the late sixties, notions such as design analysis and morphological analysis have taken their place in design education and research. On the one hand, the discourse on typology and morphology has been unfurled in the Mediterranean countries, particularly in Italy and France by Muratori, Aymonino, Rossi, Panerai and Castex. On the other, analysis of architectural structure is ongoing in the Anglo-Saxon arena in the works of Rowe, Ching, Bacon and others. Both approaches exploit drawing as a tool to analyze architectural and urban designs.

These approaches have also been a subject of study at Delft University. In the Architecture Faculty, design analysis soon followed a path of its own, emerging in its present form. Design analysis has proved to be a first-rate didactic tool in design education, and *Design and Analysis* grew out of experience gained over the years. More than just an introduction to design analysis, this book offers an outline of space design as a whole, from individual buildings to urban and landscape ensembles.

Each chapter examines one aspect of the design field. Chapter 1 describes the design process and the basic principles of design analysis, with an overview of factors to be discussed in Chapters 2 to 5. In Chapter 2 the designer's formal instrumentarium and the ordering of space and material are addressed. The third chapter explores the relationship between design and use, and the fourth

9 that between design and building technology. Then follows a chapter on typology, which establishes a connection between the order, use and structure of buildings.

The final chapter examines the relationship between design and its geographical and historical context. It takes the Dutch landscape, a man-made landscape that has grown layer by layer, as a didactic model to trace the historical relationship between context and design. An appendix documents exhaustively the practical means required to make analyses; it sets forth the various drawing techniques and relates these to subjects dealt with earlier in the book.

THUS WE HAVE ACHIEVED A THOUSAND THINGS IN EACH GENRE, AND ONE OF THE PRINCIPAL OCCUPATIONS OF SCIENCE AND PHILOSOPHY, IN ORDER TO UNDERSTAND THE REASONS FOR THEM, IS TO DISCOVER THEIR ORIGIN AND PRIMITIVE CAUSE. *QUATREMÈRE DE QUINCY*

———

ARCHITECTURE WILL NOT SIMPLY BE THE EXPRESSION OF ACCEPTED FUNCTIONAL OR MORAL STANDARDS. RATHER ACTIONS, WHETHER FORBIDDEN, OR NOT, WILL BECOME AN INTEGRAL PART OF ARCHITECTURE. AS A RESULT, CONVENTIONAL PLANS WILL NO LONGER SUFFICE AND NEW TYPES OF ARCHITECTURAL NOTATIONS WILL BE DEVISED. *BERNARD TSCHUMI*

I
Design and analysis

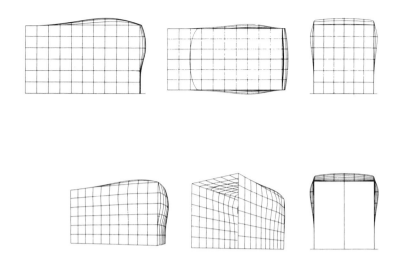

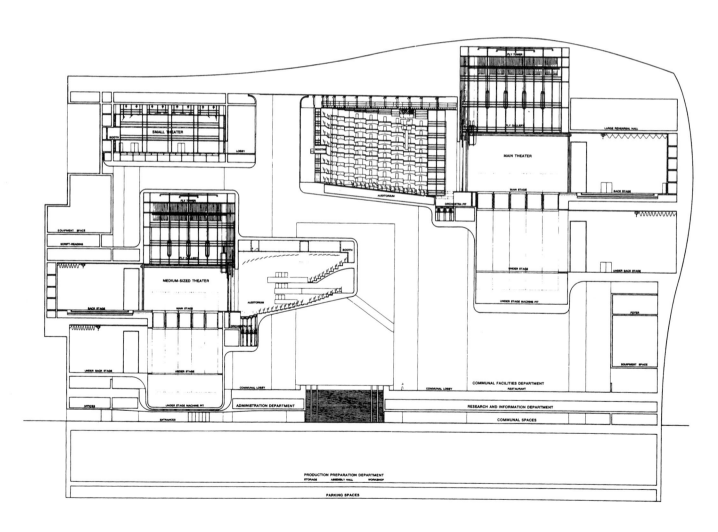

Jean Nouvel, competition design for a Tokyo
opera house, 1986. Computer drawings of the
mass

Section

1.1 The design

Whoever makes a design, whether it be a building, part of a town or a park, is basically concerned with a given program and a location or site. The program can be fixed beforehand or determined as the design progresses. Much the same applies to defining the site. Additionally, designers are faced with a series of fixed precepts and unwritten demands informed by a particular culture or convention. Finally, designs must satisfy conditions of usefulness and construction. Generally these aspects do not arise in a fixed, logical order; designing is not a linear process, with a specific task leading to one and only one possible solution. Knowing how to fulfill all these requirements and expectations is one of the main problems facing designers with each project. All relevant aspects need to be subjected to critical scrutiny. Based on their considerations, conclusions and viewpoint, designers must interpret the task and adjust the relative importance of the various requirements and expectations. This act of *interpreting* is a preliminary step when embarking on a design.

Next, the designer's view of the task leads to a *concept*. A concept need say nothing about the form the design is to adopt. Above all, it expresses the idea underlying a design and gives direction to design decisions, organizing them and excluding variants. There are a wealth of forms a concept can take; it can be a diagram, an illustration or a text. At the office of the French architect Jean Nouvel, for example, before a single line is drawn extensive discussions between designers and specialists in certain sub-areas take place. Drawing begins only when a description of the project—a concept— is clearly formed. This working method presupposes both a vast knowledge of the possibilities and an active imagination.[1]

An example of such verbal concepts is Nouvel's competition design for an opera house in Tokyo (1988). Based on a series of discussions within the office, the choice fell on the metaphor of a large carrying case for a musical instrument. The building's exterior would have a smooth black finish, curved somewhat at the main theater. Inside, the gold-colored theaters would stand free in the space, like instruments in a case.[2]

Quite another method of working is exemplified by the Expressionist architect Erich Mendelsohn.

When designing the Einstein Tower in 1920 at Potsdam, he began with a visual concept, a rapid sketch illustrating how the observatory was to look. The power of this sketch lies less in its correct application of perspective than in the lines giving the primary expressive elements. Sometimes the concept involves a sketch of the section through the building, sometimes a few lines indicating the main form of the plan. The sketch made by the Finnish architect Alvar Aalto for the Neue Vahr apartment building (1963) in Bremen is an excellent example of the latter category. In what at first seem to be childish scribblings lies the essence of the design— the dwellings fanning outward, and the resulting compact circulation space, and an undulating frontage line with units oriented for maximum exposure to sunlight. This sketch also shows that Aalto, while drawing, was searching for the right shape for the curving façade; it is a remarkable registration of one particular moment in the design process.

Again, the idea behind a design may be fixed in a diagram. The famous drawing by Ebenezer Howard in 1898 of the garden city can be conceived as such.[3] Although Howard did set a scale below it, his diagram provides information about relationships only, with no implications for the actual shape of the city.

Erich Mendelsohn, design sketch for
the Einstein Tower, Potsdam, 1920

Einstein Tower, Potsdam, 1920

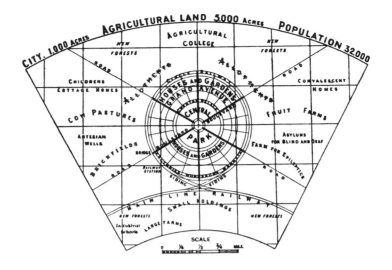

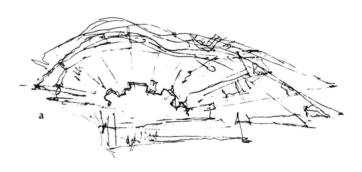

a

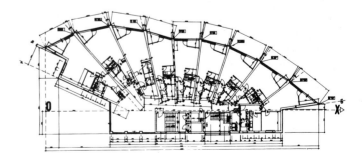

Alvar Aalto, design sketch for the Neue Vahr
apartment building, Bremen, 1958–1962

B. Parer and R. Unwin, plan of Welwyn Garden
City, 1902, a garden city based on Howard's
diagram

Ebenezer Howard, diagram of garden city, 1898

Plan

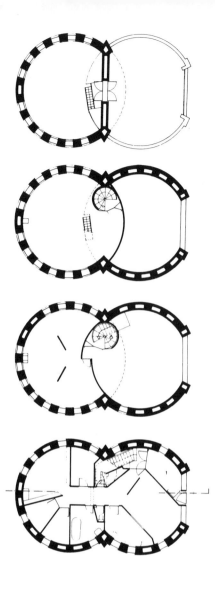

The design process

Thus, developing a concept is the first step towards making a design. Between the abstract concept and the concrete design lies an entire process. This is not a simple question of translating one into the other; rather, it is a creative operation in which designers formulate a possible formal elaboration, test it against the requirements, and possibly reject the solution or adjust it for further testing. It is a repetitive process whose course is partly cyclical and partly directional, through which it continually gains depth. At every step the designer examines the possible consequences for subsequent steps and creates margins for solving whatever unforeseen problems may occur. At each step he or she also looks back to see whether the original concept still holds or requires modification. Setting various possible solutions side by side for comparison can be important at this stage.

Form

At a certain point in the process concepts crystallize into a final form for the design. But how does the designer arrive at a form? Is designing comparable to solving a problem whose solution (in this case the form) is encapsuled in the task? This issue has caused a great deal of ink to flow. Usually it revolves around the question of whether the demands made of a design, particularly in terms of usefulness or construction, generate a form, or if the form can be derived from another source. Is it possible, for example, to derive the shape of a room explicitly from the pattern of lines of movement through that room; or can a span derive directly from the bending moment diagram? And if a line of movement can generate form, should the form of the structure then determine that of the space, or vice versa?

The different points of view adopted in practice regarding the relationship between design and use on the one hand and design and structure on the other are dealt with in Chapters 3 and 4 respectively. Here, suffice it to say that programmatic and structural requirements are not exclusively able to yield the form of an object or component.

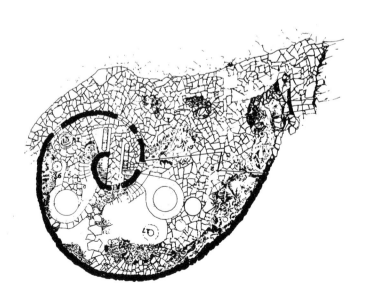

K. Melnikov, house, 1922, composition of two interlocking cylinders

Bruce Goff, design for a spiral-shaped house

Typology

If form is not deductible from these requirements alone, then, broadly speaking, there are two possibilities: designers must either draw on experience or come up with a new form. Basing form on experience is the customary procedure. Where a comparable task in similar circumstances has brought satisfying results, a designer may decide to apply it again. To be able to resort to experience, designers must have considerable knowledge of comparable solutions.

For example, they must be acquainted with many kinds of stairs, windows, doors, auditoria, building forms, dwellings and urban layouts and be able to name them. These are what we call *types*. More will be said about working with types in Chapter 5.

The need to produce an original form may present itself: after all, every type was first given shape at one time or another. To create a new form for, say, a city space or a theater, the designer usually begins with abstract geometrical shapes, cubes, prisms, pyramids and the like. These primary geometrical forms are intellectual constructions (the so-called *Platonic solids*). The designer might also derive a form from nature, living or dead, such as a tendril, kidney, snail's shell, and so on. To be able to master these organic forms, they too are translated into Euclidean geometry when it comes to the actual construction of a building.

Bearing in mind the type of task, the designer chooses a form he surmises to be a suitable basis for the design. Thus, a snail's shell would not be the most popular shape for a theater auditorium, where it would undoubtedly raise problems of sight lines. For a public lavatory, however, it is a proven means of organizing the transition from public to private, as any visitor to Amsterdam will know. The above remarks about form hold as true for the individual parts of the design as for the compilation of those parts, the complete building or ensemble. Here too the designer can choose between embellishing the familiar (the type) and introducing a new abstract or natural form.

Composition

Designing is more than just choosing a form. Preparing a meal is not merely a matter of bringing together the ingredients but rather of how they are processed, mixed and cooked. Similarly, in design we have a "black box" in which the design is "prepared." In it the material forms and spaces are arranged into the final composition, the definitive design. At this stage each element ends up in its proper place according to the principles of composition. Without this ordering process the result would be chaos. The method of ordering and the concept employed ultimately dictate the character, appearance and style of a design. Here is where decisions are made, and the designer's personal preference will prevail. Chapter 2 takes a closer look at what goes on in this "black box."

Context

A design task basically comprises a plan (set down in a brief) and a site. The site is a component of the broader notion of "context," in which a design is set. As the place where the future design must be executed, the site is the most palpable part of this context. In its broadest sense "context" includes the history of the site, the background to the design task and the social processes informing the design.

Understanding these issues enhances the design task and appreciation of the site, enriching in turn the design's potential.

Once a design is realized it presents a new whole in combination with its surroundings. How designers regard the given context and how they respond to elements present there is the subject of Chapter 6.

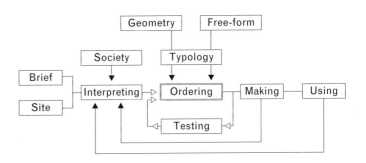

Schematic diagram of the design process

1.2 The analysis

One way of gaining insight into the process of designing is by analyzing existing work. Such analyses we designate with the term "design analysis." If designing is a creative process that produces something that did not exist previously, analysis begins with the outcome of that process and then attempts to get at the underlying ideas and principles. This analysis, it should be pointed out, is predicated on hypothesis; it is not our intention to reconstruct the design process.

Analysis is a means of developing insight into the profession, yet it can also prove useful when researching a given site, a building to be converted or a urban area to be transformed. Though the results of a design analysis can take the form of a written text, in most cases this will be accompanied by drawings, models and computer simulations. In making an analysis it is not our task to faithfully reproduce the object under scrutiny but rather to examine those of its components crucial to the analysis such as its composition, the relationship between design and context, and that between design, construction and usefulness.

Bringing out such aspects is done by reworking an existing drawing or model. This can just as easily involve omitting as adding information. In the remainder of this chapter we will examine the possibilities design analysis can offer using the perfect medium for the purpose, the drawing.

Processing the drawing

Whereas a model can provide three-dimensional representations, a drawing will never be more than two-dimensional. It is possible, though, to suggest on paper a third dimension. For this we enlist an array of geometrical projections, from various types of parallel projection through oblique projections to perspectives. The appendix ("Drawing techniques to aid analysis") looks more closely at the technical aspects of projection drawing.

The basic material of analysis almost invariably consists of orthographic or flat projection drawings of the design. These might be sketches, working drawings or drawings obtained by measurement, yet drawings made for presentation can serve the purpose equally well. The information stored in these drawing types varies with the objective of the analysis though all represent an abstraction of reality. The greatest measure of abstraction is usually obtained in presentation drawings, in which the object is generally reduced to solid matter versus space. Unlike working drawings, those made for presentation purposes are frequently devoid of references to material and construction methods. Often even the principal measures are lacking, and the scale of the drawing may have to be guessed at. However, the lucid and clearly organized information they provide can be useful for some types of design analysis.

When analyzing part of a city or an element of landscape our most important tool is the topographical map. Drawn by surveyors, such maps provide detailed information about buildings, green space, roads, water and so forth. Differences in level are charted using contour lines. For the purpose of analysis this basic material can be processed in several ways.

Reduction

The most elementary technique is reduction. We use it primarily to disclose the structure of a design, whether the morphological, typological or physical structure. To expose the structure means omitting from the drawing all information bearing no relation to the main composition of space and material. In a typological reduction this means leaving out such particulars as irrelevant oblique corners and physical projections in the design. This modus operandi is equally applicable to bringing out the load-bearing structure, though then it is of course restricted to material playing a major structural role. To avoid losing altogether the analyzed object in the reduction drawing, the contours of recognizable parts of the design are often included as a frame of reference. Thus in a reduction drawing of a city on a river, the river is included as a reference.

Addition

Addition involves introducing information into the drawing that is either non-visual or non-architectural. It may be information about function or use, or tell us something about the underlying geometrical system, such as axes and zones. Generally speaking such information is added once the drawing has been stripped of as much superfluous and distracting data as possible (i.e. has been reduced).

Démontage

Drawing the object for analysis as though it had been taken apart can bring out the relationship between components or aspects of the design. Juxtaposing or superimposing drawings, giving complementary information, can be helpful when examining the relationship between different systems in the design, whether these be several stories or several layers in a plan. It is also possible to draw the object as though it had been blown apart. Graphically termed an exploded view, this type of drawing helps to provide insight into the relationship between many elements.

Giambattista Nolli, map of Rome, 1748, re-markable in that it makes a distinction between public and private space. Nolli shows not only the street as public space but freely accessible interior space as well

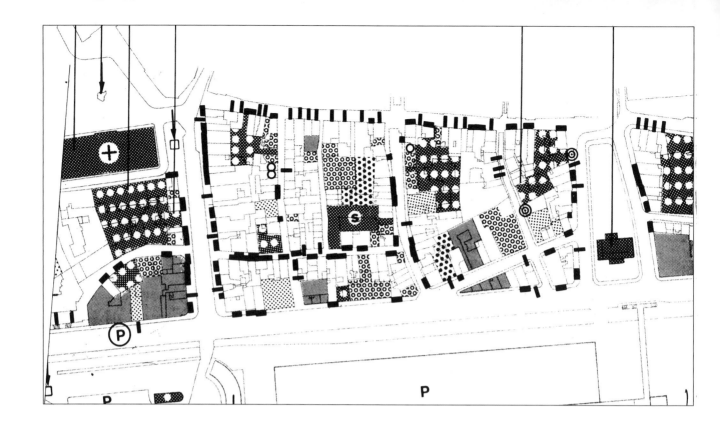

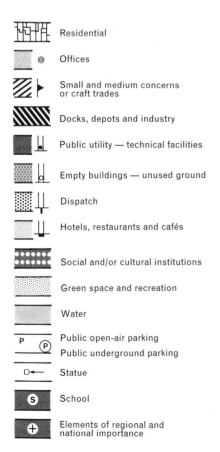

Residential

Offices

Small and medium concerns
or craft trades

Docks, depots and industry

Public utility — technical facilities

Empty buildings — unused ground

Dispatch

Hotels, restaurants and cafés

Social and/or cultural institutions

Green space and recreation

Water

Public open-air parking
Public underground parking

Statue

School

Elements of regional and
national importance

Antwerp, city block distinguishing functions

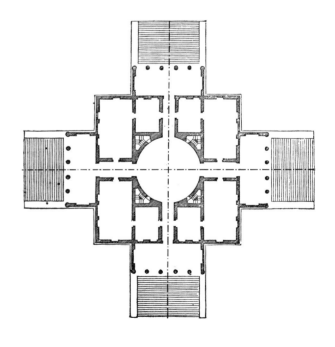

Palladio, Villa Rotonda, 1566–1567.
The drawing includes the axes determining
the direction of interior space

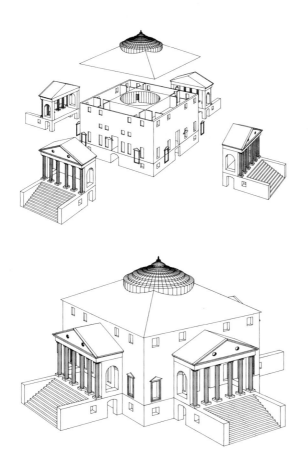

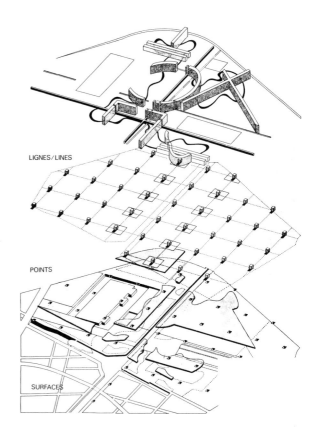

LIGNES/LINES

POINTS

SURFACES

Palladio, Villa Rotonda, 1566–1567.
Exploded drawing of elements showing the
separate elements of the villa's composition

Bernard Tschumi, design drawing of Parc de la
Villette, 1983. To illustrate the underlying concept Tschumi shows the design in its conceptual
layers

2
Order and composition

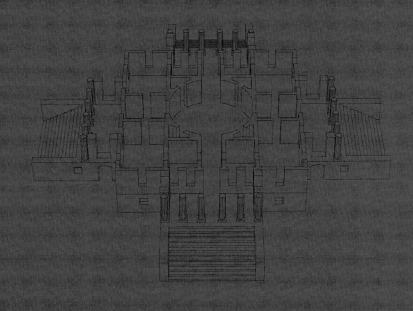

2.1 Introduction

In Chapter 1 we examined the broad lines of the design process. We saw how aspects such as form, type and context affect the ordering of a design, a process described as the "black box." Chapter 2 takes a look inside this black box.

Material and space

Whether designing a house, part of a city, a garden, a park or a landscape, the design is predicated upon a composition of spaces and material. In a house these are the rooms as against the exterior and interior walls, in a park the open spaces, paths and lawns as against the trees, and in a city the open spaces of streets and squares as against buildings and trees alike.

Activities take place in the spaces; this is where the *program* is situated. Broadly speaking, form, place and the nature of the material dictate the qualities of that space. Thus the quality of a square is governed by the form, place, nature and function of buildings around it, and the form, nature and quality of the enfolding materials determine the quality of a room in a house.

When designers or critics must describe how a design is composed without the aid of drawings, they resort to technical terms. The Danish architect Steen Rasmussen, for example, describes Palladio's Villa Rotonda thus: "Most famous of all the villas was the so-called Villa Rotunda, an almost square block with a large, colonnaded portico on all four sides. Ascending the broad flight of stairs to one of the porticoes you are aware of the same composition of rooms as in the *School of Athens* (a fresco of 1508 by the Italian renaissance painter Raphael which shows a building with a like spatial composition — ed.). From the broad, open portico you enter the barrel-vaulted hall, which leads you into the circular domed chamber in the center. From there the axial line continues through a new barrel-vaulted hall out to the portico on the other side."[1]

The design by the Swiss architect Bernard Tschumi for the competition for Le Parc de la Villette in Paris has been described as follows: "The plan is characterized by the regularly disposed follies, all on the same principle but each with its own program of activities. In composition the scheme is a 'plan libre' based on three autonomous systems.

A points grid of 120 × 120 meters with a folly at every point, a grid also there to relate to the surrounding urban fabric. Then there is a system of lines, a covered axial intersection as main access... and a fanciful *promenade architecturale* along the theme gardens. Third, there is a system of planes— larger spaces meant for open-air activities, bounded by taut rows of trees.'[2]

Both descriptions use technical terms. On the one hand, they draw on concepts that refer to the *elements* of which the design is constructed—*follies, circular domed chamber* and *porticoes*. On the other, they include terms that describe how these components are treated and arranged into a whole, such as *points grid of 120 × 120 meters* and *fanciful promenade architecturale* in Le Parc de la Villette and *axial line* in the Villa Rotonda.

Elements

Every design, then, can be broken down into spatial and material elements. Spatial elements include cupboards, rooms and urban squares, whereas door knobs, walls, building blocks and clumps of trees come under objects or material elements.

The components or elements that constitute a design are designated in part with terms referring to existing components most probably used on more than one occasion, such as the porticoes of the Villa Rotonda and Tschumi's follies. We can then speak of types (see Chapter 5).

Some elements are described in terms of their basic geometric form, such as the circular domed chamber, or a triangular space.

The fanciful promenade confronts us with an element lacking a geometrically defined form. Evidently the designer shaped this element along intuitive lines.

Instruments

The terms we employ to describe the ordering of the design can be traced back in part to the set of tools deriving from Euclidean geometry. The points grid and the axial line are just two examples. This geometry tool kit consists of the following:

- organizing lines and axial lines (e.g. symmetry axes, spatial axes and building lines, regulating lines);
- zones;
- grids (e.g. points grids, line grids, belt grids);
- systems of measure and proportion.

Some of these tools can also be found in present-day Computer Aided Design (CAD) programs.

Order

Every design is based on order. The need to order is prompted more than anything else by our general desire to arrange the world so as to make it easier to understand. This ordering takes place as much on the level of language by assigning terms and introducing classifications, as by physical interventions in the environment.

A second motive to arrange or order relates to production. Clarity of organization is a prerequisite for successfully putting a design into practice (see Chapter 4).

A third motive for ordering has to do with use. It should be clear that an organized system of streets or corridors can in principle mean greater efficiency. At the same time, ordering has a role to play in gaining a better understanding of the space around us. Ordering is a means of drawing together concrete reality and abstract thought. In a city whose order is unclear we only tend to get lost.

When imposing order, designers use not only the geometry tool kit, but also other principles. For example, the course of an action, a movement or a narrative can dictate the order of a series of objects or buildings. Principles of pictorial composition derived from painting can also play a part.

Thus, several ordering principles emerge. The difference in programs and building methods, changing circumstances and interpretations of these circumstances—varying from place to place or even from person to person—give a rich perspective on centuries of space design, with many styles evolving over time.

Architectural system

When we speak of style, we generally think first of the appearance, the form of the elements and the differences in decoration. Yet style has a second, more fundamental system that forms a leitmotif in this chapter. The art historian Emil Kaufmann calls it the architectural system.[3] An architectural system describes the structure of designs considered to belong to a particular style, the way the elements are to be combined, the set of design tools to be employed and the manner of their employment.

Architect and CAD specialist William Mitchell draws a parallel in this respect between language and architecture. He compares architectural elements with words, as being ordered to satisfy the conditions of an architectural idiom or system.[4] Just as words are declined in abeyance to such conditions, in architecture these rules dictate how its elements are to be *transformed*. Every language must have a *vocabulary* of elements and a *grammar* or collection of self-imposed rules.

In principle, then, every element is subject to manipulating, transforming or *deforming* to take its place in the arrangement or composition. This processing is at times no more than an adapting to scale, dimension and proportion. At others, processing is more drastic, with elements being rotated, distorted or truncated.

Although Kaufmann and Mitchell developed their ideas with architecture in mind, these principles are just as applicable to urban design and landscape architecture.

The way designers over the centuries have ordered their designs, the vocabulary and the tools they have used and the rules to which they have adhered—all have been influenced by social and cultural change. The following analyses of examples from ancient Greece to the present day illustrate how designs and design tools have developed through the ages. These particular examples have been chosen because they clearly exhibit certain ordering principles, and not for the sake of historical completeness. They should in no way be regarded as an attempt to present the history of architecture.

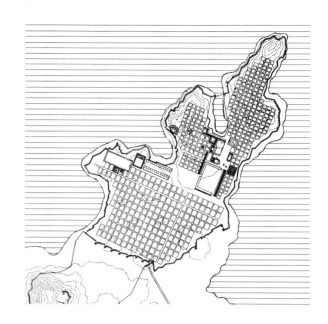

Aerial perspective of Priene

Plan of Miletus after its destruction in 479 B.C.

2.2 The basic instruments of classical architecture

One of the oldest tools for creating order is the *grid*. This ordering principle is a proven resource for laying out cities. Miletus is often regarded as the first city to be designed with a grid, yet this principle can be found earlier in Asia Minor and Mesopotamia, and in ancient China cities were already built in this way.

Grid

The special role assigned to the Ionic city of Miletus is probably due to Aristotle (384–322 B.C.) who in his book *Politica* presented the architect Hippodamus of Miletus as the originator of the grid-city. By postulating that the grid's equal, non-hierarchic division into blocks ("insulae," or islands) best suited the ideals of democracy, Aristotle gave the grid-city an ideological charge.

The new plan for Miletus that emerged after the city's destruction in the conflict with the Persians, is based on a square grid. This grid, which can be conceived as a system of equidistant and intersecting axial lines, sets the center line of the spatial element, the street. Where the situation dictated, the fields of the Miletan grid might be smaller or larger, rectangular or square. A number of blocks were kept free in the city center to site the main civic buildings and the forum. That the Greeks regarded it as an organizing principle without direct aesthetic intentions is evident from the way it is draped over the uneven ground.[5]

Harmony and proportion

In about 30 B.C. the Roman architect Vitruvius wrote what is arguably the first handbook on architecture. It gives a clear idea of the aesthetic aims of classical antiquity. Not only did a building have to satisfy *firmitas* (firmness), *commoditas* (commodity) and *venustas* (delight), architecture for Vitruvius meant *order*, *hierarchy*, *appropriateness*, *economy* and *symmetry*. The last concept in Vitruvius refers to *harmony*, not to the mirror-like connotations the word "symmetry" has today.[6]

These ideas gained concrete form in Greek temple architecture. One of the most famous Greek temples is undoubtedly the Parthenon (c. 449 B.C.).

Sitting atop the Acropolis in Athens, it dominates the ancient city. From the front, the temple's composition is quite basic. On a large platform or *stylobate* stand eight *columns*. Above the *capital* crowning each of these is a great stone beam, the *architrave*. This assemblage of elements is welded into a whole by the *tympanum*, the large triangular end of the saddleback roof.

The elements in this composition are on equal footing. A number of fixed ratios serve to harmoniously order the elements (i.e. symmetry) in a *system of proportion*. This system relates as much to the measurements and proportions of an element as to those of the entire composition. The Greeks regarded the system of proportion as "frozen music," and the absolute proportions it comprises are in fact derived from musical harmonies. However, the various theories on this matter usually have been found to conflict with the evidence of the actual measurements. The Renaissance architect Alberti (1404–1472) describes the phenomenon as follows: "We define harmony as that consonance of sounds which is pleasant to the ears. Sounds may be low- or high-pitched. The lower-pitched a sound, the longer the string that emits it; the higher-pitched, the shorter the string. From the different contrasts between these sounds arise the varying harmonies which the ancients have classified into set numbers corresponding to the relationships between the consonant strings... Architects employ all these numbers in the most convenient manner possible: they use them in pairs, as in laying out a forum, place, or open space, where only two dimensions are considered, width and length; and they use them also in threes, such as in a public sitting room, senate house, hall, and so on, when width relates to length, and they want the height to relate harmoniously to both."[7]

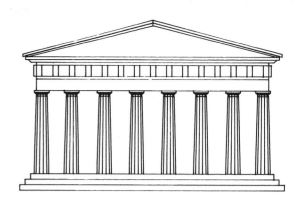

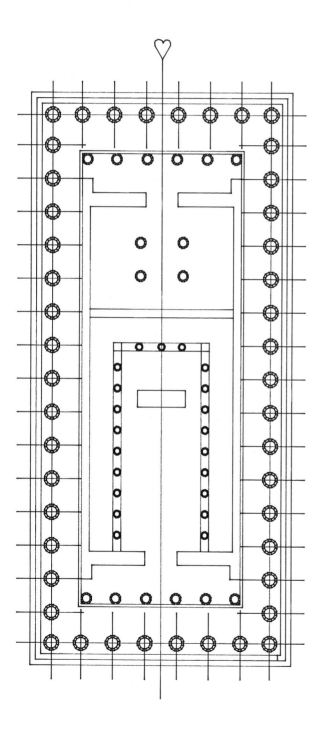

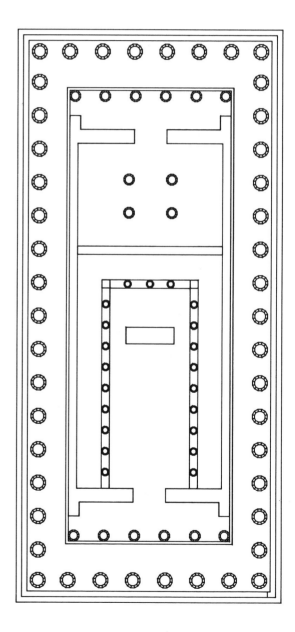

Front elevation

Plan

Plan of the Parthenon showing bays and axes

Material system

The floor plans of these ancient temples are likewise clearly arranged. Pillars line the edge of the oblong stylobate, which can be entered on all sides from three steps. In the center of the temple is a walled space, the *cella*. At the front and back of this two-roomed cella stand a second row of columns. Columns inside the cella are also set in a row.

Though the temple is a plastic and spatial object, designers describe it in terms of material elements which together define the temple's composition. A system of imaginary lines or *axes* regulate the positioning of these material elements. We can distinguish two types of axes used to do so: the *symmetry axis* and the *material axis*. A symmetry axis along the length of the temple regulates the mirror symmetry of the temple. The positions of the neatly ranked colonnades are determined by material axes, organizing lines that run through the center of the columns.

This entire array of material elements (columns, tympana, architraves) and the tools used to order them (axes, systems of proportion), comes under the heading of material system.

Bay

The distances between the axes dictating the position of the columns are called bays. This bay measurement derives from the thickness of the column, depending on the proportional system used. The bay, which in Greek temple architecture related only to the center-to-center distance between columns, took on far greater importance in Romanesque and Gothic architecture. The emergence of the groin vault gave rise to a system whereby the bay regulates the composition of the building. In Gothic cathedrals the columns adhere to a grid of material axes. Thus, a bay can be defined as the zone between two material axes.

Renaissance

In the fourteenth century the cities of central and northern Italy developed into mighty republics. Their wealth was based on the tempestuous developments in trade and industry during this period. The rise of commercial prosperity brought profound changes to the social structure of the proud city-states. The monopoly on the transfer of knowledge that the Church had held for centuries crumbled. With the emergence of the city academies, the sphere of influence the monastery had had on the development of religious and philosophical ideas shifted to the academy. Not only did the Church's influence on thinking gradually diminish, but also that of religion as a whole.

Man developed an ever stronger position at the center of the world-view. This gradual transition from a feudal Europe to a new social order was echoed in the shift in major architectural commissions. Now, not only did churches determine the history of design, but also town and country houses, gardens and urban plans of the thinking urban elite.

Patrons' tastes reflected more than anything else the examples of Roman, and as much as was then known of Greek, antiquity. This rebirth of the lost ancient civilizations takes the French name Renaissance.

Following the line of the ancients, geometry took a prominent position in Renaissance architecture. Elementary geometric systems and precise systems of proportion were regarded as an objective medium between the divine model to be emulated and human creation. "The square, the cube, the circle, the sphere, for example, were regarded as being among the elements of the divine model, thus the necessity to apply them in the configuration of buildings. This belief, which can be found in the writing of the Pythagorists, Plato, several writers of antiquity and the Bible, was invigorated and reinforced during medieval times and especially during the Renaissance."[8]

From then on man was looked upon as the measure of all things, as a "cast" of the divine model. Man took over from music as the basis of the proportional system. Various geometric devices were developed to transform human measurements into proportional relationships. One of the best-known examples is the drawing made by Francesco di Giorgio Martini in 1492 showing a plan of a church based on the proportions of the human body.

Hierarchy

Besides elementary geometrical forms, the Renaissance architects used hierarchy to control the ordering of space and material. Kaufmann asserts that just because classical antiquity and the Renaissance used the same vocabulary and the same forms does not mean that they shared the same architectural system. In his book *Architecture in the Age of Reason*, Kaufmann describes the difference between the architectural system of classical antiquity and that of the Renaissance (and the Baroque) as follows: "The ideal of quantitative perfection lived on in the Renaissance. We know how much thought its theorists gave to the 'correct' measurements. But more important, and far more significant than the reintroduction of ancient forms, was the rise of a new compositional principle: the parts now should be presented not only in aesthetically satisfying relationships of size and in mathematical reciprocity, but they should be differentiated as superior and inferior components. Such differentiation would have been strange to antiquity... at any rate within the individual building. The postmedieval composition which emphasized the different values of the parts made of the whole a hierarchy of well-disciplined elements."[9]

In order to examine the ordering principles of the Renaissance, two villas have been chosen as the object of our analysis. The internal composition is the main focus in the first of these, the Villa Rotonda. The second, the Villa Medici at Fiesole, is examined mainly in terms of the geometric order and composition of the garden.

In the mid sixteenth century a new type of country house emerged in northern Italy. Such houses were attached to a large farming enterprise and served as a retreat for rich town-dwellers from their wheeling and dealing in the city. (See also the Villa Emo in Chapter 3.) The Renaissance architect Andrea Palladio contributed much to this development. His severe though pellucid ordering has made the Villa Rotonda, whose construction began in 1567, one of the paradigmatic examples of Renaissance architecture.

On the exterior of the villa, Palladio controlled the composition of material using symmetry and proportion. To effect the required hierarchic composition in the elevation, some elements of the villa dominate the composition more than others. For

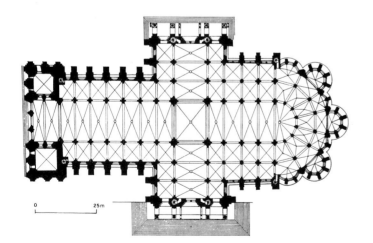

Isometric from below, drawn by A. Choisy

Plan of Chartres Cathedral, 1194–1220

instance, the porticoes derived from Greek temple fronts are stressed by being set on the four sides of the block on the symmetry axes as self-sufficient elements.

On the interior, the material is primarily the counterform of the spatial composition—the residue left after the spaces have been defined, where the structural components of the building are to be found. Yet the surface of the material figures prominently here too, not just in defining the space-form but as a bearer of imagery and meaning. The magnificent frescoes painted later on the plaster surfaces give the interior an extra dimension.

Space system

In the quote at the beginning of the chapter, Rasmussen describes the Villa Rotonda as a block. He then goes on to describe the place of the porticoes in terms of this block. Rasmussen takes his exploration indoors through one of the porticoes. If his description of the exterior dissects its composition into objects, inside Rasmussen distinguishes spaces: the barrel-vaulted hall and the circular domed chamber in the center. From it we can conclude that unlike the Parthenon, the composition of the Villa Rotonda is based as much on space as on material. Because the ordering of material and ordering of space adhere to their own set of rules, designers distinguish two distinct systems that together shape the composition: the material system and the space system.

In his description of the villa, Rasmussen remarks that the rooms in Palladio's building can only be seen one at a time. You are either in one room or in another—the rooms are distinct entities. To organize the discrete rooms (the spatial elements) in the composition as a whole, Palladio resorts to perspective with a central vanishing point, one of the major discoveries of the Renaissance. The Villa Rotonda strings rooms in sequence along an imaginary axis, the *space axis*. Such a concatenation of spaces we denote by the expressive French word *enfilade*. The space axis, like its counterpart the material axis, in principle divides the element (the space) into two equal parts. Two such axes organize the basic layout of the villa and tie it in with the surrounding landscape. Thus, Palladio brought to bear a perspective framed in the door openings of the surrounding landscape.

The sequence of rooms set about the circular hall are arranged along a secondary system of axes. In the original design these axes ran through the heart of the rooms. In the design as built they were shifted off center, freeing the middle of the rooms for circulation lines.

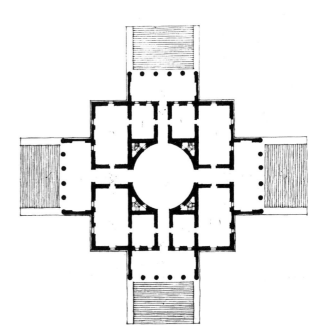

A. Palladio, Villa Rotonda, plan

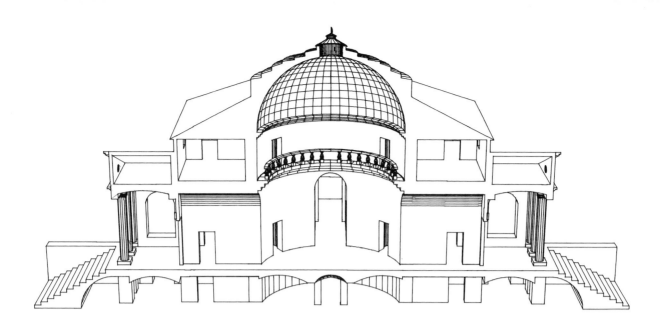

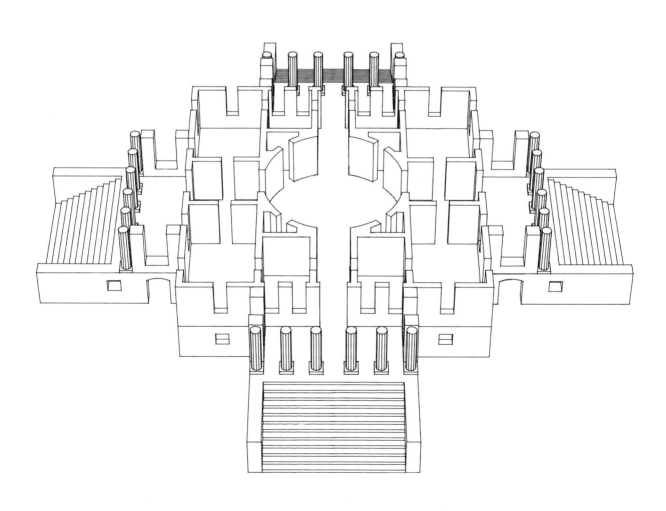

A. Palladio, Villa Rotonda, 1566–1567.
Sectional plan and elevation

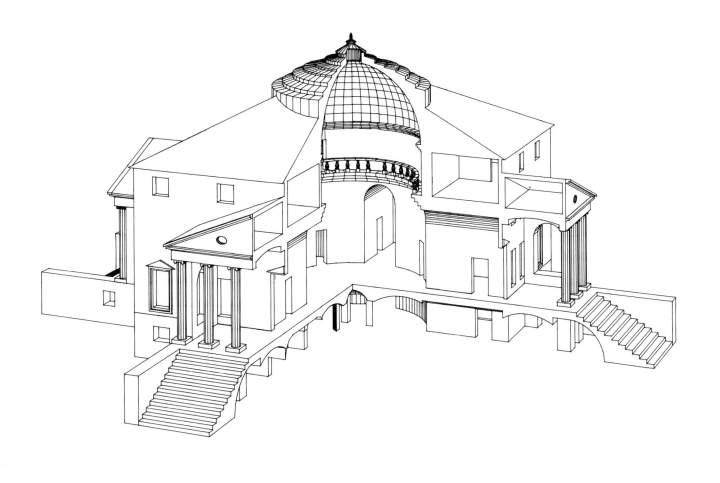

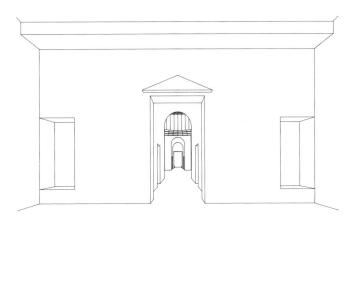

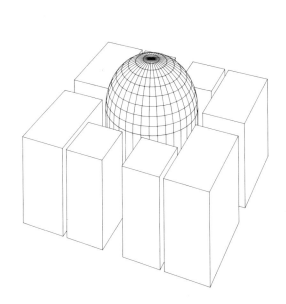

Planometric reduction showing spatial
composition of Villa Rotonda

Villa Rotonda, cutaway perspective

Perspective drawing of enfilade through
Villa Rotonda

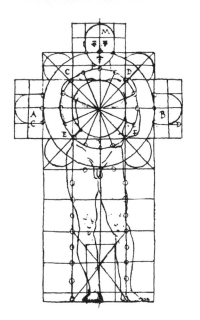

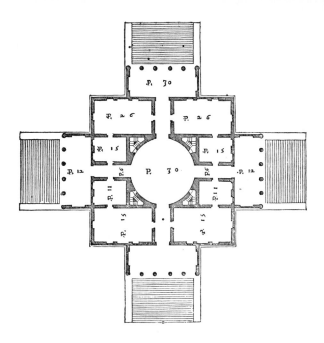

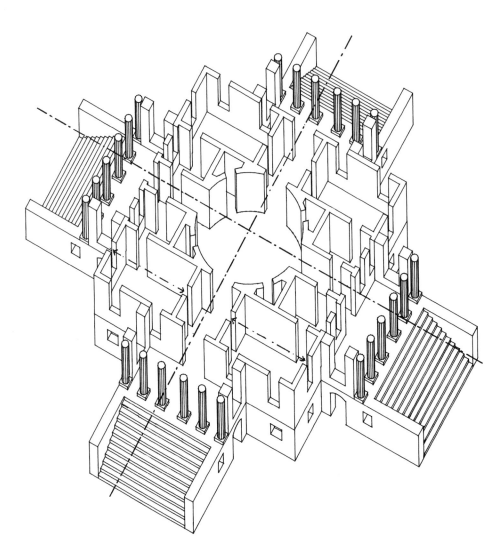

Francesco di Giorgio Martini, diagram of a
church plan derived from the proportions of the
human body

A. Palladio, Villa Rotonda, 1566–1567.
Cutaway isometric showing axes

Villa Rotonda, Plan showing proportions.
From *The Four Books of Architecture*

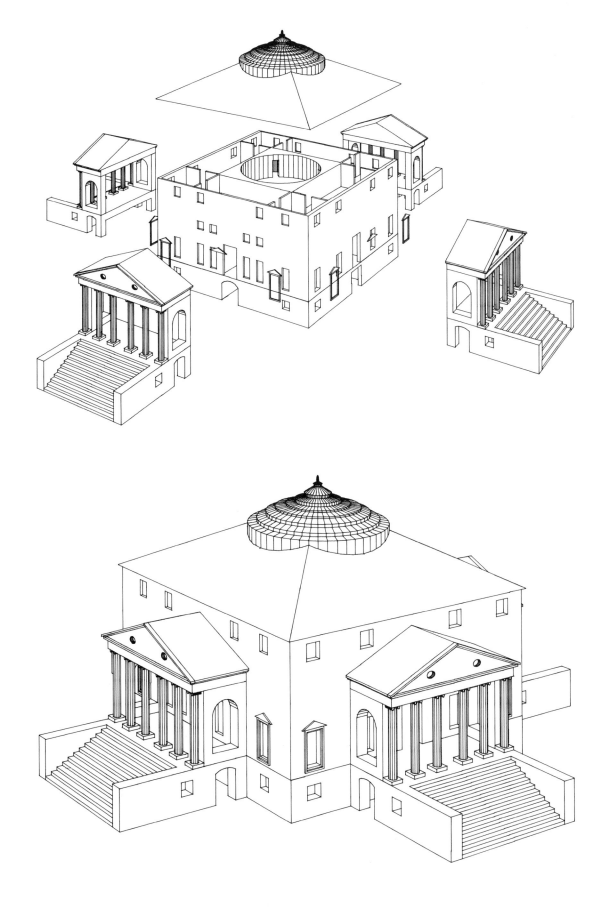

Villa Rotonda, exploded view reducing it to its
determinant elements

Geometry

Building up a design from elementary geometric forms themselves subdivided into smaller secondary elementary forms, gives rise to a hierarchic and usually centralized composition founded on a *geometric system*. Representing the geometric structure, this system uses Euclidean geometry to regulate the space and material systems, and thus the geometry of the whole composition. The great value accorded geometry in the Renaissance gave it a major role at that time.

In Palladio's villa this arrangement of the spatial elements or space system divides the cube-shaped block into a number of elementary geometric spaces. The two symmetry axes stress the centralized composition.

In his treatise *The Four Books of Architecture*, Palladio expounds on his proportional system and argues for simple ratios (1:2, 1:3, 1:4 etc).[10] In the many floor plans of his designs illustrated in the *Four Books*, the proportional measurements are converted into real ones expressed in Vicentian feet and designated with a P for *piedi*.

The geometry of the renaissance garden

Early in the Renaissance it was customary for wealthy citizens to have a house outside the city. In Florence the members of the rich and powerful Medici family of bankers had various villas built for them in the vicinity of the city. One of these is the Villa Medici (1458–1462) at Fiesole, set on a slope. The first stone of this villa was laid more than a century before the Villa Rotonda was built. The garden attached to the house descends the slope in two large terraces. In discussing Palladio's Villa Rotonda, we concentrated on the internal organization of the composition. The well-preserved garden of the Villa Medici prompts us to turn to the ordering principles of the Renaissance garden. In brief, such gardens had a geometric layout based on a grid whose spatial organization took its cue from the panorama. Hence the geometry, derived from that of the house, organizes both garden and panoramic view.

Pictorial system

In making a landscape analysis of a garden design we distinguish two systems, the pictorial system and the space system.[11] The space system relates to the main layout of spaces, planes and terraces comprising the garden and so is synonymous with the term of that name as used in the two foregoing sections of this chapter. The pictorial system relates to the elements that dictate the image and how they are organized in the composition. In the Villa Medici these are particularly the discrete components and objects placed in the spatial system, such as fountains, lakes, clumps of trees and steps but also not infrequently "mythological" components such as caves and small temples.

There is a parallel to be drawn between this concept and that of the "material system." Both cases concern themselves with material elements; if the main focus when analyzing a building is the material as structural component, in the case of landscape architecture it is the material as bearer of image and meaning (hence the name pictorial) that features more heavily.

Garden design, too, is governed by a structuring geometric system, the system of axes and lines defining the garden's composition. The Renaissance was a time of experimenting with geometric systems whose precise measurements and proportional relationships reflected the divine model. The geometric system with its attendant proportions was laid over the existing landscape; this was the city-dweller's way of setting his stamp on the surroundings.

If we carefully analyze the garden at Fiesole we find that the measurement system can be reduced to a module of 4.9 meters.[12] The square of 4 × 4 modules can be regarded as the basis for the garden's further design. Derived from the geometry of the house, this square determines that of both upper and lower terraces.

Placed in tiers, the two terraces are primarily tuned to the panorama across the valley of the Arno and Florence. The elements of the pictorial system play a secondary part in the design, their positioning being by and large geared to strengthening the panorama-oriented composition. Thus the major pictorial elements, a spring, a set of steps and an ornamental lake, are set on a symmetry axis which crosses the terraces in the direction of the Arno.

Another important element is the long pergola
parallel to the retaining wall. Again, walking
beneath this pergola, one has only to look to one
side to have a continual view of the Arno and
Florence. The pergola simultaneously provides a
foreground and frames the view so that the effect of
depth in the landscape is enhanced. As the method
of composition of the Renaissance garden relies
heavily on geometry it has given rise to the concept
of *rational staging*.

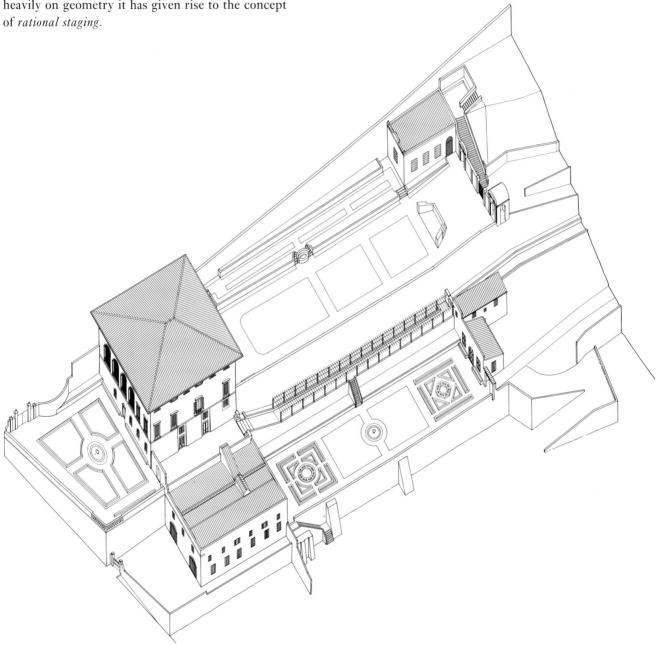

Isometric of Villa Medici

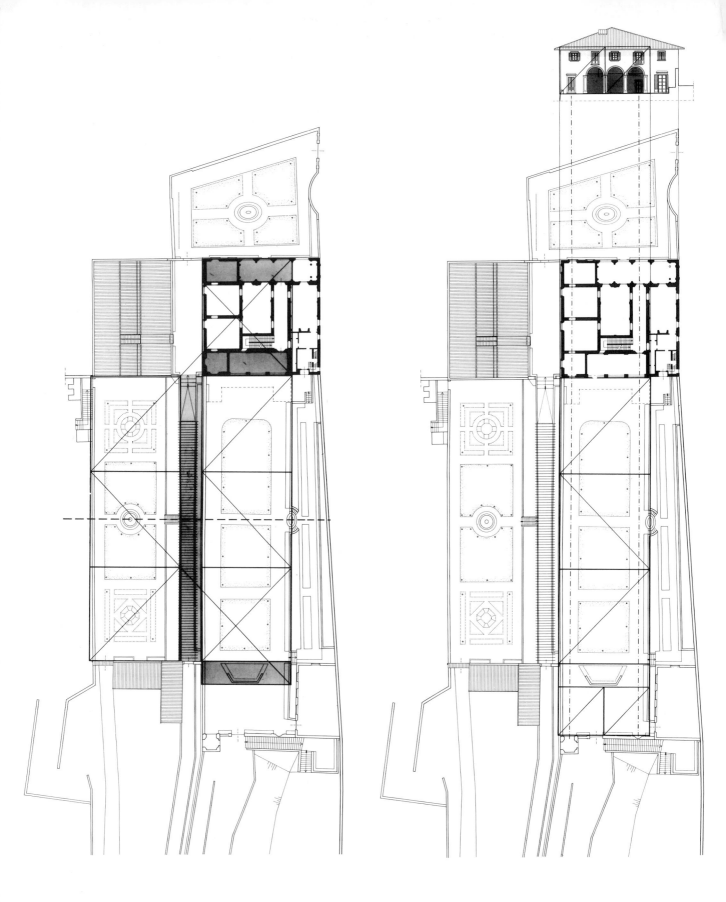

Geometry of the Villa Medici, Fiesole,
1458–1462

Plan showing geometry of house and garden

2.3 Transforming and manipulating the classical system

In 1633 the Italian architect Francesco Borromini designed the church of S. Carlo alle Quattro Fontane in Rome (1633–1667). Situated at a cross-roads with a fountain at each corner, the Quattro Fontane is generally regarded as one of the major achievements of Roman Baroque.[13] Baroque style employs the same elements as Renaissance style and even resorts to the same set of design tools; Kaufmann asserts that the Baroque and Renaissance architectural systems are basically the same. However, the Baroque set out to express something essentially different.[14]

The principal aspirations of the Baroque may be described as the desire to impress with a play of form, space and light by creating space which, unlike its Renaissance equivalent, is no longer clear-ly defined.

If we study the plan of Borromini's Quattro Fontane it is immediately apparent that the clear geometrical schema of the Renaissance has here made way for a much more complicated one in which concave and convex walls alternate, even on the façade of the church.

Transformation of geometry

The positioning of the pillars betrays nothing of a clear-cut structure based on axes and bays. The pillars are in fact incorporated into the undulations of the façade and the interior. Borromini sub-ordinates both detail and large elements such as pillars and tympana to a great movement through the space (some commentators speak of dynamics in this respect). Transformation is a key notion in understanding the Baroque—the entire system, the elements, geometry and detail, all are the product of transformation.

According to the French architectural theorist Castex, the main shape of the Quattro Fontane can be conceived as a Greek cross confronted by a rect-angle—a transformation yielding an ellipse.[15] The elliptical dome can be understood in terms of a similar transformation, in which the geometric system is elongated along a single axis. To weld together the plan and the dome on pendentives the

walls are curved and the details distorted, all elements of the composition gelling in an unbroken movement. The corners of the Greek cross are removed and furnished with a double column for the same purpose. To quote Castex, "Borromini once again resorts to the procedure of overlapping spaces whose principal feature is that all elements of the spatial arrangement spill over their boundaries. With the spatial units no longer clearly defined, all kinds of relations are possible."[16]

Because the division between its spaces is in-distinct, Baroque architecture can be read in many different ways.

Manipulation of perspective

In seventeenth-century France, during the days of absolutism, the style generally referred to as French Baroque evolved. To distinguish it from sixteenth-century Baroque, the term French Classicism has been adopted in this book. Versailles, its palace, gardens and town, is one of the most complete and coherent examples of this style in which geometry and the manipulation of perspective figure strongly.

In 1661 the French king Louis XIV decided to have his father's hunting lodge expanded into a complex without parallel in all history. He com-missioned the famous landscape architect Le Nôtre to make a new design for the garden. The extension to the palace was the work of the architects Le Vau and Mansart. To complete the complex, a new court capital was built at the front of the palace. The process of designing and building the new Versailles took more than fifty years.

Palace, gardens and town were to express the absolute power of the Sun King in a manner quite beyond compare. To this end the space-organizing system of perspective developed in the Renaissance was converted into an instrument to manipulate visual perception.

One of the most important elements of the garden design introduced to achieve this was the long visual axis. This was an open strip or vista, along which one looked out from the Grand Salon of the palace across the rear terrace, the parterre garden and the Grand Canal to the horizon.

Where Palladio employed a visual axis to link his Villa Rotonda with the surrounding fields, Le Nôtre's great axis was a means for the Sun King's palace to dominate the world. Looked at another

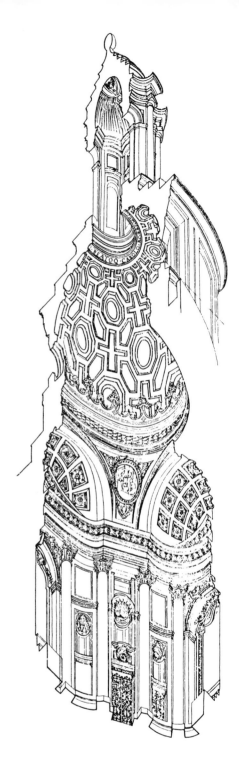

Front façade of Quattro Fontane

Cutaway drawing of Quattro Fontane with
double columns at the corners

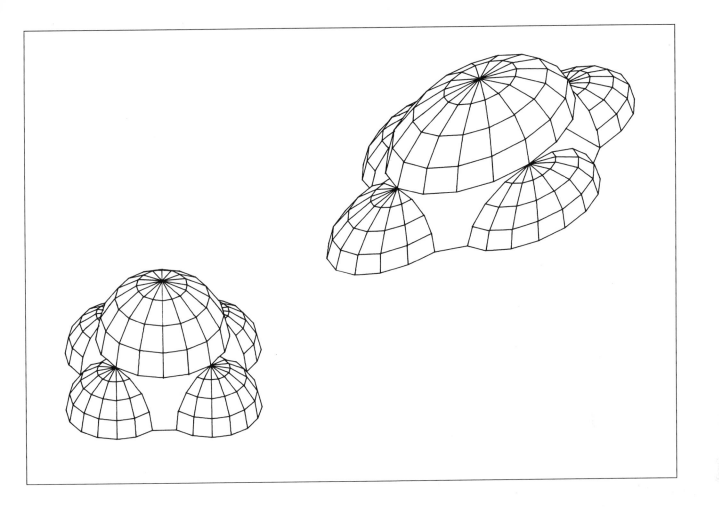

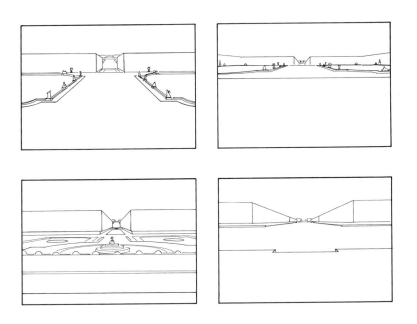

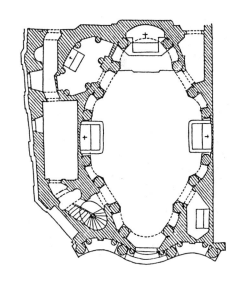

Versailles, perspectives of main axis   Transformation of the Greek cross   Borromini, Quattro Fontane, 1638

way, Le Nôtre used it to place the palace at the world's center.

The first phase of the garden largely followed the layout of the existing Renaissance garden. This part of the garden is dominated by the grid deriving from the original garden. The second phase was to dig the Grand Canal, a basin of colossal length set on the principal axis behind the palace. To increase the perspectival effect of the axis, Le Nôtre manipulated the perspective. This he did on the one hand by varying the breadth of the vista, from fifty meters at the front to one hundred and fifty at the back, giving an effect of foreshortening. On the other hand, he introduced a hill into the perspective. By having the vista terminate against the hill at the far end, the perspective effect is even further lengthened.

In the second phase of the park layout, it was the vistas that fixed the composition. Here the orthogonal grid gives way to star-shaped avenues in patterns that slice through the wooded terrain. Le Nôtre used the vistas here to bind together the various components of the park, such as the start of the Grand Canal and the more northerly Grand Trianon. The method of composition used for the French garden, one strongly oriented to the visual form, has been described as *formal staging*.

Although Le Nôtre's means differ from Borromini's, here again everything is geared toward impressing the observer through the manipulation of visual perception. Borromini achieves his aim through transformations of geometry, Le Nôtre through the power of the manipulated perspective.

The formal effect of the grid

Set before the palace in Versailles is a large square, forging a link between the palace and the town. Here too is the focal point of the trio of avenues that converge on the palace. The central avenue, a vista one hundred meters across, extends forward the great axis behind the palace. The other two diverge from it to the northeast and southeast. Together these form a so-called "patte-d'oie" or "goose-foot." This is another motif frequently used to manipulate the perception. Viewed from the square the suggestion is created that the two outer avenues are at right-angles to each other, giving the effect of looking through a wide-angle lens.

The consequence of these avenues for the town is

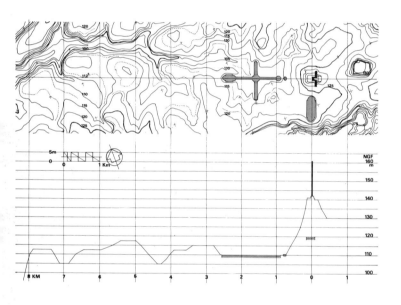

Versailles, map showing contour lines and section through Grand Canal. The vertical scale of the section has been exaggerated

that there the palace comes into view at various points, thus imposing its power on the town. The perspectival effect of the principal axis is strengthened further by assimilating it in the palace as a series of ever smaller prefatory spaces.

The town itself is built to a grid system such as that applied by the Greeks in Miletus, given that here the neutral and at times somewhat impaired grid is given a formal reworking. The new principles of creating "green rooms" such as Le Nôtre had done in the park, were carried further in the town's design. In this case not the green mass but the mass of urban buildings has been "hollowed out" to create streets and squares. The three above-mentioned avenues function as vistas and dictate the main layout of the urban composition. In addition, squares are situated at a number of intersections in the grid. When placing these spaces in the urban fabric formal arguments such as symmetry and orientation to the vistas played a major part. Superimposing this formal space system of avenues and squares on the neutral grid brought a hierarchic order to the town. The special places thus created logically provided space for key buildings.

This formal processing of the grid gave rise to a notion that would persist for many years as the *Classical* or *Baroque city*, and would influence the designs of many cities up to the close of the nineteenth century. Examples include eighteenth- and nineteenth-century Paris, and nineteenth-century Berlin and Washington.

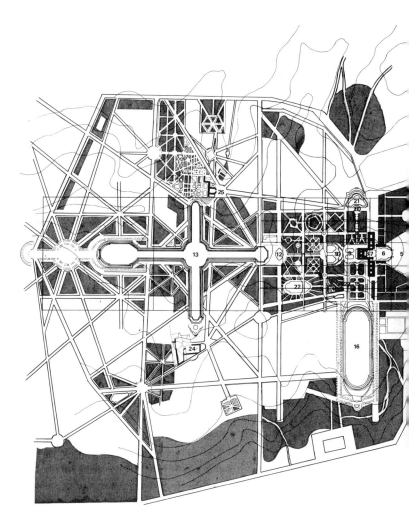

Versailles, overview of the garden

2.4 The picturesque and the narrative

While the Classical system was generally accepted and conquered Europe in countless variants, eighteenth-century England witnessed a development of great importance (if often underestimated) for the future of composition. The increased concern with nature, now regarded as an autonomous phenomenon with its own values—this was the time of Jean-Jacques Rousseau who urged that natural values be recognized—led to a tendency in landscape architecture that proceeded from natural landscape form. As the geometric ordering principles prevalent in Renaissance and French gardens had little to do with form in nature, designers sought other means. The answer came from beyond architecture, initially from amateurs in the design world. A number of English parks from the period around 1740 greatly influenced this development. Most noteworthy about these parks is that they were designed by the owners or by amateurs with no true architectural training.

One of the best preserved parks in this series is Stourhead, designed in 1741 by the banker Henry Hoare. Hoare deployed three means of arriving at a "natural" form—dramatizing existing nature, composing "scenes" using methods culled from painting, and the free-form technique.

As he wished to avoid using elementary geometry to construct the main shape of the park Hoare let the natural contour of the ground dictate the park's form. Instead of projecting a geometric system across the existing landscape he turned to *dramatizing* the nature already there. This he did by picking out existing elements in the landscape. We will return to this dramatizing of nature in Chapter 6.

The picturesque scene

In order to ascertain where the highlights figured in the park's composition, Hoare turned to painting. Inspired by the way the seventeenth-century landscape painters composed their canvases, Hoare built up his park around a series of scenes. One of these worked into the park literally brings to life a scene by the French landscape painter Claude Lorraine. The example Hoare used was his painting *Coast View of Delos with Aeneas*.

The choice of Claude was not by chance, for his paintings lucidly reflect a compositional technique that gave park designers the tools they required. The art historian and Claude expert Marcel Röthlisberger summarizes these stylistic principles as follows: Claude uses a clearly distinguished foreground and background. Between these there may be a narrow zone containing a few large masses. Large features with few details he places along the diagonal in the foreground. Highlights on one or both sides of the scene frame the composition. Claude often applies to one side of the painting

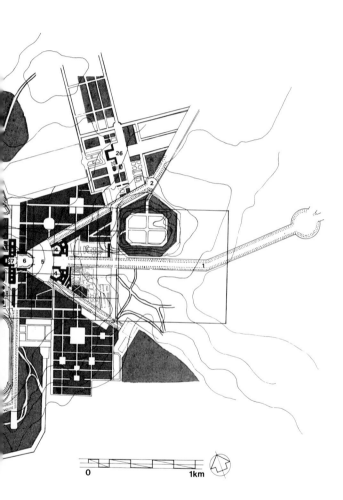

0   1km

Versailles, plan of the city

gradual transitions in tone and color from large sil-
houettes in the foreground to smaller forms in the
background. On the other hand, the contrast between objects in the foreground and background can
be extreme, as much in color as in scale. Another
stylistic principle is his wielding of simple, compact
forms.[17]

From then on, these painterly techniques of composition would become increasingly influential in
architectural and urban design as *picturesque staging*.
In English garden design these principles translated
into the staging of such scenes as described above
and the placing of objects such as temples in
relation to differences in level. The existing natural
landscape served as a backdrop to such scenes.

But simply applying this "picturesque" compositional technique was not enough for Hoare to
achieve his aim. For this method presupposes for
each component a basic premise from which the
scene can proceed. To solve this problem Hoare
looked to literary subjects.

The narrative

Hoare ordered his scenes along a route through the
park. Projected around a lake, this route illustrates
the wanderings of Aeneas as described in Virgil's
Odyssey. The surrounding hills serve to set the
scene, so that the park can be regarded as a stage or
as scene-painting in which visitors become spectators. The route leads them past various buildings
and scenes visually depicting episodes from
literature.

The route as bearer of the narrative, comparable
to the perforated strip of celluloid bearing the film,
can take on innumerable forms. Only the order is
important. The form has as little influence on the
narrative as the way a film is wound on a reel or left
lying in loops on the floor. What is important is the
form and composition of the picturesque scenes
themselves and their order over time. Staged as if
paintings, these segments of landscape serve to
unfold the narrative.

The difficulty with this method of composition is
that each component exerts an influence on the
others. Indeed, the main motif in one scene could
well be the stage set of the next. This means that
making such a seemingly free design is a long and
laborious process in which every change in one
scene has to be considered in terms of all the others.

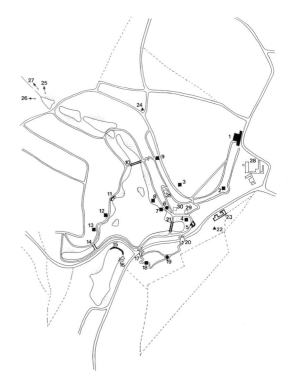

Plan of Stourhead park

Stourhead

Claude, *Coast View of Delos with Aeneas* (1672).
This painting was the model for the garden of
Stourhead

2.5 From distribution to composition

One of the leading architecture schools in Europe during the eighteenth and nineteenth centuries was the Ecole des Beaux-Arts in Paris. This school grew out of the Académie Royale d'Architecture set up during the reign of Louis XIV in 1671. The aim of the Academie was to teach a "timeless" architecture. To do so, its director, Jacques-François Blondell (1617–1686) looked back to the tenets of Vitruvius. During the existence of the Académie and the later Ecole des Beaux-Arts the ideas culled from Vitruvius underwent many modifications and shifts in response to the increasing complexity of the design tasks and the need among designers to set their personal stamp on the work. At the same time, support for these modifications was sought in the quest for eternal truths in architecture. These shifts within the classical system make the Ecole des Beaux-Arts, which is generally associated with a period in which a welter of styles were skillfully interwoven, an interesting subject for research.

As the eighteenth century progressed, the dichotomy within classicism became ever more sharply defined. Along with an architecture resting on eternal truths there were the critics of the Beaux-Arts ideas, the Rationalists. These include architects who stressed rather than played down the influences of technological progress (see Chapter 4). In France these diverging opinions were made manifest by the founding in 1794 of the Ecole Polytechnique. One of its principal teachers was Jean Nicholas Louis Durand (1760–1834). We will take a more detailed look at the Ecole Polytechnique in Chapter 4, but the present chapter follows the history of the Beaux-Arts.

One of the pinnacles of Beaux-Arts architecture is Charles Garnier's Paris Opera House. In 1857 a competition was held to design a new opera house, as part of the transformation process under Napoleon III and the prefect of the Seine department, Baron Georges Haussmann. Garnier's winning design was built in 1874.

Broadly speaking, the building has all the typical nineteenth-century hallmarks: a clearly organized plan adhering to the prevailing rules of classical composition that arranges bays of symmetrical form along a principal axis. Although the building is marked by a profusion of enfilades and ornament, the classical system seems at first to have been respected. However, certain aspects of the Paris Opera House were new at the time. They reflect a shift in the architect's concern for certain elements of the spatial composition.

Composition

The history of the Beaux-Arts brought a shift in the way the plan is organized and in the concepts used to that end. Originally the notions of *distribution* and *disposition* derived from Vitruvius were used to describe the composition and order in a design. The concept of *composition* prevalent in painting since the Renaissance entered the architectural discourse in the second half of the nineteenth century at the Ecole de Beaux-Arts.[18]

The emergence of this idea was accompanied by a new way of designing. Until then constructing the main shape of a building was largely a question of dividing up the spaces (distribution) over the entire volume in accordance with the classical pattern of bays and symmetry. The new briefs involving larger and particularly more complex programs ushered in by the emerging nineteenth-century metropolis, made new demands on designers. The sheer scope and complexity led to buildings being designed as an assemblage or "composition" of masses and spaces. The main shape of a building was no longer achieved by dividing and subdividing a single entity. Combining components, composing with elements, gained increasing ascendance.

The conceptual shift from distribution to composition has additional significance. If designs in the Renaissance were ordered to reflect the divine and only true model, the personality and individuality of the designer took an ever greater hold on the design during the centuries that followed. This fact is made evident if we consider that the many architectural competitions regarded originality as a primary condition—a development that is still with us.

Parti

Paralleling the rise of the concept of composition is that of the *parti*.[19] Derived from the French expression "prendre parti," to make a choice, it relates to the main shape or overall form of the scheme; these days the term *conceptual study* is also used to describe the initial state of a design. The term was needed to define the main shape, which by then was no longer describable in terms of total mass, number of bays and one of the classical orders.

The design for the Paris Opera House marks in some measure a transitional phase in architecture. Considered superficially we can still define it as a single volume. This picture changes if we include the added entrances on the east and west sides, the pronounced flytower and the chandeliers above the famous staircase. Seen from inside, the composition is anything but a simple distribution of rooms within a single entity. The complexity of the sequence of principal spaces including the foyer, stair and main auditorium here elevates designing to the "composing" of spaces.

Marche

A third term to appear in the nineteenth century is *marche*, which literally means where the foot is placed, a pace or step forwards.[20] In Beaux-Arts jargon it refers to the detailing of the design, the sequence of spaces considered in terms of movement through the building. The marche makes one aware of the impact of the enfilade and the shift in character from one space to the next.

In the Paris Opera House the marche is employed not only as a horizontal, linear circulation to bring out the enfilade; it is a route that undulates freely along stairs up through the building. We see here the influence of the picturesque English landscape style.

The staircase of the Opera House is the climax of Garnier's design. Encountering, seeing and being seen are here raised to the level of high drama. The famous stair up which the public strides or saunters has in Garnier's hands become a spectacle that threatens to outdo the performance onstage.

Stair of the Paris Opera House

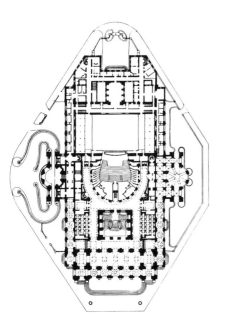

2.6 Towards a new architecture

The turn of the century saw great changes in European society. The rise of industrial capitalism triggered a fermentation process that swept the built environment along with it. Cities swelled into metropolises. The transformation of Paris at the hands of its prefect Haussmann is a good example of this process. New techniques and materials impacted on society, with cast iron, steel, glass and reinforced concrete making their entrance in building construction. The great upheavals in the economy and technology appeared to be contagious; the urge to discover a new formal idiom and new ordering principles, and the desire for a new architecture seemed greater than ever. Issues seminal to the period were deciding where to search, and assessing what value the classical architectural system had.

One of the architects caught up in this vortex of change was the Brussels designer Victor Horta, regarded as one of the major representatives of Art Nouveau. His commissions consisted largely of dwelling houses for the well-heeled. These were citizens who, having prospered in the colonies or in the first flowering of industry, permitted themselves a house of ample proportions. This upper crust of society was interested in new ideas and forms to express their elan. The Art Nouveau architecture of Horta gave them just this. In 1890 Horta even built a house for himself in the new style.

Charles Garnier, Paris Opera House, 1878

Section through Paris Opera House

Shifting axes

Trained in the Beaux-Arts tradition, Horta made systematic attempts in his work to go beyond the rules of classical architecture. At the level of decoration he largely replaced classical ornament with a formal syntax culled from the organic world of plants. But of far greater significance is that Horta attempted to change the entire system of classical architecture, foundations and all.

He examined the effects of asymmetry. His own house exhibits an intricate game of tag played between symmetry and asymmetry. The shift in the axes of the spaces gives rise to a diagonal movement in space. By building the structure of iron and steel Horta had the spaces flow freely into one another. This effect is best observed at the point where the stair arrives at the upper floor. Here the intricate play of spaces makes it impossible to gauge whether one is in the stairwell or the living room.

The façade of the house likewise reflects Horta's exploration of the symmetry-asymmetry relationship. Here, stone, wood frames, steel beams and posts and large areas of glass predominate.

Movement

By shifting the spatial axes Horta also breaks through the classical treatment of the space system. He exchanges the concatenation of autonomous spaces in an enfilade for a composition of spaces that flow one into the another.

Horta constructs a spatial composition that begs to be experienced through movement, by walking through the house. Horta strengthens the as yet quite static Beaux-Arts concept of the marche, elevated by Garnier in the staircase of the Opera House, by introducing axial shifts and interlocking spaces. Ascending the stairs, visitors to Horta's house find themselves in a riot of intermerging spaces.

Two years after Horta moved into his own house the Viennese architect Adolf Loos wrote his celebrated essay *Ornament and Crime*.[21] Published in 1908, it rails against the architecture of the Secession, the Viennese variety of Art Nouveau (see also Chapter 4). Loos cuts loose in this text on the near-tyrannical will of that movement to give shape to and decorate everything.

Despite his criticism of Horta's Viennese counterparts, we shall see that Loos adopted an avant-garde position comparable to that of Horta. The experiments Loos carried out on the fundaments of the classical architectural system were likewise applied to respectable dwelling houses, of which the Moller House of 1928 is a good example.

Raumplan

Viewed from the front, the Moller House looks like a sleek white box of harmonious proportions. Stripped of all ornament or classic formal idiom the façade nonetheless adheres to such compositional rules as symmetry, harmony and proportion. Whoever enters the house or studies the plans and sections closely is transported to quite another world. Here as in Horta's house, is a play of axial shifts and symmetry versus asymmetry. As with Horta's house again, spaces are not bordered on all four sides as in the classic style. Yet unlike the house in Brussels, the Moller House lacks any trace of ornament. The rooms seem to have fallen prey to rampant iconoclasm. Crisp block-shaped masses and spaces are visually most striking.

Another typical departure from Horta is the way Loos approaches the composition of the spaces. If the partitions between rooms in Horta's houses are eradicated by spaces that intersect, in Loos' each room remains an entity in itself. He may reduce the partition between rooms at times to a difference in level, a narrowing or a filter of columns, yet in Loos' houses there is no possible doubt about what belongs to which space.

In stark contrast to the strongly visual shielding of the interior from the outside world of the city, indoors one is constantly involved in a game of seeing and being seen. This highly visual contact between rooms and the axial shift among them facilitates this unremitting game, a staging of activities and rooms promoting the occupant to actor. Thus, you can look along a diagonal sight line from the seat above the front door through the entire house to the garden beyond (see also Chapter 3 on *staging* and use).

The way Loos constructs the space to these principles in a single volume is termed Raumplan (space-plan). Whereas the containing volume of the house stays taut and regular, the Raumplan provides every room in the house with the position and height befitting its use and the composition as a whole. The Moller House seen from outside has a classical ordering of symmetry and proportion, while from inside it amounts to a free composition in three directions of relatively autonomous rooms.[22]

Plan libre

A year after the Moller House was completed, French construction workers were putting the finishing touches to another white box, the Villa Savoye (1929) standing to the west of Paris and designed by Le Corbusier. If Horta's experiments were inspired by the potential of new materials such as steel and glass, Le Corbusier drew his ideas from the modern construction method of reinforced concrete. This technique allowed him to treat the loadbearing structure and the material required to partition off rooms quite independently. This division of the material systems advocated by him would have the greatest repercussions for modern architecture. The advantages and consequences of this solution, Le Corbusier claimed, inspired him to establish his celebrated "five points of a new architecture": 1 columns (pilotis), 2 the roof garden (toit-jardin), 3 the free floor plan (plan libre), 4 the strip window (fenêtre en longuer) and 5 the free façade (façade libre).[23]

The Villa Savoye can be regarded as a built manifesto of Le Corbusier's five points. Of these, the plan libre is unquestionably the most important. In the Villa Savoye this principle is reflected in a series of columns placed on a grid with an almost Gothic ethos.

Le Corbusier did, however, permit himself minor deviations from this grid on a few points. The arrangement of the rooms and position of the walls are free of it at times. A large wall curving freely between the columns on the ground floor reflects the idea of the plan libre the strongest. The elevations show the Villa Savoye's still fairly classical ordering, these being designed in a taut harmony, symmetry and proportion. Le Corbusier himself describes such a wall as a free façade, a non-bearing elevation than can be subdivided at will. Yet here the division of the façade is fixed by the size of the bay.

Route architecturale

Besides the plan libre Le Corbusier employs another means to organize the composition of spaces in the Villa Savoye. Concern with experiencing the design through movement, with the route as we have encountered it successively in English landscape architecture, the Paris Opera House and Horta's own house, led Le Corbusier to conceive the route architecturale or *promenade architecturale*.

This concept crops up in the Villa Savoye as a route that includes a ramp reaching through the roof. By this means he emancipated the experience through movement into a discrete element in the house's composition. By treating the route as an autonomous element Le Corbusier sidesteps the compositional problems of the English garden whereby every modification in a component influences the composition as a whole.

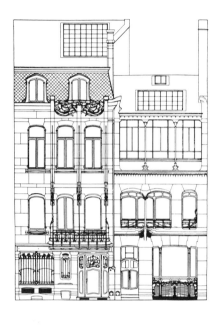

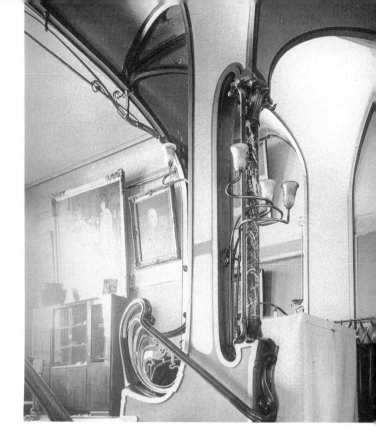

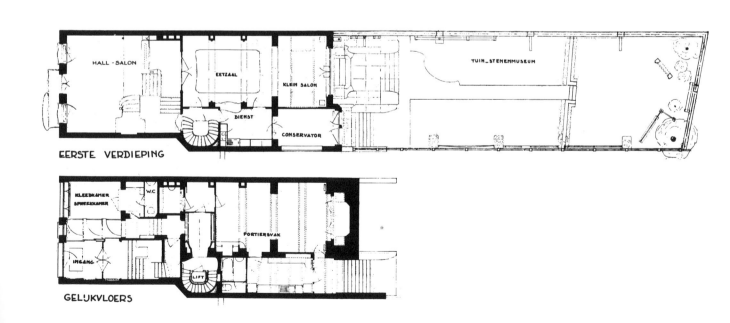

Façade of Horta House

Victor Horta, house on Amerikastraat, Brussels,
1989–1901. Upper and ground floor plans

Stair of Horta House

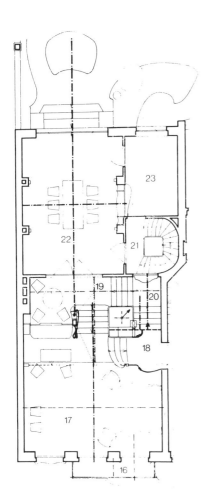

Horta House, first floor plan with shifted axes

Adolf Loos, façade of Moller House, 1928

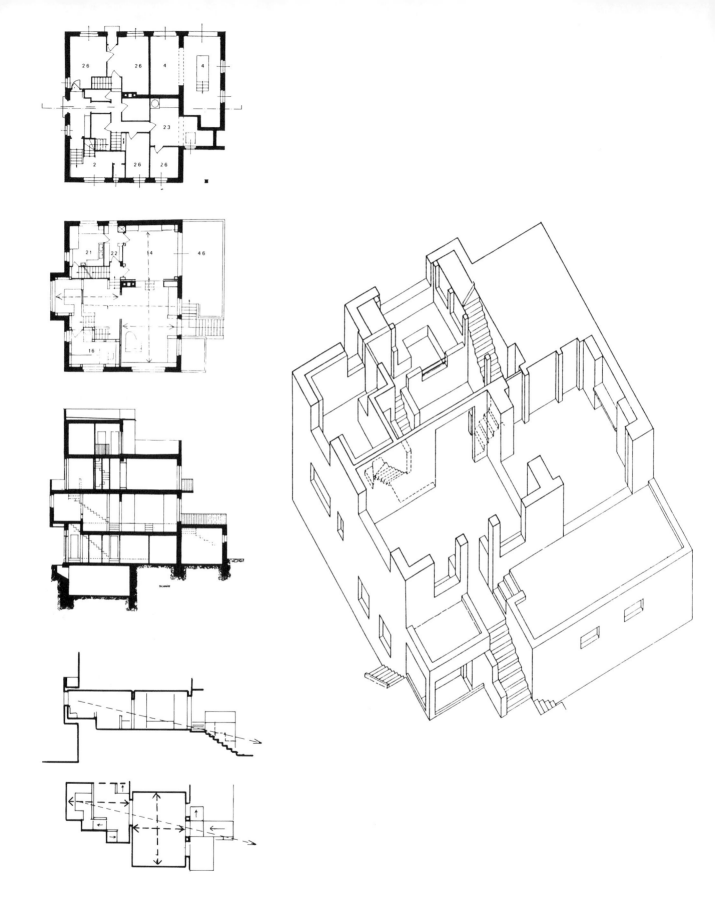

Floor plans and section of Moller House

Detail plan and section showing axes

Cutaway planometric of Moller House

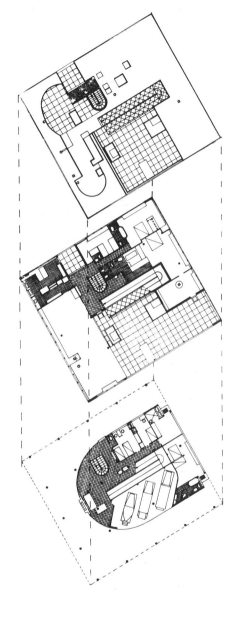

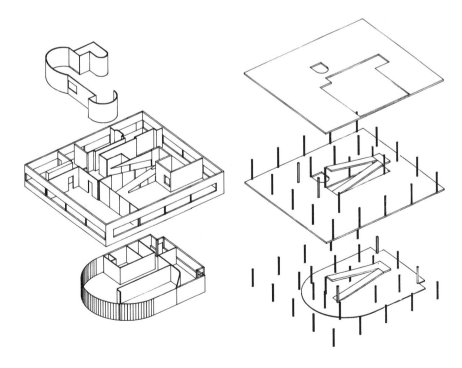

Le Corbusier, Villa Savoye, Poissy, 1928–1930

Villa Savoye. Exploded drawing divided into
spatial and structural systems

Floor plans of Villa Savoye

2.7 Unbounded space

The history of modern architecture, as with the English garden, has its own relative outsiders who, unhampered by excess knowledge, succeeded in launching new developments. Among these can be placed the architects who joined forces with painters in the De Stijl movement. One of their most important themes was "the liberation of space," the rejection of every classical confinement of space. They regarded space no longer as a unity bounded by walls but as a universal realm, part of the universe. Architecture was no longer informed by the creating of space but henceforth entailed the marking out of part of the universal space.

The conditions the new architecture had to satisfy have been described by Theo van Doesburg, the theorist of De Stijl, as follows: "The new architecture is anti-cubic, that is to say, it does not try to freeze the different functional space cells in one closed cube. Rather, it throws the functional space cells (as well as the overhanging planes, balcony volumes, etc.) centrifugally from the core of the cube. And through this means, height, width, depth, and time (i.e. an imaginary four-dimensional entity) approaches a totally new plastic expression in open spaces. In this way architecture acquires a more or less floating aspect that, so to speak, works against the gravitational forces of nature."[24]

In this text Van Doesburg breaks completely with the classical principle of a large volume divided into self-sufficient spaces. Spaces must flow into one another; the volume (the box) in which all elements are enclosed must be broken open.

Horta designed his spaces to flow together, though in his case the "space cells" sit within an overall volume. Van Doesburg hoped to achieve a "new plastic expression" in buildings. Like Loos, he distanced himself from ornament. In De Stijl it was replaced with a plastic formgiving that is wholly new. One of the finest examples of this new architecture is the Schröder House (1924).

In the early 1920s Gerrit Rietveld, architect and fellow member of De Stijl, designed for and in collaboration with Truus Schröder-Schräder, the house that bears her name. Terminating a terrace, this simple dwelling was to be of seminal influence on international architectural discourse in the ensuing years. Where exactly lies the power of this private house designed by a cabinet-maker and the widow of a lawyer? Before embarking on this examination it should first be pointed out that neither the architect nor the client had enjoyed a standard architectural education. Whereas Loos and Horta were constantly grappling with symmetry and harmony, Rietveld designed the Schröder House from the perspective of a quotidian pragmatism.

Flowing space

The house's parti is informed by planes set freely in space. It is on the upper floor that Rietveld and his client best succeeded in realizing De Stijl ideas on composition. Subdivisible with sliding panels, this living area can be conceived as one large open zone of flowing space, extended into universal space by drawing out the roof plane. Rietveld strengthened this effect by omitting the mullion of the corner window, so that when the windows of the dining area are opened this corner is entirely free.

Rietveld's space concept, in contrast to the strongly centralized geometry of the Renaissance, is centrifugal. As Van Doesburg expresses it above, "The new architecture… throws out the functional space cells from the core of the cube.'

Van Doesburg would have liked best to have eradicated gravity entirely so that all planes and volumes could literally float in space. The illusion of immateriality is an idea that has haunted modern architecture ever since.

Free composition

It should be clear that an architecture stripped completely of all classical features has no further use for a set of classical tools to order the composition. It is pointless searching the Schröder House for axes, bays, enfilade, symmetry and proportional systems. The question, then, is how did Rietveld order his design? He used two types of means to this end. The first was squared paper, a simple device resorted to by many modern architects. Rietveld, however, didn't use this ground to neatly arrange all the elements of the design on a grid of one meter. He treated it as the broadest of lines only, rather than a basic proportional system. Nonetheless, if we study the Schröder House in plan it is not too difficult to reconstruct this one-meter grid.

The composition of the house without axial lines, grid and bay is termed free composition, given that the architects had accepted the restraining influence of the orthogonal system. Rietveld was another to turn to the rules of composition in painting to handle the free composition in architecture. The Beaux-Arts academies carried these principles through into our own century, whereupon the Russian painter and Bauhaus master Wassily Kandinsky gave them a contemporary slant.

One way of controlling free composition is the pictorial or "painterly eye," controlling the composition in the way a painter would do. It is a question of the play of unity and distinction—too many similarities between the elements of the composition lead to lack of clarity, too many distinctions to chaos. What is needed is an empirical process to strike the right balance, with *clarity*, *tension* and *dynamics* the key concepts. These terms are still used in design education today.

Clarity in this context is pitted against lack of clarity and chaos. The word tension expresses the degree to which the design stimulates the imagination, and is the opposite of tedium. We come across this concept in the tasks Kandinsky set his students at the Bauhaus.

Kandinsky instructed them to make analytical drawings of still-lifes. The students began by drawing a much-reduced rendition of the subject. By drawing so-called "lines of tension" on a second layer of tracing paper, they could then make their interpretation of the project. These lines were to represent the tension between the opposing elements in the composition.[25] Dynamics is a concept we encountered earlier in connection with the Baroque. It is meant to express a suggestion of movement and change. In modern architecture, and that of De Stijl and Constructivism in particular, it designates a mode of formgiving that is not harmonious in the classical sense, an architecture that wants to express time. To this end it makes use of extreme proportions and non-rectangular corners. Asymmetry and a sense of floating are other favored themes for expressing acceleration and time.

Light, air and space

The preceding sections of this chapter might give the impression that order and composition are exclusively the domain of the large private house. This is not so, of course. Though the house has in many cases served as a "laboratory of form," the new developments in order and composition of the design have in no way been restricted to this building type. There have been shifts at an urban design level too, as we shall see.

At the end of the nineteenth century and in the beginning of this one, the concept of the classic city came under increasing attack. The appalling living conditions in the slums of the large nineteenth-century industrial metropolises were the main cause of this criticism.

Progressive architects who joined forces in 1928 in the Congrès Internationaux d'Architecture Moderne (CIAM) sought new ordering models for the city, models that would provide light, air and space. Their ideas derived on the one hand from De Stijl's notions about space, and on the other from the principles of organizing space in the work analysis conducted by the American F.W. Taylor.

The city block, like the contained space, needed opening up. Once the perimeter block had been broken open, the urban fabric fragmented into discrete objects. Looked at this way, the city ceased being a system of spaces: giving shape to the city became a question of organizing objects.

The rhythm of repetition

One of the most prototypical examples of this development is the Siedlung Westhausen, built between 1929 and 1931. This Frankfurt suburb formed part of an ambitious extension to that city masterminded by the city architect Ernst May. This extension scheme was itself a component of the social housing experiments being carried out in Frankfurt prior to 1933, at the time of the social-democratic Weimar Republic.

The design for Westhausen was made by May in collaboration with the architect H. Boehm. As distinct to the free composition of De Stijl, the Taylor organization model functions as a taut architectural system. In Westhausen an analysis of the household work provided the springboard from which to elaborate a standard dwelling in all its details. Taking the themes of light, air and space, May and Boehm developed an ideal house type, placing it in an ideal layout type so that the housing blocks stood free in "cosmic" space. A theoretically endless repetition of this layout type then produces a street, neighborhood, district and Siedlung. The measurements, dictated by functional needs, fix the distances be-

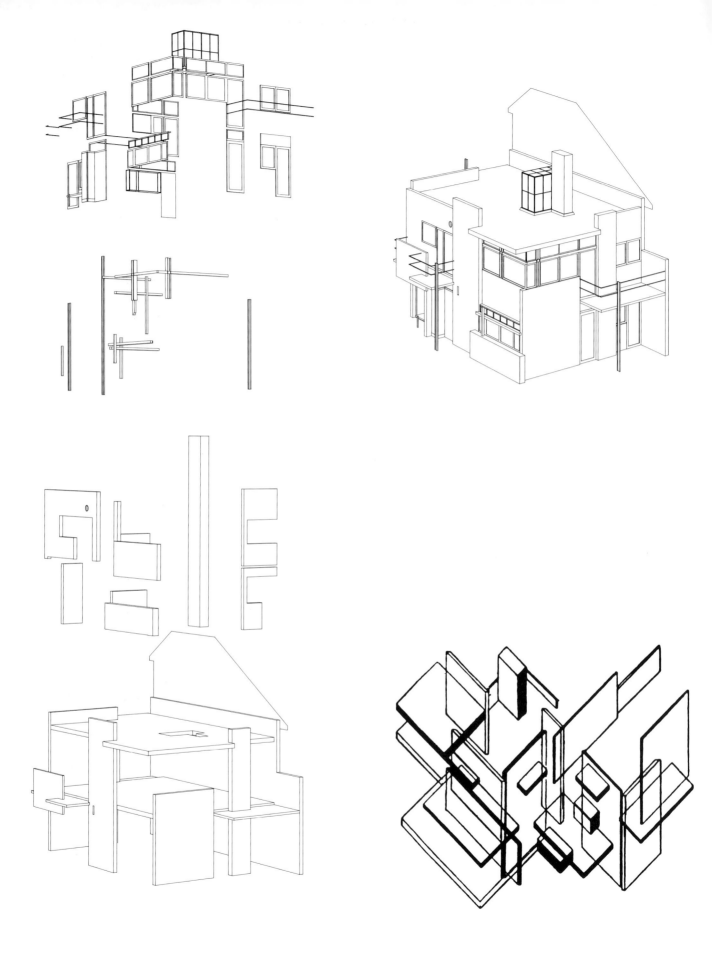

Exploded drawing of Schröder House

Theo van Doesburg, sketch for Maison
d'artiste, 1923

tween blocks. Here proportion makes way for an efficient system of the dimensions according to use.

A new aesthetic had emerged, the aesthetic of mechanical production. Hallmarks of this aesthetic are repetition, rhythm and the employment of material that is abstract and technical in appearance.

Whoever visits Westhausen will see that it is more than the Taylorized expression of an ideal. Though all units are organized in rows, the residential sector has been elevated above just filling in a line grid with blocks through the application of certain sophisticated resources.

By building up the blocks asymmetrically, May creates small discrepancies between them. This is a game played with mirror images, and groupings in odd or even numbers. He terminates the Siedlung with taller blocks of porch-accessed flats. Another factor is that Westhausen stands on a gently sloping site. The interference between the grid of row housing and the inclines in the site is a further enrichment of the scheme.

Composition of objects

Beyond a small spearhead of architects and planners the aesthetic of repetition failed to make any real headway. One of the interesting responses to the monotony of the new housing architecture is undoubtedly that of the French architect Emile Aillaud. From the 1950s on, Aillaud designed several residential areas in the periphery of Paris, such as Pantin (1955–1960).

Following in the tradition of the modern open row housing yet averse to the principles of Taylor, Aillaud designed Pantin as a composition of objects placed freely in space. The result is a play of light and shadow, planting and vistas.

The means Aillaud resorted to were limited to two types of object: porch-accessed flats and towers. The porch flats are in turn divided into two types of layout: rectangular blocks set together in squares and gently billowing configurations which can be strung together in a long elevation; this latter type is characteristic of Aillaud. This solution is found in very many of his schemes in ever varying configurations, offering an unlimited range of forms.

Aillaud took these three elements—towers, rectangular and curved blocks of porch-accessed flats—and worked them into a virtuoso composition. Pantin stands where two roads fork, with one

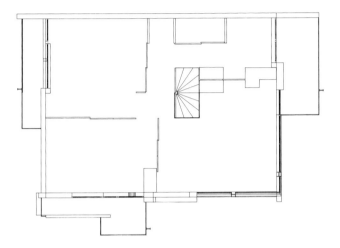

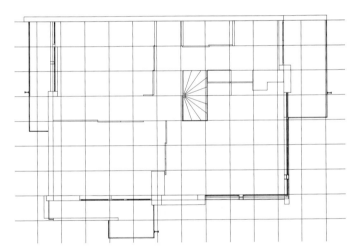

Gerrit Rietveld, plan of Schröder House, Utrecht 1925

Plan of Schröder House on 1 × 1 meter grid

prong slicing through its large green space. A winding elevation stringing together the billowing porch-accessed blocks defines the main shape of the area. This wall encircles a large central expanse of green of singular character, consisting as it does of a gently rolling lawn and scattered clumps of trees. The local primary school is situated here too. The towers stand north and south of this principal element. Finally, there is a square of housing and shops along the intersecting route.

Collage

The layout of Pantin is a typical example of a free-form composition. Whereas the free compositions of De Stijl were still restricted by the right angle, Aillaud drops the orthogonal solution entirely. Pantin's composition has much of Matisse's joyful collages or "Decoupées." Matisse painted the components of his collages himself, cut them out and assembled them into the composition he wanted. Aillaud likewise produces his own collage material; he designed his own types, his towers and curved and straight blocks. While every one of its elements is based on a geometric order, the composition as a whole can only be understood as a free-form collage whose arrangement once again turns to the principles of pictorial composition and to painting.

It is tempting to judge the composition of an urban ensemble of this size in plan, that is, from above. The user, however, will experience the district primarily at ground level. This means that if such a free composition is to be designed for maximum functioning, it will need resources that enable constant checking at ground level. In the eighteenth century they used paintings for this purpose; since then models and three-dimensional computer simulations have been added to the repertoire.

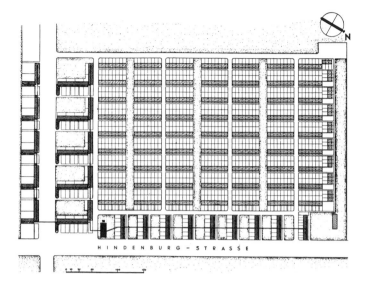

Ernst May and H. Boehm, plan of Westhausen residential sector, Frankfurt, 1929–1931

Houses in Westhausen

Emile Aillaud, plan of Pantin residential estate
near Paris, 1955–1960

Henri Matisse, *Les codonas*, collage in the cycle
'Jazz,' 1947

2.8 Giving shape to the indeterminate

In the closing decades of the twentieth century there is once again a radical shift in ideas and values, often termed *Postmodernism.* Unlike other "isms," Postmodernism is not a world view.
The word primarily refers to a system of altered conditions.[26] Hence there is no "postmodern architecture" as such, but architecture created under postmodern conditions.

Among these conditions are certain social and cultural phenomena belonging to the second half of this century. One such phenomenon is discussed under "the postwar period" in Chapter 3. Another is the seeping away of the great ideologies. The demise of the major "isms" has brought with it an increasing disbelief in the existence of a single truth. The search for one truth has given way to the realization that reality can be interpreted in many different ways, as expressed by a multiform society. Concurrent with the decay of the major "isms" is the notion that the open market is the least offensive of the ready solutions for regulating society.

In our day, design tasks are taking on ever more complex forms and programs are becoming more vague and indeterminate. Programs in the sense of predictions about the future use of a building seem to be losing their value. Every notion of a single fixed architectural system seems to repel, and flexibility, multiformity and strategy have become the key words. All styles, all architectural means to date, all forms are there for the taking. Speed, mutability, high-speed images and high-speed dissemination of information stimulate the awareness and set today's standards.

The issue now is how and with what means can form be given to this unpredictable world; how can we give shape to the indeterminate? The sheer élan generated by this quest recalls the urge for innovation in the twenties.

An arrangement in layers

In 1983, Paris witnessed a competition that kept many minds at work for a long time. As part of the so-called "Grand Projets," Paris was allowed to lay out a city park "for the twenty-first century." The site chosen was a former slaughterhouse set against an outlying superhighway on the Basin de la Villette.

The program, as provocative as it was vague, called for a whole sequence of urban activities including a museum, a music conservatory, numerous facilities for sports and games, theme gardens (astronomical, meteorological, etc), amusement centers, playing fields and a space for open-air concerts. Briefly, the program covered all inner city activities, the housing component being replaced by gardens and parkland.

The first prize was won by the Swiss-born architect Bernard Tschumi. His park design can be regarded as a number of principles discussed above, stacked in layers. Befitting the postmodern condition, Tschumi has at his disposal design resources engendered by three thousand years of Western architecture. Rather than degenerating like so many of his contemporaries into a historicizing use of architectural elements, Tschumi deploys merely the design tools and systems of bygone eras. The fascinating thing about La Villette is that it brings together the disciplines of architecture, urban design and landscape architecture.

To be able to handle the indeterminacy as well as the complexity of the program and the complicated site, Tschumi invested his park design with several systems arranged in layers. Each system has its own part to play in the design.

The large open spaces for playing fields and open-air concerts Tschumi expresses in a composition of "surfaces." This layer also defines the ground plane for the larger objects such as the science museum and the auditorium.

A second layer consists of "lines," connecting lines and linear elements such as rows of trees as well as routes. The most significant component of this layer is a meandering route extending through the park and bearing similarities to the routing system of English picturesque parks. This is undoubtedly its prime source of inspiration, with the one difference that there is no narrative element attached to it.

Sequences of imagery illustrated by perspective design sketches do suggest, however, that this route was planned as a cinematographic (filmic) series of images.

To accommodate the countless minor components of the park program such as kiosks, video pavilions, information centers and a child day center Tschumi elaborated a sequence of small bright red buildings which he calls follies. The reference to English landscape gardens would now seem to be complete. Various explanatory texts provide further evidence that Tschumi's primary point of departure in projecting the routing system and visually pictorial system of follies and rows of trees onto the existing situation was the compositional techniques of the English landscape garden.[27] However, to avoid the complexity of picturesque composition — the program was already complicated enough— he disconnected the different systems and laid them loosely one above the other.

From that moment the park's composition seemed quite simple. Routing system in the "lines" layer, large spaces in the "surfaces" layer and isolated objects in the "points" layer, each has a system of its own. Superimposing the three layers would conjure the whole.

With this act of disconnection into layers, however, Tschumi not only sidestepped the problem raised by picturesque compositional techniques, but lost control of the design instruments needed to organize the park.

Evidently Tschumi had misgivings himself about the success of this operation and endowed one of the three layers, that containing the follies, with a special property. By placing the follies at the intersections of a grid this layer took on a structurally determinative function while serving as orientation system for those using the park.

The dominant role Tschumi accords to the geometric system immediately brings to mind the Renaissance garden. As in the Villa Medici where the grid links the garden to the house, here the grid of follies is designed to relate the park to the town beyond.

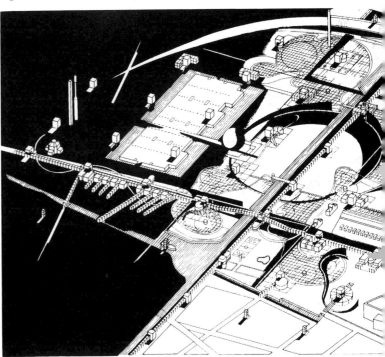

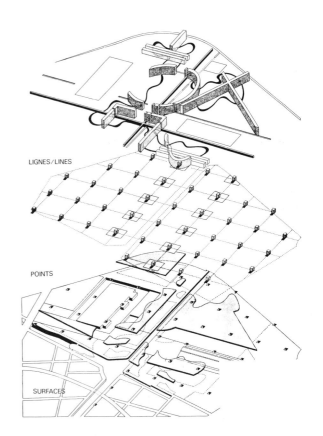

Bernard Tschumi, plan of Parc de la Villette, Paris, 1983–1993

Bernard Tschumi, design drawing of Parc de la Villette, 1983. To show the concept of his design clearly, Tschumi has separated the design into its constituent conceptual layers

An arrangement in zones

A comparable postmodern design attitude can be found in Rem Koolhaas's Villa dall'Ava (1991), also in Paris. In this villa Koolhaas combines various elements from recent architectural history. These are not direct quotes but, as in Tschumi's design, relate to the wielding of design instruments of differing origin. A basic knowledge of recent architectural history is enough to reveal a number of principles—the "plan libre," the free façade with "fenêtre en longeur," the crisply ordered glazing reminiscent of Mies, the denial of gravity derived from De Stijl and a Loosian manner of staging. Reading this probably conjures up visions of an architectural ragbag, though this bears little resemblance to the actual situation.

As Tschumi used a grid to govern the composition of his entire park design, so Koolhaas opts for zoning, an instrument sooner expected in a town-planning scheme than in a villa design.[28] Koolhaas handles the zoning by arranging the entire complex composition into three strips running lengthwise across the site. The central zone is further divided into three subzones. Strict separation among the zones is countered by a great design freedom within each. Zoning, then, is the ideal means of giving shape to the indeterminate. Setting out the composition with the aid of belts or zones is nothing new. The Foundation for Architectural Research (SAR) had already developed zoning principles in the sixties and seventies. Partly as a result, zoning became applied to schemes requiring flexibility during the design stage, as in urban plans and designs for large buildings. Influenced by the floor-by-floor division of functions in some New York skyscrapers (notably the Downtown Athletic Club) on the one hand and the layout of Dutch polders in ribbons of land and water on the other, Koolhaas has reinterpreted the zoning instrument.[29] He first resorted to it in his design for the IJ-plein residential area in Amsterdam North (1983–1988). In his OMA office's submission to the La Villette competition this means even informed the entire design. OMA's proposal divides the complete planning area into unequal strips. This way Koolhaas hoped to give shape to an indistinct program without making concrete statements about how the scheme was to be fleshed out. In principle, OMA's entry consists of just an inscription on the ground, lines to keep functions

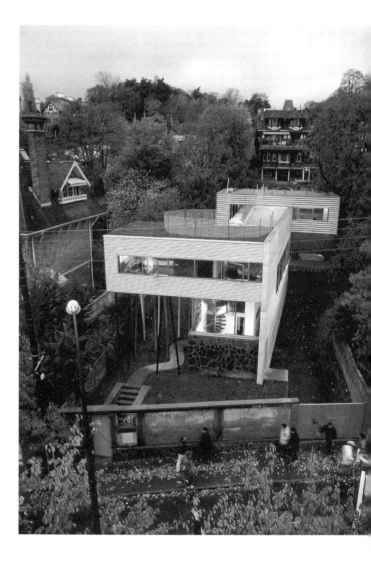

Rem Koolhaas, Villa dall'Ava, Paris, 1991

apart. Every zone has its own infill: tennis courts besides a strip of corn fields, a strip containing models of planets, and another containing a children's zoo. A walk breadthwise across the strips would be experienced as images spliced together in a film — film montage as a space-organizing principle.[30]

Using instruments closely allied to motion such as zoning, montage and staging, raises the question of whether these can be counted among instruments for regulating spatial compositions, or whether they are use-related tools. We shall return to these subjects in the following chapter.

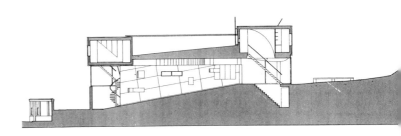

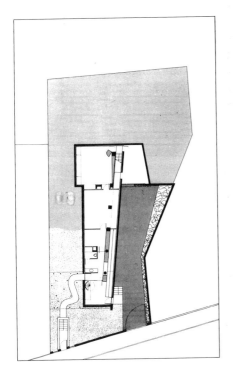

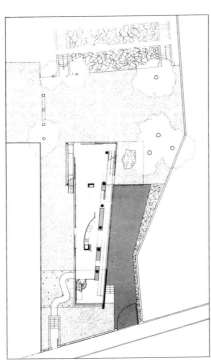

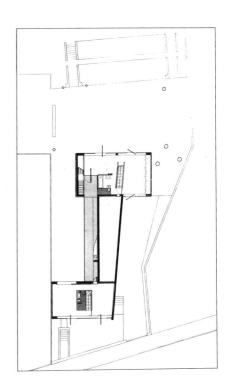

Floor plans and section of Villa dall'Ava

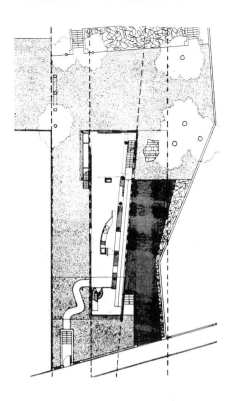

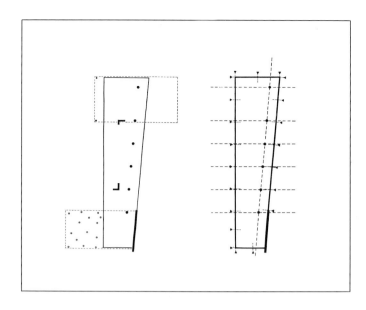

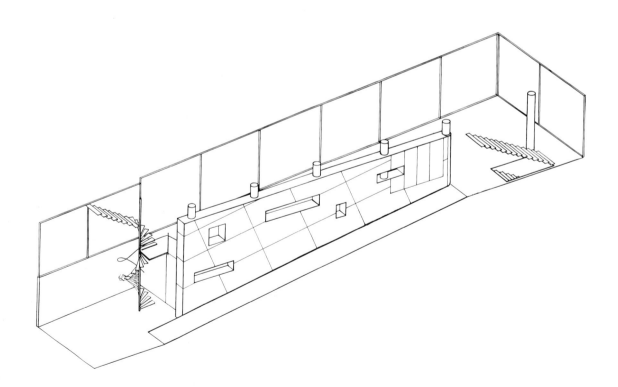

Plan of Villa dall'Ava showing its zones

Stripped-down isometric of Villa dall'Ava

Plan of Villa dall'Ava showing bay and system lines

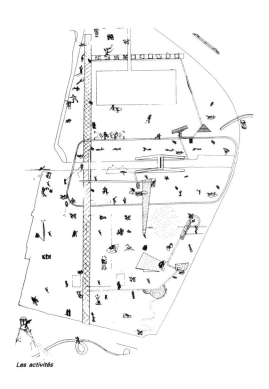

Les activités

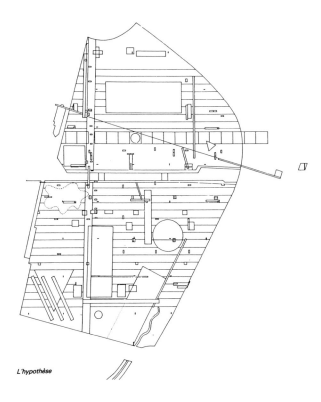

L'hypothèse

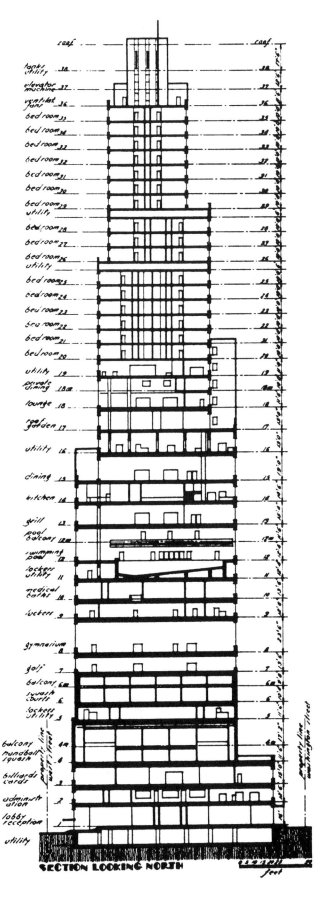

Rem Koolhaas, competition design for Parc de
la Villette, Paris, 1983

Starret & Van Vleck, Downtown Athletic Club,
New York, 1931

3
Design and use

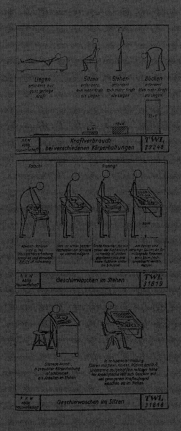

3.1 Introduction

The preceding chapter looked at various ways of ordering material, describing matter and space largely in abstract terms. It discussed how, since the eighteenth century literary, narrative themes and the perception of space have become determining influences on the development of architecture. This narrative element bridges the gap between human perceptions and actions.

This chapter examines the relationship between use of the built environment and the actual space. In the context of this book we shall focus on how social conventions and demands generated by the use of a building or a city are eventually translated into an architectural language.

John Summerson has described the relation between human activity and buildings as follows: "Architecture, by virtue of its actual limitations, can exploit our capacity for dramatizing ourselves, for heightening the action of ordinary life; it can increase man's psychological stature to an angel's. All this it does through its irrevocable attachment to function. The dramatizing of movements appropriate to architecture (and impossible without architecture), movements like entering through a door, looking out of a window—mounting steps or walking on a terrace—is something with which music has nothing to do. Here is architecture's special province which on the one hand constricts its movement and on the other intensifies its meaning."[1]

Summerson refers to architectural examples at the scale of a building. It requires little effort, however, to imagine that his description holds just as true for the space in a city or for a park. Terms like stair or window can easily be exchanged for terrace, arcade or square.

The following section looks at a number of case studies, analyzing the architectural themes that emerge with respect to their use as well as the way these themes have evolved in the history of space design.

The brief

The design process generally begins with the client or commissioning body conveying to the designer their ideas on how a scheme is to function. As discussed in Chapter 1, the practice today is usually to draw up a program or list of user requirements — the *brief*. This practice is not as automatic as it might appear. Many designs are based on a combination of requirements formulated beforehand and various demands and wishes regarded as so generally applicable as to be taken for granted.

Differentiated use

Influenced by technological and social developments such as division of labor, industrialization and increased mobility, cities and buildings have over the centuries commanded increasingly differentiated spaces to accommodate new activities. This is a process that is still unfolding today. The second half of the twentieth century is full of examples of such new activities: watching television, working at a computer or using a sauna are just three random cases of activities brought about by technological discoveries or social change.

Other acts have lost their original meaning. Whereas in earlier times producing fire was a laborious if important occupation, to turn on a gas heater or electric cooker these days is little more than a routine flick of the wrist. Some actions have undergone a shift in meaning. For instance, in Jewish tradition boiling milk and cooking meat separately was originally a question of hygiene; they could easily become contaminated in the hot desert climate. In our own century this custom has lost that particular meaning with the advent of refrigeration and air conditioning. Yet it is still done to this day, being part of the history and identity of a community. The act has gained a *ritual* significance.

Interpreting use demands in the design

The place an activity occupies in the context of society is subject to change over time. Such change is invariably of consequence for the shape of the space in which these activities occur. Space design is not just a case of translating social requirements into use; it involves the designer's interpretation of these requirements. In the following paragraphs we will be using examples from history to examine the relationship between designing, interpreting and social practice.

This modest journey through time is divided into three parts. The first discusses projects from before 1900, a period largely preceding the Industrial Revolution. Part two deals with the period between 1900 and 1945, a time span which saw the emergence of Western mass society and in which "functionalism" was a major architectural stream. The third part uses designs to examine how architects, urban planners and landscape architects have responded since 1945 to the rapidly changing needs of the highly developed societies in Western Europe and North America. This tripartition should not be taken too rigidly, however. Ideas about functional organization like those postulated by architects in the 1920s weren't born overnight, but were the outcome of a much longer process. A nineteenth-century example demonstrates that ideas about how best to configure spaces in a house influenced designing from early on, long before the "functionalist" architects committed their daylight indicators to paper.

3.2 Aspects of use prior to 1900

In the history of space design in Europe, the organization of society and the role of the individual within it have provided keys to an understanding of design. This also holds true for the Roman civilization; consider the spatial interventions carried out in large areas of Europe and around the Mediterranean under Roman rule. The Roman Empire was not just the product of one city-state's desires for expansion. Over time it became increasingly a political body that comprised the entire world as it was known then, and which bound its citizens by guarantees of safety and peace, the Pax Romana. Planning interventions—especially the laying out of an infrastructure of roads, aqueducts and defense works, the draining and parcelling of farmland and the founding of new cities—played a decisive role in achieving that aim. Such operations enabled Rome to keep order across a vast region and to evolve a flourishing urban culture.

Strict rules for setting up Roman colonial settlements issued from considerations as much practical as religious. The shape of these cities was usually rectangular. Their circumference was fixed at a ceremony in which the priest described by walking the line the city wall was to follow. Contrary to the Greek notions about how a city should be laid out (see Miletus in Chapter 2), the Roman idea of order embraced every facet. It had to involve all levels — the rectilinear layout of streets, the parcelling of farmland, the simple organization within the city walls, even the internal subdivision of private houses. The same spatial relationships were striven for at all these levels, relationships that in turn were an expression of the cosmic order of the gods.

Thus, the cities were laid out in a checkerboard pattern. Two main streets—the "cardo" running north–south and the "decumanus" east–west— dictated the alignment of the entire city grid. The point where these main streets intersected, preferably in the middle of the city, gave the position of the city center. At this intersection stood the forum and the temples, the other civic buildings often being arranged along the two main streets. Lining these streets were shops reached from arcades and colonnades. That blueprint was as

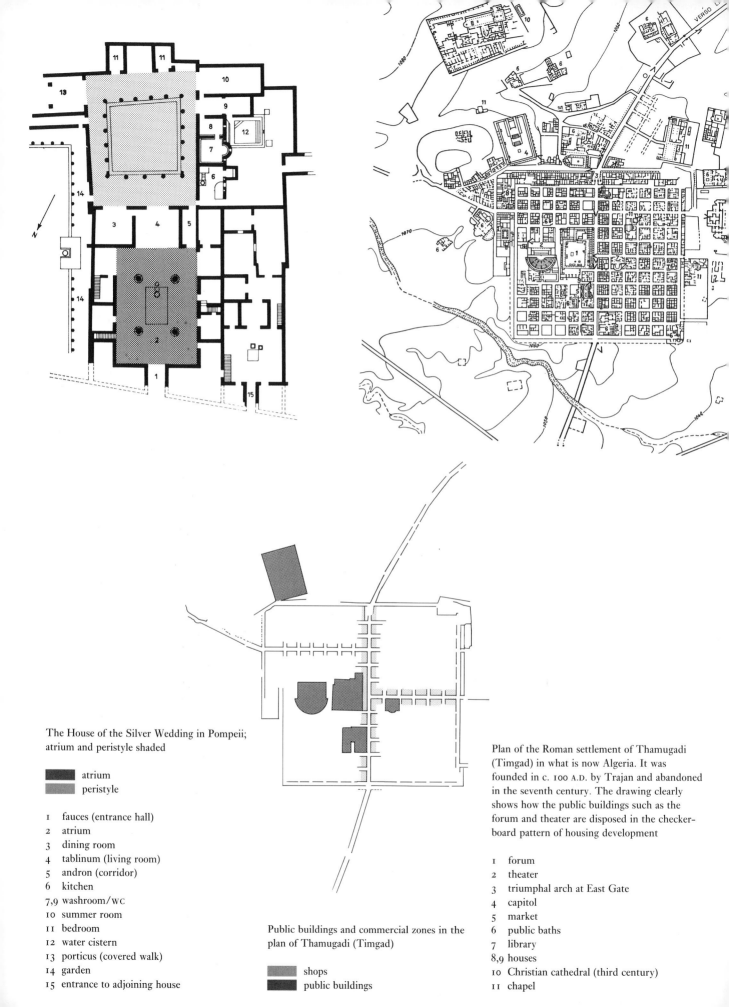

The House of the Silver Wedding in Pompeii;
atrium and peristyle shaded

- ▓ atrium
- ▓ peristyle

1 fauces (entrance hall)
2 atrium
3 dining room
4 tablinum (living room)
5 andron (corridor)
6 kitchen
7,9 washroom/wc
10 summer room
11 bedroom
12 water cistern
13 porticus (covered walk)
14 garden
15 entrance to adjoining house

Public buildings and commercial zones in the
plan of Thamugadi (Timgad)

- ▓ shops
- ▓ public buildings

Plan of the Roman settlement of Thamugadi
(Timgad) in what is now Algeria. It was
founded in c. 100 A.D. by Trajan and abandoned
in the seventh century. The drawing clearly
shows how the public buildings such as the
forum and theater are disposed in the checkerboard pattern of housing development

1 forum
2 theater
3 triumphal arch at East Gate
4 capitol
5 market
6 public baths
7 library
8,9 houses
10 Christian cathedral (third century)
11 chapel

Transitions between public and private

The layout of streets, like the use of colonnades, is a good illustration of the great interest the Romans took in effecting gradual transitions between one urban territory and the next. Vitruvius devotes an extensive passage to the ways of preventing unhealthy and cold winds from blowing down the streets, and the chronicler Libanius who in about 360 A.D. described several Roman cities in Asia Minor, emphasizes in his report the gradual transitions between individual houses, civic buildings and the street space. "As you walk along them [the main roads] you find a succession of private houses with public buildings distributed among them at intervals, here a temple, there a bath establishment, at such distances that they are handy for each quarter and in each case the entrance is in the colonnade. What does that mean, and what is the bearing of this lengthy description? Well, it seems to me that the pleasantest, yes, and most profitable side of city life is society and human intercourse, and that, by Zeus, is truly a city where these are found."[2] This gradual transition between city and individual dwelling, between public and private, seems also to have been the ruling principle for organizing the "domus," the house of the well-to-do Roman citizen.

Perhaps we should first look briefly at the origin of the word "private." It derives from the Latin verb "privare," meaning to deprive of. For the Romans, the private realm was the space of which society at large was deprived. For them space was initially common property from which individuals could partition off small units for their own needs. The traditional Roman city house was an almost literal translation of this idea. Vitruvius describes it thus: "We must… consider the principles on which should be constructed those apartments in private houses which are meant for the householders themselves, and those which are to be shared in common with outsiders. The private rooms are those into which nobody has the right to enter without an invitation, such as bedrooms, dining rooms, bathrooms, and all others used for the like purposes. The common are those which any of the

people have a perfect right to enter, even without an invitation: that is, entrance courts, cavaedia, peristyles, and all intended for the like purpose.'[3]

The original Roman city house as it existed from the fourth century B.C. onwards throughout Central Italy, consisted of no more than a handful of small rooms clustered around a larger, open-roofed space, the "atrium." In the atrium was a domestic altar, the fireplace and dining table; the smaller rooms served as bedrooms, living rooms and storage space. Movement through the house was organized along a longitudinal axis. The visitor entered the atrium through the "fauces," a narrow passageway between the shops on the street. Behind the atrium lay a small walled garden reached by a passage.

From the second century B.C. on, this elementary principle of a central open space surrounded by rooms was extended at the rear with one or more "peristyles." These were large, similarly open garden rooms to which the family could withdraw. The peristyle began life as a space accessible to the public. This second large gathering space for the family can also be conceived, however, as an element that brought out more than before the private nature of the house. If the atrium conveyed to the outside world the tradition and social status of the family, the peristyle was an informal domestic space. Another result of the altered relationship between public and private was that the transition from house to street was formalized by introducing an entrance hall, the "vestibule.'

Representation and utility

The last example places the emphasis on the difference between public and private spaces. Other aspects are neglected as a result, such as the aligning of rooms with respect to the wind that Vitruvius writes about, or the position of the ancillary spaces —the kitchen, for instance.

In the next example, which takes us almost 1500 years closer to our own time, the focus is on quite another aspect. At the end of the fifteenth century the greatest source of income of the Venetian patricians shifted from overseas trade to farming on the mainland of the Veneto in northeast Italy. Most of this lowlying boggy area had just been conquered by Venice and required both pacifying and draining. The new ruling class of colonizing citizens needed outposts to proclaim abroad the new order as well as

Villa Emo, view through loggia pillars and along
axis bisecting farm lands

Villa Emo, broad steps and loggia of central
pavilion

facilitate control of the immense areas of farmland. These outposts took the shape of villas which other than, say, the country houses of the Florentine nobility and citizenry and in direct contrast with the Villa Rotonda described earlier, were not places for healthy rural diversion. In the villas of the Veneto the ideal of country life was confronted with the demands made by agricultural enterprise, namely an overview of the entire area and the visual presence of its new owner.[4] In these houses, there was greater emphasis on representation and the staging of practices that reflected the social status of the incumbents than on the distinction between public and private. These ideas show that activities, construction and architecture alike were organized in a deliberate move to express the new social balance.

The Villa Emo (1559–1565), designed by Andrea Palladio, consists of three parts, two of them wings housing the more utilitarian spaces. Here are the kitchen, wine cellar, stables for the horses and tool-sheds as well as rooms for storing grain and cages for the carrier pigeons used to communicate with the city of Venice, where the owner had his political obligations.

Yet the most striking part of the building is the central pavilion where the members of the owner's family lived when not in the city. This pavilion sits neatly on the axis several kilometers long that both bisects and accesses the estate. The central position of the residential block along this axis represents the relation of landowner to agrarian population as well as visualizes the unification of local and cosmic orders. Unlike the Roman town house, the central pavilion exhibits little difference between the publicly accessible and private zones. All spaces are representative reception areas and as such reflect the owner's social position. This holds most for the rooms set on the building's axis: the "loggia" (a colonnaded gallery) and the "sala" (main hall) entered in that order from a broad and extremely drawn-out flight of steps. The estate was managed from these rooms and the local population was received here. The other rooms in the pavilion have a representative character too, yet were used in a great many other ways—for dining, sleeping and so on.

Whereas the disposition of spaces in the ancient Roman town house brought with it the dichotomy

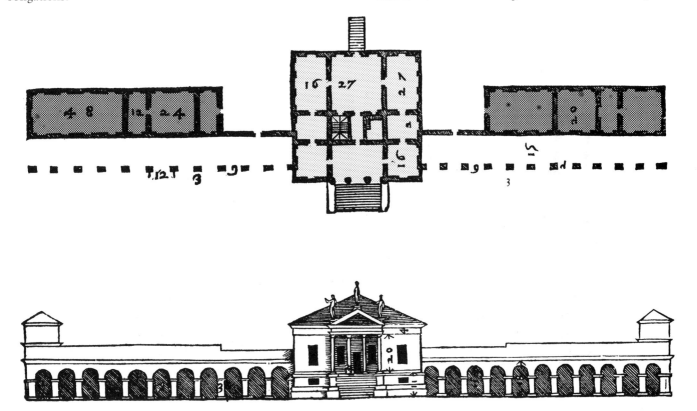

Andrea Palladio, Villa Emo (1559–1565).
Plan and elevation

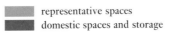

representative spaces
domestic spaces and storage

of a private zone and a ceremonial sequence of entering, Palladio's sixteenth-century villas commanded a representative program. This was expressed architecturally by organizing the building so that the domestic spaces were located in the wings hidden behind rows of pillars.

The city at the dawn of the new era

During the Middle Ages the European city underwent a slow but steady process of growth. Most European cities developed by the accretion of irregular extensions. The shape of the city was usually determined by the topography of the landscape. Urban activity underwent a similiar pattern of differentiation and organization, one that had been shaped by years of practice. Often this was paralleled by the social structure and division of labor in the urban community. Citizens were subdivided into professional groups: potters, tanners, drapers, turners, carpenters, and so forth. These distinctions and the activities pertaining to one or other group can still be found today in the names of streets. Workplaces that might have been a source of disturbance in the densely built-up cities were located on or beyond the periphery. In Amsterdam, the shipping companies could be found in the harbor area, a district at some distance from the center. The areas in which buildings for religion, city administration, discipline and education were concentrated constituted discrete elements in the city. Chapter 5, which examines the growth of medieval Amsterdam, includes several drawings that illustrate this process of splitting up urban activities.

This path of steady growth was radically disturbed from the fourteenth century on. For this various factors are to blame. The development of European trade, the breakthrough of the banking economy and from the sixteenth century the rise of overseas trade—all these brought about fundamental cultural and social change that would greatly affect the evolution of the European city.

In the previous chapter we examined the path taken by design through the Renaissance and early Baroque periods. We will now concentrate on the way activities in the period 1550–1650, whether new or reinterpreted, had an impact on urban form. Here, by way of illustration, we will look more closely at two examples that are paradigmatic of the developments in European countries: Rome, the hub

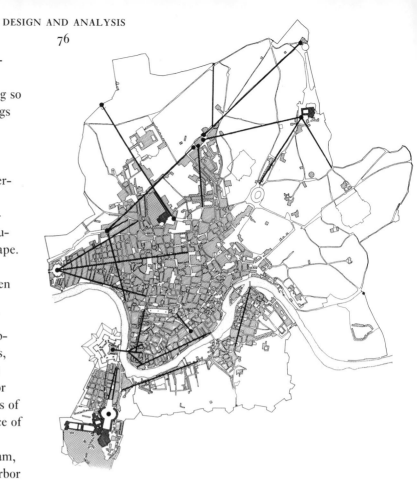

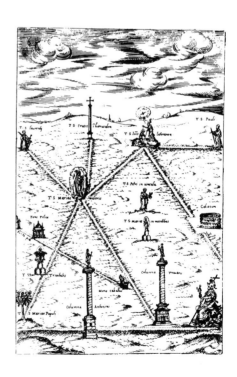

Rome, eighteenth-century city plan; the old roads and main streets laid out during the reign of Sixtus have been marked

Rome, drawing from 1588 showing the new connections between monumental buildings of the Counter-Reformation in the Catholic Church, and Amsterdam, the early bourgeois merchant city par excellence.

This tale of two cities shows that two distinct driving forces can have a decisive effect on city planning during one and the same period. But it will also show that the interventions and the means employed are directly related to these forces. To put it in the simplest terms: in Rome's case there were plans to reinstate through architecture and planning the authority of the Church, undermined as it had been by the Reformation. Amsterdam, by contrast, underwent a thorough transformation during the seventeenth century which would ultimately unify the aspect of use and the need for representation among the new urban upper classes.

Expressing church authority in the Holy City

When Pope Sixtus v assumed office in 1585, there was little left of the illustrious past of ancient Rome other than a handful of ruins and memories of better times. Since the aqueducts had fallen into disuse, the medieval city had been restricted to the area along the Tiber. The hills with the ancient "fora" and temples lay in waste save for a pilgrim church or two.

The plan embarked on during the pontificate of Sixtus (1585-1590) had a number of resolute aims. One was to create a new economic basis for the by then impoverished church state. This was effected by resuming irrigation of the hills and stimulating industry with a few well-aimed interventions. The most famous aspect of the plan, however, had quite another objective. By laying out an ingenious system of links between the seven major pilgrim churches, Sixtus and his successors made Rome what it still is today: the center of the Catholic Church.

The pope exploited certain existing elements. First of all, there were seven churches visited by pilgrims that lay scattered over the unbuilt area outside the medieval city though within the wall built by the emperor Aurelian in 271 B.C.

Another point of departure was an old *ceremonial custom*, the procession, which was reinterpreted in this context. In many cultures communal events are accompanied by processions of a religious or secular nature. This is an extremely ancient phenomenon, a story illustrated in a pageant sometimes involving actors and sometimes images carried in the procession. This pageant took the form of a linear movement between certain points in the city or its surroundings. Main protagonists, supernumeraries, spectators—all had a part to play in the public performance. This tradition reached back in Western civilization at least as far as antiquity, as can be observed in the architecture built to accompany such processions. At the Forum Romanum, for instance, we can still see the series of triumphal arches through which the returning victorious warriors passed. In the Middle Ages, mainly religious processions were transformed into routes, and these were exploited in the new plan for Rome.

Sixtus and his successors adopted a strategy in small stages. First, they positioned obelisks at key points and places of pilgrimage, as a common attribute. These included the entrance to the city at the Porta del Popolo, the church of Santa Maria Maggiore, the cathedral of St. John Lateran and St. Peter's. The obelisks, set as they were at an important locus in front of each building, together provided an as yet invisible network of points in the city lying on the pilgrims' way. In the next stage, this network was visually imprinted on the form of the city by joining the obelisks with a system of routes. Urban squares were subsequently laid in place around the obelisks. With these interventions the church secured for all time the open spaces within the walls which only later would become part of the city proper. As the new streets followed a straight line, the continuity of movement along them was visible to the pilgrim at all times. More than that, the new links were suited to a brand new mode of transport, the horse-drawn carriage.[5]

Sixtus v's plan was no haphazard pattern but a response predicated on use. The new system of routes served to channel the movements during processions from one place of devotion to the next. Major points of intersection between routes now combined with the dead-straight streets and the obelisks into a tight-knit, easily read system. The character of Rome had changed for good, and henceforth would remain in the hands of the Church.

Living and working in the mercantile city

In contrast to Rome, the development that Amsterdam would undergo during the seventeenth century did not spring from the will of a ruler. The driving force behind the process of change lay in Amsterdam's new role as center of commerce. Burgeoning port and commercial activities and the influx of refugees from the southern Netherlands, Spain and Portugal caused a dramatic population increase at the end of the sixteenth century. In 1585, work began on extending the city with three new canals, influenced by urban ideas from the Renaissance about beauty and geometric regularity. The medieval tradition had played a major part in shaping Amsterdam the mercantile town.[6] This tradition yielded the smallest built component of the new extension: long deep plots much like those in the older parts of town were laid out along the new canals.

The evolution of the canal house shows clearly how the wishes and hopes of the rising merchant class were translated into the floor plans and the architecture of these dwelling houses.

At the dawn of the seventeenth century the type of town house being built in Amsterdam still adhered to the medieval tradition. Most were very simple in design, and also served as warehouses and shops. The long, narrow shape of plot suggested an organization whereby the front section of the house (the "voorhuis") contained the business premises and the back section (the "achterhuis") the living quarters. Sometimes the latter was raised up on a basement. Size of the plot permitting, a second "achterhuis" was often built on at the rear for additional living or storage space. The upper stories of the "voorhuis"—usually no more than two or three above the ground floor—could be used for work or storage as well as dwelling. The dividing line between living and working was anything but sharply demarcated and made its way through the middle of the house.

As the prosperity of the new republic grew, the new urban elite came to expect a domicile befitting from and reflecting its recently acquired status. As a result, the floor plan of the merchant house evolved in leaps and bounds throughout the seventeenth century. The house built in 1639 on Keizersgracht to Philips Vingboons' design is a typical example of the ever greater distinction drawn between functions, in which can be seen the physical division into dwelling and work (the business). In the tall "voorhuis" is a small room separated off for the manager

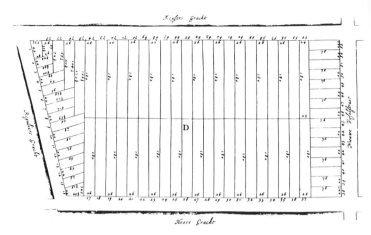

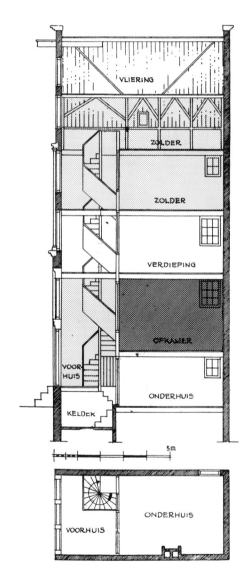

Amsterdam, drawing of plots laid out between two canals

Amsterdam, section through a typical early seventeenth-century canal house

working
dwelling

to do the administration undisturbed, the side-room or comptoir (office). The "achterhuis" is reached along a new element, the corridor. This *circulation space* skirts the interior court, delivering light into the living quarters at the rear and the upper stories of the front section. The internal subdivision by function can be clearly read in the façade. The canal house's double-height front space and characteristic lifting beam are a reminder of its commercial origins.

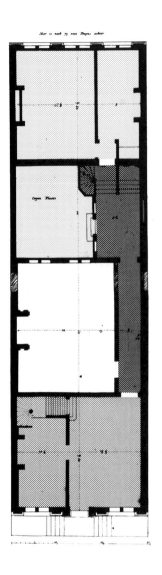

Philips Vingboons, house at Keizersgracht 319 in Amsterdam (1639), elevation and plan in original state. The plan clearly shows the office as a distinct, slightly raised space in the front section of the house

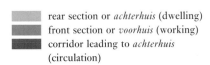

rear section or *achterhuis* (dwelling)
front section or *voorhuis* (working)
corridor leading to *achterhuis* (circulation)

Pilot schemes for work and dwelling

In 1594 the Dutch engineer Simon Stevin wrote *Van de oirdening der steden*, a treatise expounding the first and most important town planning theory posited in the Dutch language. In it Stevin also proposes a number of ideal diagrams of a mercantile town with an inland harbor that accurately reflect the way cities really were used at century's end. At the same time the diagrams recall plans for ideal cities drawn up before then, particularly in Italy. Stevin's diagram is predicated on function and on the Dutch town as it existed at the end of the fifteenth century. It abandons the idea of a radial or centralized configuration, a feature of most Italian ideal-city plans. This was a logical step in that in Dutch mercantile towns commerce occupied a far more important place than the question of defense. Rather than being radially disposed, his diagram links residential and commercial buildings to three canals that slice lengthwise through the town. Square to this system of canals is a zone reserved for communal spaces and buildings for administration, education and commerce. Here are the principal market, the church, the school, the poorhouse and—on the very edge—the royal court. All other public facilities serving the quarters of the town are set on four squares distributed evenly across the town and doubling as specialized markets.[7]

In its characteristic simplicity, Stevin's schema has been of seminal influence on urban expansions in the Netherlands and Northwest Europe in general. This is because it responded to the functional requirements of the new larger-scale commercial networks of the seventeenth century and provided a clear framework allotting a logical place to major urban activities. Moreover, the diagram can be extended in all directions and is eminently suited to mercantile towns, one of whose properties is expansion. Not only important because of the influence it has had on town planning practice, the treatise gives us a picture of changing ideas on the disposition of functions in the seventeenth-century town.

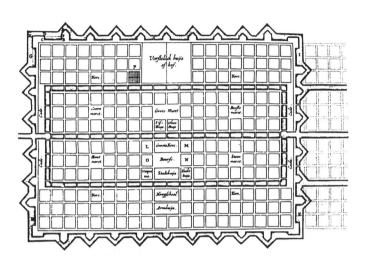

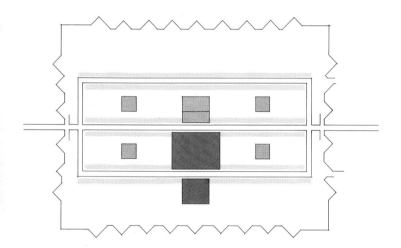

Simon Stevin, diagram of a mercantile town (from *Van de oirdening der steden*)

Functional organization of the town

commerce
markets
civic buildings

Rooms versus circulation

The villas of Andrea Palladio were a major source of inspiration for architects in other European countries. England was a particular case in point; there the old landed gentry and the new class of affluent merchants became intermixed in the seventeenth and eighteenth centuries. The rise of this new social group ran parallel to the emergence of a new building type that would prove of seminal influence on English architecture during the next three centuries: the country house.

Proceeding from what were then "modern" classic examples and Old English internal arrangements, the country house underwent a major change in the seventeenth century. If the northern Italian villas exhibited no clear-cut subdivision into public and private rooms, the English country houses were informed by ideas on different degrees of "publicness." As can clearly be seen in the plans of the Villa Emo and the Coleshill House designed by Pratt in 1650, the English made a distinction between rooms belonging to the house-owners and the circulation space. Other than in the sixteenth-century Italian villas and much like Vingboons' canal houses the separation into rooms was integral to the English country house. A distinction was made between servants and the owner's family and this was expressed in the spatial layout. The architect himself posited that the central full-length corridor was there to prevent an occupied room from being disrupted by people using it as a way through. And in the rest of the house the servants, Pratt continues, should not be seen performing their duties.[8]

Thus arose a far more differentiated floor plan of corridors and rooms. In the seventeenth century these rooms—as in Palladio's villas—were still closely interlinked, but later they achieved greater independence to ultimately become accessible only from a corridor. The spaces became more and more like rooms in the present-day sense, with the result that each was increasingly intended for a particular activity. Thus, the typical English country house emerged in the eighteenth and nineteenth century: a large rural residence the names of whose rooms already tell us they were for one kind of use only. A house of this type is a sum of rooms for specific activities and ambiences dictated by *convention*: the dining room, the breakfast room, the library—and the drawing (originally withdrawing) room for the ladies to retreat to from the smokescreen produced by the men.

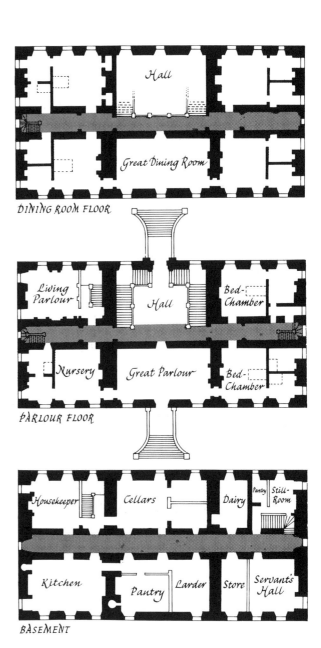

Roger Pratt, floor plans of Coleshill House (1650)

▨ corridor

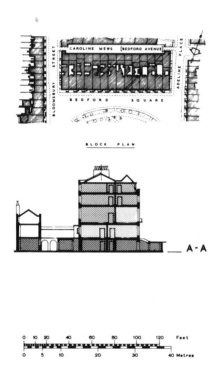

BLOCK PLAN

A-A

0 10 20 40 60 80 100 120 Feet

0 5 10 20 30 40 Metres

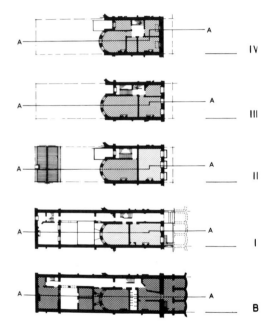

London (Bloomsbury), Bedford Square (1775–1780), south elevation. The plans and sections of one of the houses show the internal organization of a typical London townhouse for the well-to-do citizen of the eighteenth century. The basement extending below the pavement of the square contains the kitchen, the cellars and servants' quarters. The dining room was usually on the ground floor. The first floor is taller than the others and contains the drawing room which overlooks the street. The rest of the house is given over to bedrooms

representative living rooms
bedrooms
domestic rooms

Standardization and specification

In eighteenth-century English town houses, the same changes are observable in the relation between dwelling and circulation areas as in the villas of Palladio. At this time too, these houses clearly exhibit another tendency which was to gain in strength during the next two centuries. Town houses in London, Bath or Edinburgh were commissioned not by individuals but by building contractors who built for a market, and indeed often speculated with these houses. The new houses had to satisfy generally accepted expectations; they could no longer be geared to individual users because at the time of building it was often not known who the occupants would be. The upshot was a greater tendency towards uniformity and *standardization* than in the case of the large freestanding house. The usability of a house was gauged by the presence there of specific, differing spaces for the different activities associated by a complicated system of conventions with the social status of the occupants.

These facts are evident in the floor plans. Whereas in most of the earlier named examples of houses the floor plan consisted of rooms without any further designation of function, in the English town house the rooms were not only explicitly named but provided with dimensions stipulated by convention. The point of departure of building for a *market of anonymous buyers*—and users—compelled builders (from now on building *contractors* and *developers*) and architects to express dwelling pleasure or comfort in measurable terms and figures. The example of the English house shows clearly how requirements of usefulness and feasibility, fire regulations and the change in principals led to a new kind of dwelling.[9]

The building of large residential districts in London introduced to Europe the distinction between the City (the center of commerce) and the suburbs reserved for dwelling. This brought with it radical changes in the townscape. No longer possessing a clear boundary, the town gradually closed with its surroundings by way of the lower-rise and less dense development of the residential areas. The middle-class move from the city center coincided with its perceived lifestyle as a protected interior of homely warmth, kept apart from the rawness of urban reality. Interiors like these ushered in the notion of comfort. The German writer Walter Benjamin would later describe this development thus: "For the private individual, the dwelling space is now in opposition to the workplace. The first coincides with the interior. The office is complementary to this space for dwelling. In the office the individual takes reality into account. He now requires of the interior that it should sustain him in his illusion."[10] This development marked the beginnings of the residential district, a *monofunctional* area from which every type of disturbance is excluded.

Dwelling and comfort

In the nineteenth century the English ideas of comfort continued to be developed and refined. While industrial development in London and the other large cities generated new building tasks (stations, office buildings, factories and the like), the suburbs grew with the expansion of the railway network and the arrival of the underground. The demands made on dwelling comfort by the rich citizens and the middle class expanded likewise; still more facilities were invented to make home life more amenable. Dwelling comfort thus became a subject of study for architects.

Exemplary in this respect are the sunlighting diagrams made by the architect Charles Voysey at the beginning of this century. In them, Voysey indicates how the various activities taking place in the home could best be arranged in the interests of *optimum sunshine*. One design of his in which Voysey exploited the diagrams was the celebrated country house in the Lake District. The sunlighting and the view of one of England's most famous lakes, Lake Windermere, spawned a division into dwelling spaces with a fine prospect, and a service wing. The bipartition is expressed in the house's arrangement as two adjoining volumes, in which the service wing occupies a position subordinate to that of the volume containing the residence.[11]

3.3 Functionalism

With the turbulent development of the industrial metropolis in the nineteenth century, housing became a social problem. Large groups of people had to be given accommodation in a short space of time.

Until then, house-builders had fallen back on a general consensus on functionality. Moreover, the tasks such as those in our examples were straightforward, and often involved providing single solutions for wealthy individuals. This changed in the nineteenth century, and large estates of rapidly erected unsanitary dwellings were ample proof of this change. As the means for housing the industrial worker were limited, all attention became focused on what was strictly necessary and *functional*.

Separating the functions

The rise in the nineteenth century of the big industries and new forms of transport made new demands on the way cities were laid out. With the arrival of the railway, for example, there was a new mode of transport which could not simply be slotted into the existing urban fabric, but sliced through it instead. As industry increased in scale and non-residential business centres sprang up—another phenomenon first encountered in London—these dictated the appearance of this and other cities in Europe and North America. Gradually the industrial areas and commercial centers became separated from the residential districts. This development was largely due to market mechanisms; the cost of land in the commercial centers rose so steeply that few were in a position to live in these areas.

After 1850 the quality of housing came in for increasing concern in the wake of epidemics that included cholera and tuberculosis. In a bid to solve the problem of *hygienic* residential areas for the urban masses, the Modern architects united in CIAM (Congrès Internationaux d'Architecture Moderne) advocated a distinction between areas for living and working. This point of departure was reworded and systemized by Le Corbusier in the *Athens Charter* (1933) in which he set down the strict division into *Dwelling*, *Work*, *Recreation* and *Transportation* as the objective of urban planning.

In 1935 Amsterdam's physical planning agency led by Cornelis van Eesteren drew up a General

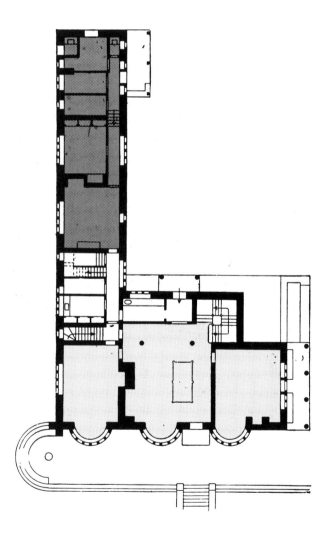

Sunlighting diagram

Charles Voysey, house on Lake Windermere (1908). Plan

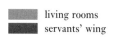
living rooms
servants' wing

Extension Plan (AUP) based entirely on the CIAM proposals. The scheme took as its starting point the calculated future growth of Amsterdam. This growth was accommodated by developing a number of suburbs separated from one another by green zones. Each residential area had its own daily facilities directly derived from the function of dwelling; there was no commercial center there. It was assumed that the male residents worked elsewhere in the city, in the new western docks, for example.

Recreational areas such as Sloterplas and the Amsterdamse Bos were an important element of the plan. Both continue the tradition of the so-called public parks, parks in which recreational use plays a special part in the design. Thus the Amsterdamse Bos includes a rowing course, an aquatic sports center, a playground, an open-air theater, a bridle-path and a farm.

Functional relations and movement

Taking their cue from American scientists such as F.W. Taylor, the originator of scientific management, the functionalist architects made investigations in the 1920s into how to divide up a floor plan to give it maximum objectivity. But they took things a step further. Not only did they organize functions; they set out to determine the *minimum dimensions necessary*. Form and function were one and the same, they declared, or rather the function produced the form, and the old principles were no longer applicable. "Form follows function," the credo of the American architect Louis Sullivan, long served as a catchy slogan.[12] This body of ideas crops up in the approach taken by Grete Schütte-Lihotzky, the designer of the "Frankfurter Küche" (1926), a model kitchen for social housing. She conceived her design as a *machine*. Her ideas issued from the above supposition that a function implies a form. In her kitchen all actions were predetermined and developed out of ergonomic requirements.[13] *Ergonomics* is the study into the most healthy and least tiring postures for the human body in different activities. This research developed during the quest for efficient production techniques in industry but was soon seized upon by architects and translated into the shape of the space. The surface needed for a prescribed activity can thus be defined quantitatively. Activities serving a common aim, such as the preparation of food, are brought together in functions

and described in quantitative terms. It is then possible to fix beforehand the requirements for use in a (functional) program. Design research subsequently turns to the size and position of the space these activities demand.

Gustave Doré, impression of a working class area in nineteenth-century London

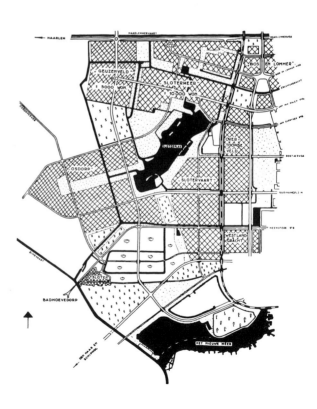

Amsterdam, General Extension Plan
(AUP, 1935)

Amsterdam-West, detail of AUP

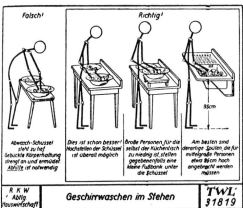

III. Küchen und Hauswirtschaft.

1. Die Küche:

In allen Wohnungen ist die sogenannte **Frankfurter Küche** von Frau Architekt Schütte-Lihotzky mit einigen Variationen eingebaut worden (Typ in Bild 25, Ansichten in Bild 26–29).

Bild 25. Frankfurter Küche.

Teil-Abdruck von einem Frankfurter Normenblatt. Die Küche ist 1,87 m × 3,44 m groß und enthält:

1 = Herd mit einer Abstellplatte.
2 = Schubladen für Mehl und Salz.
3 = Kochkiste.
4 = Schubladen für größere Vorräte.
5 = Heizkörper.
6 = Gewürzgestell.
7 = Speiseschrank.
8 = Tisch mit Rinne für Küchenabfälle.
9 = Abtropfbrett.
10 = Tellerabtropfgestell.
11 = Zweiteiliges Spülbecken.
12 = Vorratsschrank.
13 = Geschirrschrank.
14 = Topfschrank.
15 = Müll- und Besenschrank.
16 = Schiebelampe.
17 = Bügelbrett.

Alle Möbel stehen auf 10 cm hohem Betonsockel, mit Platten bekleidet, der 4 cm zurückspringt.

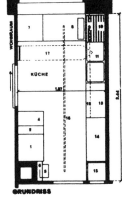

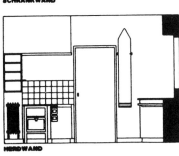

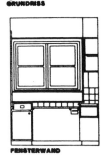

Illustrations of ergonomic studies into energy consumed during domestic activities

Frankfurter Küche (Grete Schütte-Lihotsky, 1926)

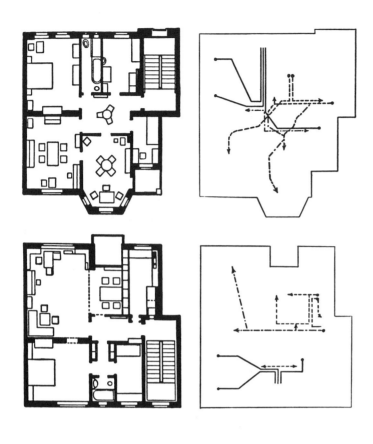

Day and night use

The above studies into the most functional of kitchens illuminate just one aspect of mass housing. Other researchers have tried to map out even more systematically the activities that take place day in day out in a house. A familiar example is the series of diagrams made by Alexander Klein of how a house is used. Klein proceeds from the fact that movements and activities can be distinguished depending on whether they occur by day or by night. By fixing exactly when particular actions take place, he hoped to be able to say something about the bare minimum of space required. An example that illustrates this approach well is the scheme J.H. van den Broek submitted in 1935 to the influential competition for low-cost workers" dwellings. The use is stipulated with great precision, even for different times of the day. The various functional units, living room and bedrooms, kitchen and bathroom/WC are grouped with a maximum objectivity. However, this objectivity only pertains if the space is used as the designer envisaged it.[14]

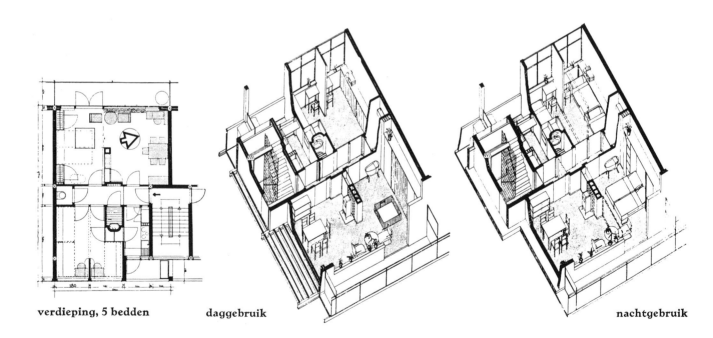

verdieping, 5 bedden   **daggebruik**   **nachtgebruik**

Studies of lines of movement in a traditional and a modern plan (Alexander Klein, 1931)

J.H. van den Broek, entry to competition for low-cost workers' housing (1935). Furnished floor plan

J.H. van den Broek, entry to competition for low-cost workers' housing. Isometric drawings showing day and night use

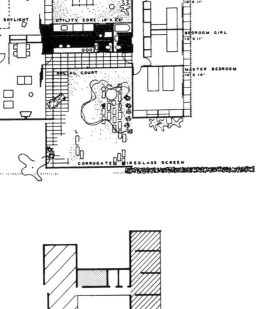

The utility core

During and immediately after World War II in America, the country where Taylor did his research, architects began designing literal "machines à habiter." A major point of departure in doing so was that such houses generally contain facilities (say for cooking and ablutions) whose placement is dictated by pipes and ducts. Against these *servant* spaces are set a number of *served* living rooms or bedrooms whose form is much less fixed. The difference between servant and served informs the design made by J. and N. Fletcher in 1945. A mechanical or utility core containing the requisite services sits literally in the center of the house which has everything of a diagram of functions come to life.

The prefabricated bathroom that Buckminster Fuller designed in 1938 is arguably the most extreme example of a design concept in which *product rationalization* and ergonomics are enlisted to determine the shape of part of a building. The off-the-peg unit is calculated exactly in accordance with the space assumed necessary and can be transported to any site without difficulty.

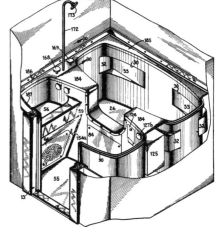

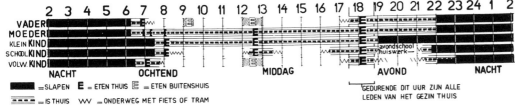

J. and N. Fletcher, plan of core-house (1946)

Core-house, relationships and functional organization
Light hatching: living rooms
dark hatching: bedrooms
services

Mart Stam, diagram of daily schedule per family member (1935)

Buckminster Fuller, prefabricated bathroom (1938)

Design research and practice after World War II

After the Second World War the ideas of the functionalist avant-garde became more part and parcel of general building practice. This certainly held for North America when, during Roosevelt's presidency, government plans for housing large sections of the population were drawn up for the first time. Yet the ideas on mass housing and urban planning developed by prewar architects were of far more lasting influence on developments in Western Europe. In Scandinavia, Great Britain, West Germany (as it was then) and the Netherlands in particular, these ideas and the quest for the conditions for an "Existenzminimum" were crucially important for the practical task of rebuilding those countries.

Some years before the war the German architect and engineer Ernst Neufert published a weighty volume entitled *Bauentwurfslehre* (1936). This book, a veritable treasure trove of information on the surface areas necessary for every imaginable daily activity, grew during the fifties into a standard opus still consulted today by many architectural practices. Neufert and his team measured everything, from the dimensions of the smallest dovecote and the most efficient hotel room to the measurements necessary for optimum circulation in a large indoor car park. Permeating the *Bauentwurfslehre* is the idea that thorough analysis of a building's functions is almost certain to produce an objective design. Though other writers may have worded this optimistic technocratic train of thought along more visionary lines, Neufert's book has been of inestimable influence on the way architects think. The functionalist body of ideas also made inroads into the *laws* and *standards* set by government such as the "matjes," the minimum surface areas in force in Dutch social housing.

To solve the problem of mass reconstruction, a prodigious quantity of research was done into maximizing the design, mutedly taking its cue from functional requirements. Also of growing influence on design during the fifties and sixties were the social and natural sciences. Decision-making mechanisms and maximizing processes had been investigated before then as part of the war effort, and this continued into peacetime. The design was now postulated as an arrangement in three dimensions that could be reproduced in strictly empirical and rational models. Form was no longer the self-sufficient category it had been; thinking in forms prevented designers from adopting a purely scientific attitude untrammelled by tradition or personal sentiment. We can include in this development the work of Christopher Alexander, who brought in new techniques from mathematics and computer science to attain an abstraction of traditional architectural concepts. The hypothesis behind this line of thought was that kitchen, bedroom, garden and the like evoked too rigid a picture that ruled out all but a predisposed attitude and made it impossible to make a "pure" analysis. Thus, in his book *Notes on the Synthesis of Form*, Alexander sets out to find a generally applicable approach to solving design problems. A design problem he defines as the "requirements which have to be met.'[15] Between these requirements, he asserts, are interrelationships that make them difficult to fulfill. Alexander introduces scientific methods to trace and then analyze these relationships, so that the structure of the problem is brought out and the solution presents itself logically.

3.4 The postwar period

While Alexander proceeded from the principle that a purely scientific analysis of human needs and activities, seasoned with psychology and experiential learning, can produce a good design, this technocratic optimism would be criticized in the period following 1950. The stinging criticism of younger CIAM recruits such as Aldo van Eyck and Peter and Alison Smithson was directly mainly at the blind faith in progress harbored by the inheritors of prewar functionalism. Van Eyck would write: "They (the 'modern' architects of the postwar reconstruction—ed.) have put their aspirations for social reform on a par with architecture and have irreversibly subjugated architecture to their rational way of thinking…They have wanted to tune the false notes in the scale of life and remove the notes they didn't want to hear. But there is something wrong with the way they are going about it, as too many notes have been removed and the rest are all tuned the same."[16] The stance adopted by the functionalists of postwar reconstruction reduced space design to a machine geared to progress though with no regard for man's less quantifiable needs.

The question of how to relate the use and form of a scheme resurfaced and has been with us ever since as a key issue in the discourse among architects and between them and the public. Today, it is impossible to nail down the exact nature of this relationship. The following examples look at two lines of approach variously followed by postwar designers. On the one hand, they kept trying to put into perspective the obsessive nature of a "pristine" functional order by appealing to flexibility. On the other, they regarded researching the cultural context of an activity to be one of the points of application from which to reinterpret, rework and exploit the functional program.

Dutch housing standards (1944)

The universality of use

An eloquent example of just such a search for the meaning of human activity is the work of the American architect Louis Kahn (1901–1974). Kahn rejected the idea that to objectively organize functions was enough in itself to produce a meaningful building. He tried to transform the program of a building into an *essence* which he called "the building's will to exist." He put this idea powerfully into words in his text "Order is" of 1960. It includes the following:

"The nature of space reflects what it wants to be
Is the auditorium a Stradivarius or is it an ear
Is the auditorium a creative instrument
keyed to Bach or Bartok
played by the conductor
or is it a convention hall?
In the nature of space is the spirit and the will to
    exist in a certain way
Design must closely follow that will"[17]

Kahn distills the task of designing a building into an archetypal category of human activities. These include the workplace, the study, the house, the street and the gathering space. Against these "served" spaces where daily life is enacted he pits the "servant" spaces—the washroom, plant rooms and the like. This distinction is crucial to interpreting the plan. In Kahn's view the building's "will"—in functionalist terms, the essence of the program— together with that of the building material, generates a form. What at first glance seems a refining of the ideas of the functionalists he interprets in such a way as to engender a modus operandi almost diametrically opposed to theirs. The essence of the program not only reflects that which is required for efficient use but resonates with the deepest desires and wishes of people for freedom and security. An example of this train of thought is the idea that the servant spaces "demand" a cylindrical form and that the served should be rectangular.

In his design for the Salk Institute at La Jolla, California, Kahn pushes this quest for the essence of the task into the very heart of the building program. The institute subdivides into three complexes, each serving a principal aspect of the research institute: the private dwelling sector, the semi-public buildings of the research laboratories and the publically accessible Salk meeting center. In the design, these three complexes of buildings (the meeting center was never built) are distributed across the site so that movement from one to the other necessitates passing through the research sector. The prominent place accorded to both dwelling and meeting complexes, reviewing each other across the expanse like two medieval castles, impresses on every visitor that the research sector is in no way the dominant element. The impression, if anything, is that the designer wished to inform the scientists that their research work is only part of a larger social entity and indeed should take up a servant position as much towards the community as towards the individual members of that community.

In the research building itself the "servant" spaces (in this case the not inconsiderable utilities) are made subordinate to the "served" laboratory area. Nonetheless they are, as in so many of Kahn's buildings, highly articulated and resolutely present. On this occasion he achieved this by integrating them with the structure, the subject of the next chapter. This integration process generates above each laboratory level a solid services floor whose height is specified by the "vierendeel" system of open girders comprising it. The vierendeel spans the entire laboratory, leaving below it a "served" space utterly flexible as to internal subdivision.

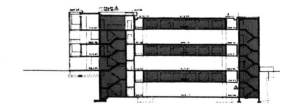

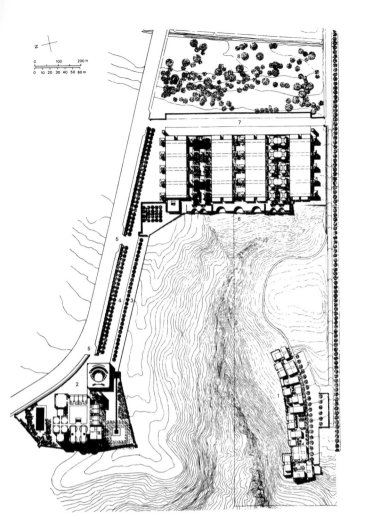

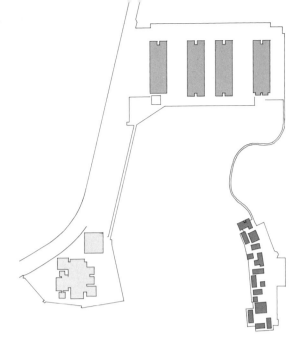

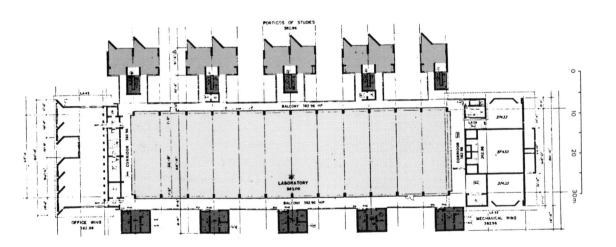

Louis Kahn, Salk Institute, La Jolla, California
(1959–1965). Plan of the original design including residential village, laboratory complex amd
meeting center

Salk Institute, plan and section of laboratory
    laboratory space
    study cells
    stairs and services

Salk Institute, the three main sectors
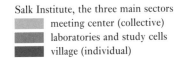
    meeting center (collective)
    laboratories and study cells
    village (individual)

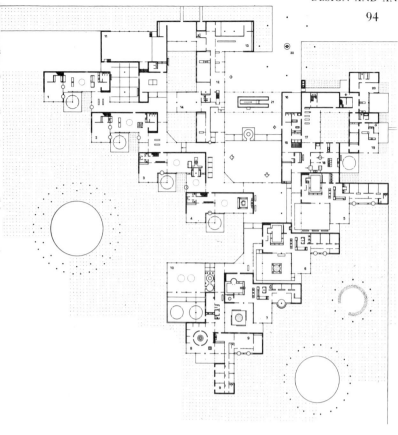

Twin phenomena

One of the most outspoken critics of dogmatic functionalism as it manifested itself in the fifties was the architect Aldo van Eyck. In those years he was one of the young members of CIAM who would later achieve fame as Team X. In his writings and buildings he attempted very early on to overcome the one-dimensional, all too clear-cut approach propagated by the functionalists.

In the Orphanage in Amsterdam (1959) Van Eyck designed a configuration of *places* that were at once contained and overlapping. What concerned Van Eyck in this building was the relationship between opposites or *twin phenomena*: open–closed, inside–outside, small–big, much–little, many–few. It was his aim that each unit should function autonomously yet also as part of the larger unit containing it. Van Eyck considered the unbroken relationship between components—or "isolated functions" as this was construed by the CIAM architects—to be as important as the components themselves. By laying stress on these relationships and on that between activities and built form he succeeded in making every such space a "place" with more than one meaning. Van Eyck uses the term *polyvalence* to denote that each spatial element carries two or more meanings that can be perceived simultaneously.

A good example of how he puts this into practice is the entry zone to the orphanage. The visitor passes beneath a raised wing of the building which leads him to a loggia. A minor modification in the paving pattern and two low stair treads announce the building proper. These gestures serve to demarcate and give form to the space between the Orphanage and the outside world. The transition between exterior and interior is softened further by a semi-public hall beyond the main entrance that beckons to the world outside yet simultaneously makes clear to the visitor that he is entering a children's world. The entire building then can be regarded as a series of transitions that ultimately lead to the fully contained dormitories on the upper level. The space forms add to the impact of these sequences. A limited number of architectural elements fix the building's form: dome-like roofs, circular roof lights and partition walls of brick and glass in many variations but all set in an orthogonal pattern. These together with the concrete stairs, differences in floor level and mirrors at unexpected

Aldo van Eyck, Orphanage, Amsterdam (1959).
Plan

Orphanage, entrance court with access to cycle shed

places, construct a complex system of polyvalent spaces intended to encourage children to appropriate every corner of the building for their own ends.

Scenarios of use

In their designs Kahn and Van Eyck seem on each occasion to be in search of deeper meanings to the activities of everyday life. They allude to the universal, timeless quality of these activities, referring us to archetypical or historic examples in architecture. The writings of Van Eyck in particular often describe the relation between built form and daily rituals as these occur in non-Western societies to draw attention to the ceremonial or ritual nature of what might seem purely objective activities in Western society. This emphasis on the cultural significance of an act allies him with designers who at first sight seem headed in quite another direction, Bernard Tschumi, for example, or Rem Koolhaas. If Van Eyck looks to the universal meaning of an act, Tschumi and Koolhaas are mainly concerned with questioning blind acceptance of a given function. To this end they resort to techniques such as those developed in Russian theater and film in the twenties by directors like Eisenstein and Meyerhold. In the work of these two men everyday acts not that exceptional in themselves were isolated, magnified, staged and linked by montage to other acts. The impact of such montages stems from the fact that the excerpts from life they contain at first seem quite unrelated, imbuing them with a new, dramatic meaning.

In *The Manhattan Transcripts*, a sequence of drawings made in 1981, Tschumi draws attention from this vantage point to the relation of architecture to use. Such concepts as confrontation and disruption—phenomena which strict functionalist analysis decreed should be barred—take center-stage in his argument. As he writes in his introduction to the Transcripts, "they aim to maintain these contradictions in a dynamic manner, in a new reciprocity and conflict," resorting to the above techniques used by Eisenstein. In a proeess of *defamiliarization* he draws new and surprising parallels between fragments which, though strange and forced to the unfocused eye, ultimately reveal once more the all too familiar patterns. Tschumi describes his modus operandi thus: "By going beyond the conventional definition of use, the *Transcripts* use their tentative format to explore unlikely confrontations."[18]

In the mid-eighties Rem Koolhaas entered —as did Tschumi—a large-scale competition for a new park on a former slaughterhouse site in Paris, the Parc de la Villette. Koolhaas's design takes a planning tool wielded by the functionalists —zoning—and reinterprets it. The impact of this strategy is that it brings into view a tool that until then was never directly visible. This he does by introducing differences in hard surfaces and in planting. The zones of use are defined and visualized by clear dividing lines. Thus, the visitor has no trouble taking in more than one activity simultaneously, in that each has its own distinct visual attributes. The image conjured up by a particular use is underpinned by simple formal means; in this case these might be the differences between the grass of the sports field, the various types of hard surface and the red or green rubber floor of the training circuit. That belts designated for quite disparate activities are placed adjacently only adds to the dramatic effect. This allies Koolhaas with the world of film where the montage technique is used to present sequences of actions and observations as isolated events run in rapid succession.

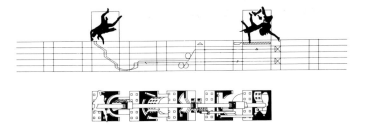

Bernard Tschumi, The Manhattan Transcripts (1981). Drawing of a sequence

Form and flexibility

In the developed western world, made dizzy by the sheer speed of technological and social advances, architects are increasingly confronted with a dilemma. The built environment has in itself a character of permanence, with the building material effectively fixing the use of a building or urban ensemble and creating conditions for the actions in and around it. Between the life span of a building and the transience typifying human activity there lies a fundamental contradiction. In the design process this contradiction can be termed the *unpredictability of the program* for the designer. Once a building or part of a city has been completed it will almost invariably be filled in other than is suggested in the brief. This unpredictability, diagnosed by certain functionalist architects as early as the thirties —take the mobile mechanical core discussed earlier in this chapter—has led in some areas of design to demands for a greater flexibility in use.

The term flexibility presupposes a number of objectives. First, the placement of the material should not obstruct future modifications in use. In addition, the issue of recycling existing built structures—in view of the desire for durability in consumer products—has become increasingly relevant in the last decades and is now often a consideration when designing a new building or district.

This striving for flexibility can lead to a multiplicity of often wide-ranging solutions of which only a few have some bearing on our argument. Despite this diversity we can make out a number of principal lines. In this limited survey, three responses are particularly worth mentioning:
– the postponing of decisions on the placement of material until the last stage of the design process;
– applying standardized and therefore replaceable building elements;
– making a distinction between fixed (bearing) elements and replaceable ones.

These approaches are not mutually exclusive and can often be found together in one and the same project.

How the desire for flexibility is expressed and then translated into a design depends almost entirely on the nature of the task. For designing a building composed of large spaces (e.g. for industrial fairs and sporting events) flexibility means something quite different than it does when applied to housing. In the following sections, we will use this difference in internal arrangement to illustrate how various built works deal with this desire for flexibility.

Flexibility in housing

Flexibility is not a new theme in housing. The prewar avant-garde regarded freedom in use as a prime objective. Le Corbusier's plan libre can be seen as one of the early examples in which freedom of internal subdivision is achieved during the design process by quite deliberately drawing a distinction between the loadbearing structure and the wall partitions. The designer could then take decisions about the shape of rooms at a comparatively late stage, when the structure and the composition of the façade had in principle long been fixed.

Rietveld's Schröder House is a perfect example of an attempt to replace the coercive fixed division of the house with a flexible plan. Dwelling for Rietveld was a conscious act requiring an active attitude. This conviction underlies the arrangement of the living floor of the Schröder House. Each facet of dwelling—washing, sleeping, eating—requires making a choice; on each new occasion the

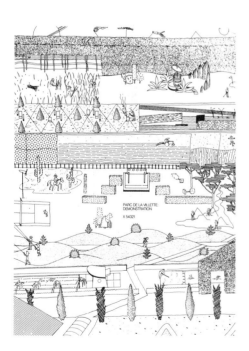

OMA/Rem Koolhaas, design for Parc de la Villette, 1981. Presentation drawing

occupants need to decide and then act on that decision. Thus, the bathroom is revealed by opening a folding partition, and tables and beds can be folded away. All this is an illustration of Rietveld's attempt to exploit with the greatest efficiency the limited space available: bedrooms become part of the living room during the day and sliding partitions rule out the idea of a single permanent subdivision. Only the stairwell, service shafts and sanitary facilities are fixed.

This treatment allows the interior of the Schröder House an astonishing number of possible uses for a surface area of ten by seven meters.[19] And yet a design as rigorous as this would not have been possible if the client, Truus Schröder-Schräder, had not also been co-designer, and if she and Rietveld had not shared the same ideas on dwelling. Certainly in 1919 such an interior would have been unthinkable in mass housing. At the end of the twentieth century the example of De Stijl proves to be as relevant as ever, to judge from some recent housing projects (see the illustrated example by Duinker, Van der Torre in Amsterdam's Dapperbuurt area). In most cases the designers choose to concentrate the services of the house in a core. This core is positioned so that the occupants can furnish the remaining space as they see fit.

Again, mass housing is one of the areas in which architects have tried to augment the possibilities of later adaptations by employing standard elements. Of relevance here are the attempts in this country by the Foundation for Architectural Research (SAR) who from 1964 pushed through a program of applied research into the possibilities of prefabricating loadbearing elements and sets of detachable units. In SAR's solution the distinction between bearer and infrastructure—both of them the community's responsibility—and individual infill kits is accompanied by standardization of the elements required. SAR proposed a support several stories high whose floor plans are left unstructured. Only the position of the entrance, the kitchen and the bathroom are fixed beforehand; it is up to the occupants to furnish the living space.

SAR developed a precision *zoning system* designed to ensure optimum use of the house. This zoning took its cue from the nature of the rooms and their position in the loadbearing structure. The result is a subdivision per house into three zones set parallel to

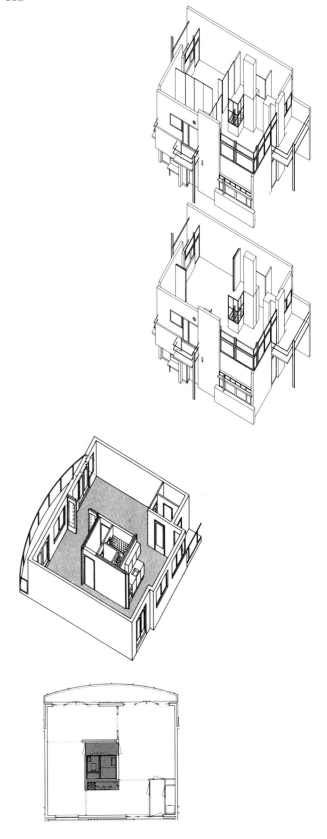

Gerrit Rietveld, Schröder House, 1919. Isometric drawings of the living level. Sliding partitions subdivide the space and increase use potential

Duinker, Van der Torre, Dapperbuurt housing, 1986–1988. Plan and isometric the façades. The two zones actually on the outer walls are used as is customary for the living rooms. Between them and the third, inner zone containing services is a strip, a "margin" in SAR terminology, allowing for flexibility in the zones" dimensions. The position of wall partitions and service shafts adheres to a measurement system that enables the detachable units to be placed according to the occupants" wishes. This means that occupants are drawn into the design process; it also goes some way to achieving the desired freedom of choice within an industrialized housing system.[20]

Flexibility in utilitarian building

In domestic construction the drive to flexibility brought both a distinction between loadbearing structure and infill and a radical standardization. This strategy is no less important for the building of offices, in which the relationship between column grid and infill is usually the point of departure for the entire design.

Then again, the need for flexibility may arise in cases when large spaces obtain rather than a string of smaller ones. To close this chapter we will examine two examples whose freedom of subdivision has to do with providing an *artificial climate*. One of the most spectacular of such cases is the geodesic dome proposed by Buckminster Fuller in 1962 for placing over Manhattan to protect it against air pollution. In this apocalyptic vision the enveloping structure is no more than a skin enfolding urban life and separating it from the hostile climate outside. Fuller's proposal pushes at the very

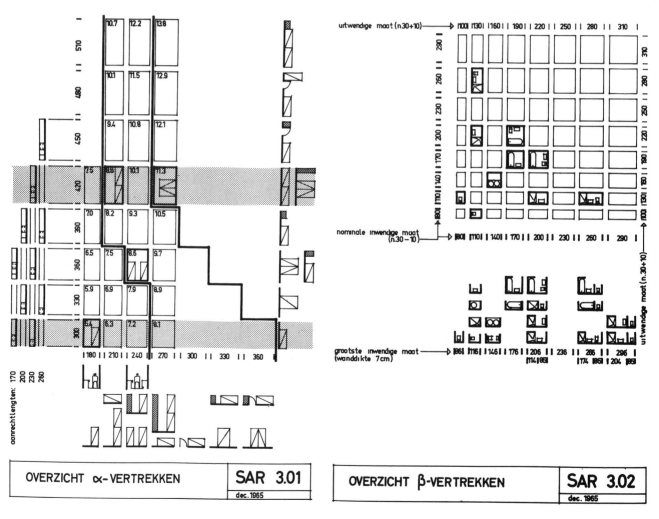

OVERZICHT α-VERTREKKEN   SAR 3.01
dec. 1965

OVERZICHT β-VERTREKKEN   SAR 3.02
dec. 1965

Overview of SAR measures stipulated for living
and sleeping zones in a single dwelling unit, 1965

frontiers of architecture. The entire program is limited to one aspect of a building, protection against the encroaching climate. Nothing further is said about the use of the dome.[21]

This preoccupation with technique to create an even climate returns in the work of the English architect Norman Foster, who worked with Fuller on a number of projects in the early 1970s. Here it is accompanied by a fine focus on the relationship between freedom in use and placement of the construction materials. Foster often realized the flexibility he strove after by designing a *serviced shed*, an undifferentiated container of steel, aluminium and glass.[22]

A good example of how this point of departure combined with a state-of-the-art construction and climate control can produce a building is the Sainsbury Centre for the Visual Arts in Norwich (East Anglia). This arts center brings together in an enormous hangar an exhibition gallery for the vast Sainsbury art collection, a space for special exhibitions, the school of fine arts of the local university, a meeting room and a restaurant. The open space with a floor surface area of 112.4 m × 29 m is spanned by steel portals. This structure constitutes a single zone able to house all services, sanitary facilities and the necessary stairs. Given this skin providing a uniform indoor climate the hall is, in

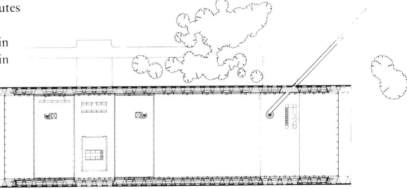

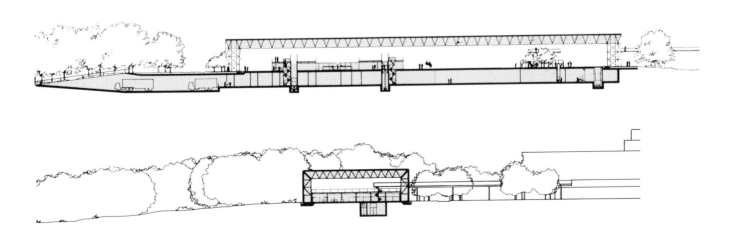

Norman Foster, Sainsbury Centre for the Visual Arts, 1978. Plan and sections

 facilities

Buckminster Fuller, geodesic dome over Manhattan, 1962

principle, freely subdivisible. Thus, the lecture halls
of the school of fine arts are set independent of the
main structure; they could be enlarged or even
removed without the need to alter it. This holds
equally for the separation of the kitchen from the
restaurant. All other components of the program
occupy the main space. The generous volume and
great height keep activities from interfering with
each other unduly. The whole comes across as an all
but empty, perfectly crafted assembly hangar offering an artificial environment for a collage of widely
diverse activities. All in all, the Sainsbury Centre is
an eloquent example of a building in which the
desire to give spectacular form to the unpredictability and transience of its use has led to a unique
structure which when seen from a distance has
much of a Greek temple.

Sainsbury Centre for the Visual Arts. Interior

4
Design and structure

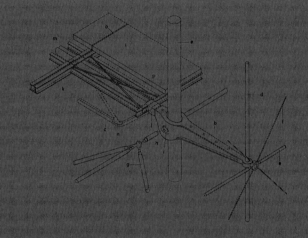

4.1 Introduction

The way that designers approach the material at their disposal lends itself to a variety of interpretations. Theories asserting that architecture derives unequivocally from the demands made by the material have been as fervently announced in the past as postulations claiming exactly the opposite. The influence the building structure has upon the design process can be described using one or other angle on the demands structure makes on the design.

Structure

In a general sense structure refers to those parts of a building that take up the *loads* on the building and carry them down to the foundations; partitions, on the other hand, serve to separate spaces into wet and dry, warm and cold, dark and light.

In Western architecture, civic buildings were for a long time built of brick and stone. As a rule these materials combined the functions of support and partition in the same structural component. During the last 150 years, however, since the rise of *skeleton construction* in steel and reinforced concrete, the bearing component, measured in material, has steadily decreased. If the principal structural issue when building in brick and stone was how to make openings, with steel and concrete it was the opposite. How were the openings in the structural frame to be filled in? Often the cladding and wall structures were not primarily loadbearing. Since then this distinction between supports and non-bearing walls has become general. In order to describe all facets of the relationship between design and structure we require the broadest possible definition of the concept structure. In this chapter we will understand it to mean the entire *material aspect* of a building as determined by the functions of support and partition.

Ideas

If we are to consider the significance of building technology and structure in current ideas on design, this can scarcely be done without due regard for developments that began with the Enlightenment and the Industrial Revolution. The evolution of science and the technological progress issuing from this evolution have been of inestimable influence on architecture. The scientific attitude adopted by many theorists and architects nurtured the ideal of a rational architecture, an architecture dictated by understanding and reason. To give tangible shape to this ideal a solid, objective design fundamental was required; this was found by regarding structure as the essence of built form, with an objective and efficient use of the means available. From then on a building could be described and designed in terms of function and economy.

New advances in building technology were accompanied by a surge of excitement about the achievements of technology and an unshakeable faith in progress. That technology and science would subsequently become part of our daily life lent the concept of structure a certain ideological charge, with efficiency and economy its implicit conditions. A thorough knowledge of applied mechanics, heating, ventilation and the like, and of materials, would thus become an indispensable element of the architect's daily practice. The last few decades of this century have seen increasing doubts as to the boundlessness of technological and economic progress. As a result, building technology and structure are back under professional scrutiny though now in a much more variegated perspective.

4.2 Unity of form and structure

When analyzing the relationship between design and structure, the link between structure and built form is probably the most logical place to begin. This link is determined by the extent to which the built form satisfies the *transfer of force* in the structure. The following examples illustrate the relationship between the form and the play of forces in the structure.

Additive and integrated structure

The Greek temple discussed in Chapter 2 is an example of a building in which the ratio between built form and transfer of force is somewhat complicated. Its design was dictated less by the *strength properties* of the material than by optical and formal considerations. For example, the marble of which the temple is built is scarcely if at all capable of taking up *bending moments*, so that to have the architrave span the distance between two pillars is mechanically not the most logical solution. Using the architrave as a span puts it under tension.

However, by making the architrave exceedingly heavy and placing a large number of supports (the pillars) at short intervals so that the span width is kept down, the tension stress is itself kept to a minimum. The enormous mass of the stacked elements (basement, pillars and architrave) means that the temple, viewed from a distance, compresses into an all but impenetrable volume that stands out in bold relief against its surroundings. What was initially considered a difficult relationship between built form and structure is of great significance in the sculptural impact of volumes so typical of Greek architecture.

The Pantheon in Rome, which we can regard as structurally the counterpart of the Greek temple, is one of the impressive results of the principles of building in stone as developed further by the Romans. It was built in memory of Caesar Augustus in 118 A.D. Characteristic of Roman architecture is its deployment of *vault and dome structures*. Because of their form, there is little if any bending stress in these structures, enabling large spans in stone and in the concrete developed by the Romans (not the reinforced variety). This enormous technical leap forward enabled the Roman master builders to erect buildings with vast spaces free of supports.

In the Pantheon the circular dome spans 43 meters —an achievement that would long remain unequalled.

Accepting that the stone material used could only be put in compression, this span was only made possible by applying the principle of the arch. In such spans the transfer of force is derived from the qualities of the material. In an arciform structure there is in principle only *compression*. When only compression and/or tension occur in a structure, we can speak of a unity of form and structure.

With the arrival of arciform spans the distinction typical of Greek temples between support (pillar) and load (architrave) gradually disappeared so that span and support became one. This fusing of elements we call an *integrated* structure. This is the opposite of the *additive* principle on which Greek temple building was based. Centuries later, in the Middle Ages, the integrated structure would reach a provisional peak with Gothic cathedral building. The transfer of force in stone structures had a very direct influence on the form of the cathedrals. In the Gothic period the objective was to build as high and as lightweight as possible. The resulting cathedral spaces the Gothic builders saw as illustrating the Divine on earth. The medieval master builders succeeded in building such tall and lightweight spaces only by having the built form accurately satisfy the play of forces in the structure. This principle of an unambiguous relationship between built form and structural transfer of force, eliminating a maximum of material from the built form, would in the nineteenth century provide the groundwork for a wholly new architectural ideal.

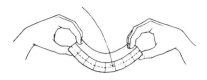

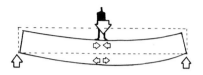

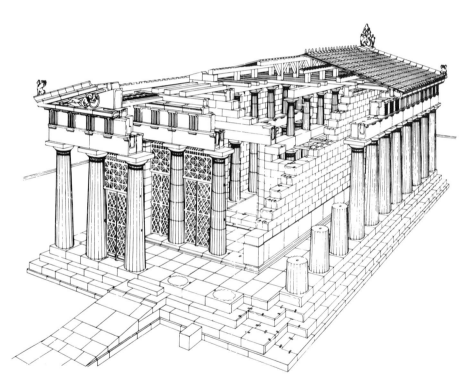

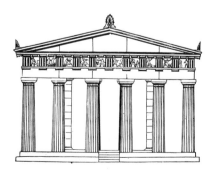

Elastic strain

Beam in simple bending

Pushing a material puts it in compression

Arch construction

Temple of Hephaestus, Athens

Material study of Greek temple

Front elevation of temple, showing emphasized distinction between support and load

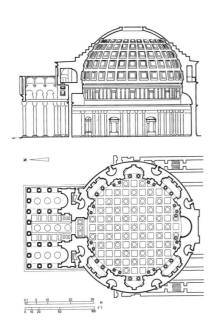

Pantheon. Material study

Beauvais Cathedral. Material study

Pantheon. Plan and section

Beauvais Cathedral, 1247–1568. Interior

4.3 Structure and truth

It would be difficult to overestimate the significance of the French theoretician Eugène Viollet-le-Duc in nineteenth and early twentieth century discourse. His work was of seminal influence on such diverse architects as Antoni Gaudí, Victor Horta, Hendrik Petrus Berlage, Auguste Perret and Ludwig Mies van der Rohe. In his major tract, *Entretiens sur l'architecture* (1863), he describes the Gothic-based rational design method in which the designing of buildings is predicated entirely on structural considerations. Expounding with great clarity how the form of a building can proceed from the solution to a structural problem, he proclaims the methods of construction to be the essence of built form.

The Gothic cathedrals had been largely the result of empirical conditions. But now, according to Viollet-le-Duc, the evolution of the science of applied mechanics and materials in the eighteenth and nineteenth centuries had paved the way for an objective foundation for architecture, one rooted in considerations wholly subject to scientific verification. A major condition was that the material be treated objectively and efficiently. This ideal of a rational architecture could be realized by responding truthfully to the demands made by the building on usefulness and construction:

"In architecture there are two necessary ways of being true. It must be true according to the program and true according to the methods of construction. To be true according to the program is to fulfil exactly and simply the conditions imposed by need; to be true according to the methods of construction, is to employ the materials according to their qualities and properties... purely artistic questions of symmetry and apparent form are only secondary conditions in the presence of our dominant principles."[1]

Viollet-le-Duc is generally regarded as the first to categorically reject the primacy of classical antiquity (see also Chapter 2) as the source of all architectural form, because this was not based upon rational principles. Yet if we study more than a hundred years on, the designs in the *Entretiens* that Viollet-le-Duc used to illustrate his theories, the question will probably arise as to what these illustrations have to do with a rational, truthful architecture. This is the moment to take a take a closer look at the term "rational architecture." In an essay entitled "Viollet-

18

Viollet-le-Duc, design for a concert hall, actualizing the lines of force throughout the building

le-Duc and the rational point of view," John Summerson approaches it thus: "For what do we mean by a rational architecture? We may mean two things. We may mean an architecture which aims at fulfilling certain specifiable functions with the nearest approximation to absolute efficiency and economy. Or we mean an architecture which seeks to express its function dialectically—to offer a visible argument to the spectator. The first sort of architecture depends wholly on the extent to which function can be mathematically stated; the second sort depends on the architect's personal interpretation of function. The first sort is ruthless in its application of means to ends; the second sort adapts both means and ends to a game of its own. The first sort of architecture is, as a matter of fact, almost impossible of conception since the total requirements of a building can never be mathematically stated: it is the mythical 'functional' architecture of the day before yesterday. The second sort of architecture is a perfectly feasible one, the only proviso being that the function of the building be considered as of sufficient emotional interest to make this dialectical mode of expression significant."[2]

Summerson makes quite clear that those who argued for a rational architecture were not primarily concerned with defining the built form in entirely objective and mathematical terms, even though their utterances would often have us suspect otherwise. The goal of nineteenth-century aspirations towards a rational architecture was in fact an architecture whose aesthetic considerations sprang from demands made by the method of construction. So the essence of designing retained its roots in beauty, though this was to enjoy an "extremely specific relation to material and technology.'[3]

Engineers' architecture

Viollet-le-Duc's ideas on truth in structure were less influential at schools of architecture than among engineers at the technical colleges. It was French engineers in particular at the Ecole Polytechnique who, inspired by the enormous influx of new technical advances, took up rational design principles. With newly developed materials such as cast iron, drawn sheet glass and reinforced concrete, the engineers gave shape to new building types necessitated by the Industrial Revolution. The last decades of the nineteenth century in particular saw

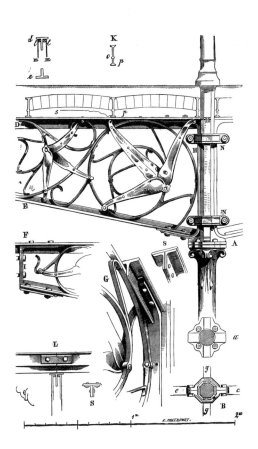

Viollet-le-Duc, details of cast-iron structures

Gustav Eiffel, drawing of the Statue of Liberty, New York

Engineer's architecture: Cottancin and Dutert's Galerie des Machines, Paris, 1889. A slender structure accompanied by a cascade of light gives an illusion of weightlessness.

Gustav Eiffel, Eiffel Tower, Paris, 1889. 'In the nakedness of the construction is contained the condition for an aesthetic; this reflects an economic response to the laws of nature; gravity and the load-bearing capacity of materials.'[5]

the design and construction of many bridges, factories, railway stations, market and exhibition halls and department stores.

The design methodology of the engineers was highly experimental by nature. New techniques and materials were subjected to extensive testing, forging a direct link with developments in technique and industry. The technical schools attended by engineers provided the impetus to apply material as efficiently and economically as possible so that each new building or structure would set out to push back the boundaries of what was structurally feasible. Fuelled by a staunch faith in technological progress, engineering architecture made rapid steps forward. It was generally felt that technical possibilities were limitless and that "new problems raised by industry and technique, could be solved by objective organization and advanced technology."[4]

The engineers" design principles were founded on ideas about objectivity and clarity of structure. To them, the rhythms and perspicuous articulation of the iron and glass structures symbolized the speed of modern life. Engineering architecture as a result was vehemently opposed to the classical ordering principles such as those taught at the Académie des Beaux-Arts (see section 2.5). Concealing the structure and adding ornament were regarded as reprehensible acts. The basis for order and composition, the engineers argued, had to issue from the statics and loadbearing structure of the building.

As the twentieth century dawned, more and more traditionally trained architects took to using technology expressively. One of the first to do so was Hendrik Petrus Berlage.[6] His Amsterdam Exchange of 1903 is generally regarded as the most convincing example of a building designed to the principles of Viollet-le-Duc. By contrast with the Paris Opera House of Beaux-Arts architect Charles Garnier (see Chapter 2) it is immediately apparent how the Exchange is constructed. If the Opera House makes a clear distinction between the representative spaces and the spaces where problems of construction have been resolved, nothing of the Exchange's structure is kept from view. Its materials—brick, cut stone, cast iron—rather than being hidden away behind plasterwork or ceilings as was then customary, are exposed for all to see. In the huge hall of the produce exchange, the vast expanse of floor surface and

the slender iron roof structure are the most immediately eye-catching elements. The floor of this exchange served as a stage on which the dynamic rituals of trade could happen at will; the roof was lifted wholesale from the canon of structural engineering.

The building's material follows to all intents and purposes the laws of matter and mechanics: there is brickwork where the span is not too great and the floor plan differentiated; the much more slender and sturdier iron is used to span the wide halls of the produce and grain exchanges where much light is required. Thus, the material properties have a great bearing on the structure of the Exchange, and the way these materials are applied and combined is decisive to its image and ornament alike.

H.P. Berlage, Amsterdam Exchange seen from the Damrak

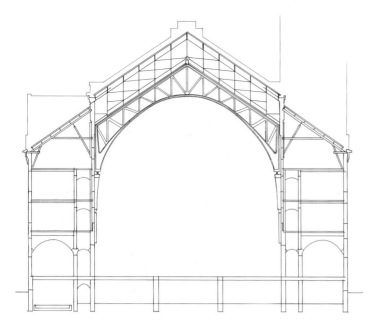

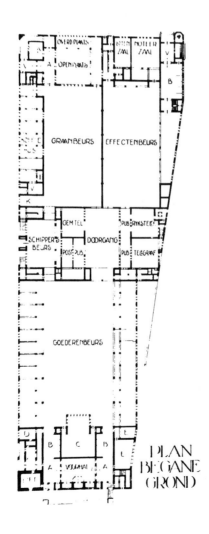

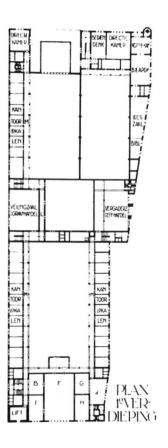

Berlage, Amsterdam Exchange.
Plans and section

The hall of the produce exchange. Both lines
of force and mode of construction are rendered
legible. Nothing of the building's structure is
kept from view

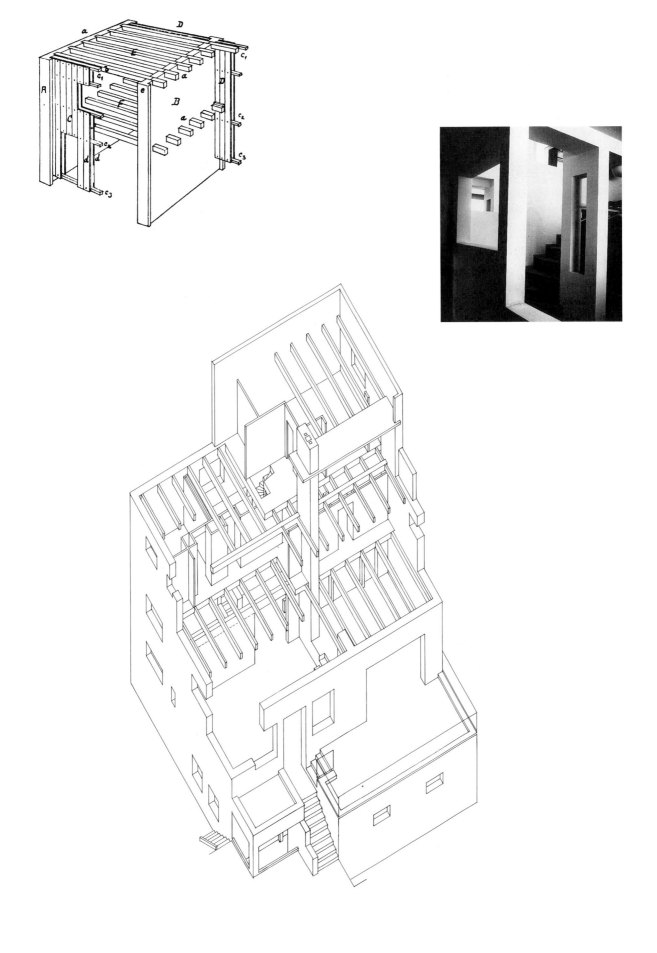

The principle of loadbearing walls   Moller House. Material study   Interior of Moller House

4.4 Structure and cladding

112

In 1908 the Viennese architect Adolf Loos publish-ed a polemical essay that gave a new direction to the discourse on "truth" in structure. In *Ornament und Verbrechen* (*Ornament and Crime*) he asserted that an excessive use of ornament is tantamount to criminal waste. In doing so he made no distinction whatever between Beaux-Arts designs and ornament based on functional-structural considerations by the followers of Viollet-le-Duc. Both forms, claimed Loos, inevitably lead to craft slavery and for that reason should be rejected.

Loos argued that "most modern building tasks were appropriate vehicles for building rather than architecture."[7] On that account he called for an unemphatic, restrained design in which good work-manship, and not artistic considerations, should set the tone. In his architecture the beauty of the industrial process prevailed over that of the ornament: "Rich material and good workmanship should not only be considered as making up for lack of decoration, but as far surpassing it in sumptuous-ness."[8] Loos felt that the preoccupation in archi-tecture with style and means of expression were in fact long outmoded by the day-to-day reality of industrialized society. "The modern style is nothing other than the product of industry: what we need is a civilization of carpenters. If the makers of applied art would restrict themselves to making paintings or sweeping the street, we would have attained that civilization."[9] Built in Vienna in 1928, twenty years after the publication of *Ornament und Verbrechen*, the Moller House illustrates Loos's rejection of any-thing tending towards an aesthetizing of structure.

In the Moller House structure is wholly sub-ordinate to space. In 1898 Loos wrote: "The archi-tect's general task is to provide a warm and livable space. Carpets are warm and livable. He decides for this reason to spread out one carpet on the floor and to hang up four to form the four walls. But you cannot build a house out of carpets. Both the carpet on the floor and the tapestry on the wall require a structural frame to hold them in the correct place. To invent this frame is the architect's second task."[10]

The Moller House could not bear out this statement more clearly. Closer inspection of the spatial and material properties reveals that Loos regarded solving the problem of structure (in this case the loadbearing structure) not simply as less important than making the house "warm and liv-able." He considered it to be of a different order entirely. For Loos structure was no more than a logistic issue to be solved independently of the other design premises. In his view, what was hidden behind the wallpaper had nothing to do with architecture.

Such an attitude was encouraged by his develop-ment of the *Raumplan* (see Chapter 2). Given the traditional structural principle of *loadbearing walls* applied by Loos it was quite impossible to implement this spatial idea "truthfully." The interrupting and shifting of spaces in the Moller House accordingly produced a structure both complex and—from Viollet-le-Duc's viewpoint—chaotic.

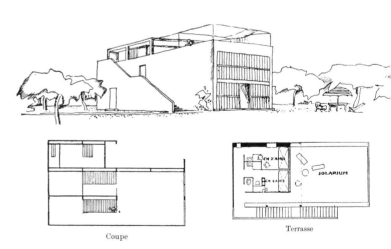

Coupe

Terrasse

Le Corbusier, Maison Citrohan

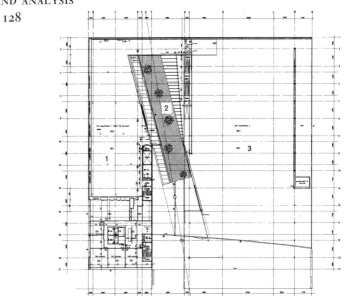

is to turn every logical connection between form and distribution of forces on its head. The forces follow a path almost impossible to plot and "will certainly not accord with the laws of nature" but give the exclusive impression that this building has no truck with gravity.[23]

Just as with many buildings we have examined in this chapter the Kunsthal stretches at the limits of what is structurally feasible. This has absolutely nothing to do with efficient and economic use of material or a lucidly built structure. Here knowledge of building technology takes second place to the creating of theatrical effects, with the loadbearing structural principles changing with each space like a set change for each new scene in a play.

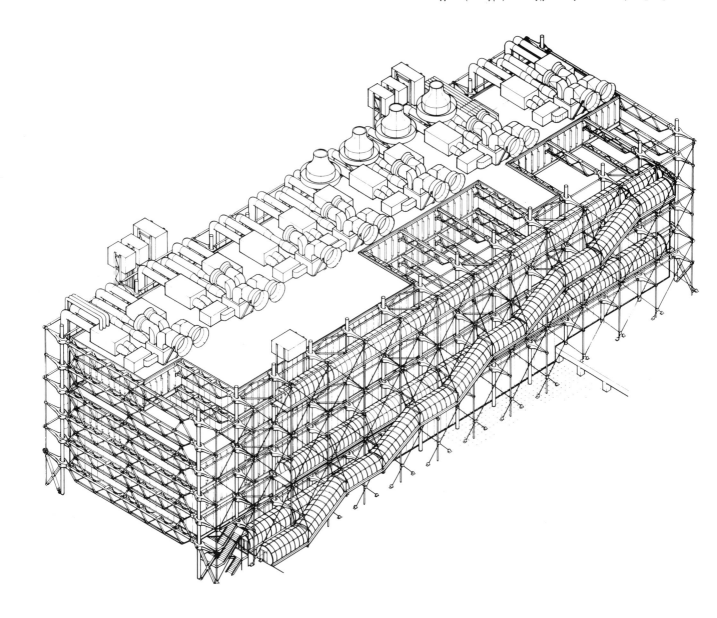

Material study of Centre Pompidou

OMA, Kunsthal. Plan

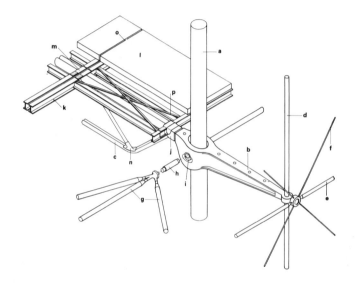

Cast steel consoles in production, each weighing
10,000 kilograms

Column-girder joint attached to console

Girders conveyed to the site by night

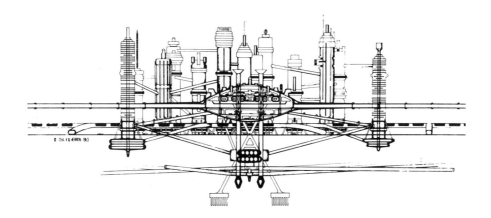

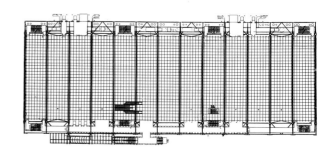

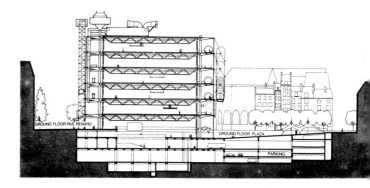

Richard Rogers and Renzo Piano, Centre
Pompidou

Archigram, "Interchange City" project, 1963

Rogers and Piano, Centre Pompidou.
Plans and section

4.9 The dramatizing of technology

In the 1960s Archigram, a group of English architects, introduced new ideas about the significance of new technologies for the architectural idiom. In a string of utopian designs they sketched a picture of the modern city that seemed to have renounced for good the idea of a static architecture. The city of the future they presented as a vast communication network which milks the potential of technology and mass media, and subjects society to an unremitting process of change. Proceeding from a general optimism towards technological progress, Archigram portrayed a future society whose principal supports were themes typical of sixties pop culture such as mass communication and mobility.

What is remarkable about the schemes of Archigram is that they make almost no attempt to contribute to technological progress as such. The group was almost exclusively interested in the expressive potential of technology, more particularly "the seductive appeal of space-age imagery," the principal source of their ideas.[22]

The images sketched by Archigram were themselves highly seductive, and did much to contribute to a renewed public interest in the technology of building. With the completion in Paris of the Centre Pompidou, a building generally considered to be indebted to Archigram's ideas, there was indeed a mass enthusiasm comparable to the reception given by the general public to the glass palaces and engineers" buildings at the end of the nineteenth century.

Completed in 1977 to a design by Richard Rogers and Renzo Piano, the Centre Pompidou is a cultural center containing exhibition space for modern art, a library, centers for industrial design and music as well as office spaces and a cafeteria. Just as in the Sainsbury Centre, the brief called for a flexible building; to design one Rogers and Piano turned to the mediagenic imagery of Archigram.

The Centre Pompidou has much in common structurally with the Sainsbury Centre. Both proceed from the principle of the serviced shed. The Parisian building consists of a steel skeleton construction with lattice trusses each spanning the entire floor area leaving an unobstructed floor area on each level of 166 × 45 meters. All comparison fades, however, when we examine the organization of the services. If Foster's building tucks these into its skin, Rogers and Piano with a fine sense of irony, drape them around the exterior, as if to give spectators a glimpse of the building's innards.

The tubular structure containing the escalators are slung from the steel skeleton by colossal poured steel consoles specially designed for the project. These solve a problem raised less by the brief than by the architects themselves. Putting the technological and structural aspects of the Centre Pompidou on display is not of practical use. In a certain sense technology here is treated as decoration, is dramatized in order to give the building a face of its own. Other than with the Sainsbury Centre, the Parisian building, through its countless allusions to industrial processes and its machine aesthetic, evokes unmistakable associations with familiar images. Without direct reference to the building's program or context Rogers and Piano give it the aspect of an oil refinery.

Another example of a building which dramatizes the structural features is the Kunsthal of Rem Koolhaas's OMA office. Completed in 1993, this Rotterdam building is home to many temporary exhibitions. It is distinguished from other museums by not having a collection of its own. This shifts the focus from amassing and managing a collection to responding flexibly to the most immediate trends in the arts, with the accent always on the intensive experience of the exhibited work. Interlinking the rooms is a complex circulation system, a labyrinth confronting visitors with a succession of surprising and contrasting experiences.

Externally the Kunsthal is a flat box shoved up against the dike terminating the park in which it stands. A service road along this dike and a ramp leading from the dike down to the park, slice through the mass, dividing the box into various spaces, each distinguished in terms of structure. The differing principles involved are often juxtaposed with no transition at all. For instance, the entrance hall and auditorium directly adjoining the ramp slope in exactly the opposite direction to the ramp itself. This effect is brought out further by having the columns in the entrance hall adhere to the tilting floor, so that this space seems to float as an independent element within the building. The effect

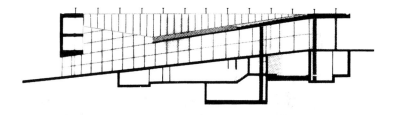

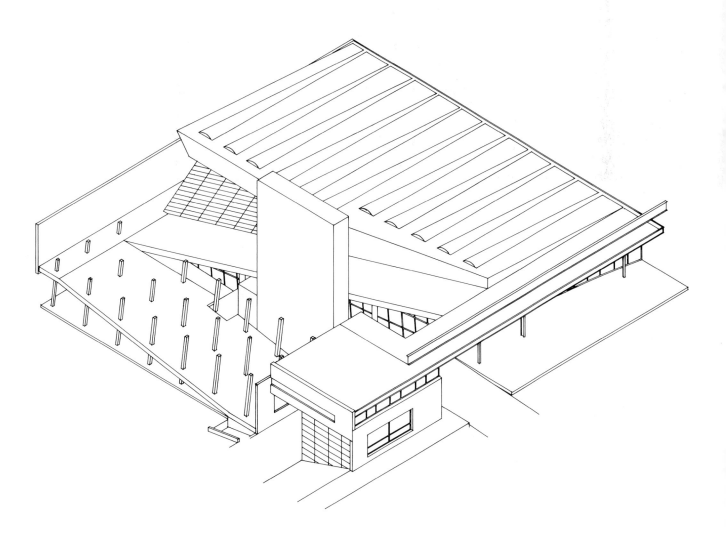

Material study of Kunsthal   OMA, Kunsthal. Section

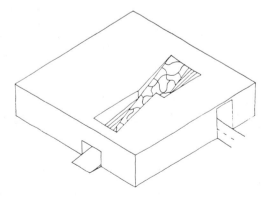

The Kunsthal under construction

Ramp and access road slice through mass

5
Design and typology

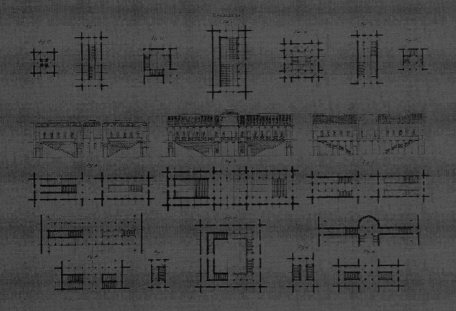

5.1 Introduction

Every science needs words, a language, to be able to exist. It is impossible to communicate in a field of study without establishing a language and defining terms. Such terms are a prerequisite if that field is to be developed scientifically. Thus, defining and classifying concepts serves to structure knowledge and give insight into a particular discipline.

There are several ways to classify architecture and urban design, depending on what we want from it. Estate agents generally use divisions relating to the housing market. Designers, on the other hand, often base their classifications on spatial and formal features. This rather more specific form of subdivision usually features the concepts of type and typology.

Within the design disciplines there are at least two reasons besides communication for turning to a typology of building. The first stems from the need to be able to analyze and discuss the existing production; the second is in the interests of designing. Though both are related to form and are themselves closely linked, lack of insight into the differences between these two typologies can lead to misunderstanding.

A typology tuned to analyzing the design — analytical typology—should give researchers the means to name the various elements of a building or city and describe how these elements fit together in a composition.

Designers, on the other hand, will primarily need a typology on which to base possible design decisions. For such cases Philippe Panerai uses the term generative typology.[1] We might regard such a typology as describing the reproducible system of related design choices. A type in this sense can be used, depending on the situation, to generate a new design. A type can be stashed in the "memory bag," transported elsewhere and unpacked. Looked at this way, a type can be defined as the bearer of design experiences pertaining to a similar issue—a standard solution, if you like. Designers, depending on their experience and the studies they have done, look to a generative typology. We are less concerned with different classifications as such than with the principles of classification.

5.2 The development of "type"

"Type" derives from the Greek word "typos," whose extremely wide-ranging meaning is indicative of, and applicable to, many nuances and variations of the same idea, such as "model," "matrix," "impression," "mold" and "relief."[2]

From the eighteenth century on, type is used as a classifying tool, as in Linnaeus" famous plant classification system. There plants are arranged or classified into families with common characteristics.[3]

Quatremère de Quincy

The notion of type entered the architectural discourse based on this meaning. In his encyclopaedia, the architectural theorist Quatremère de Quincy (1755–1849) defines type as follows: "The word type is also used synonymously with 'model,' although there is between the two a difference that is easy enough to understand. The word 'type' presents less the image of a thing to copy or imitate completely than the idea of an element which ought itself to serve as a rule for the model… The model, as understood in the practical execution of the art, is an object that should be repeated as it is; the type, on the contrary, is an object after which each (artist) can conceive works of art that may have no resemblance. All is precise and given in the model; all is more or less vague in the type. At the same time, we see that the imitation of types is nothing that feeling and intellect cannot recognize, and nothing that cannot be opposed by prejudice and ignorance.

"This is what has occurred, for example, in architecture. In every country, the art of regular building is born of a preexisting source. Everything must have an antecedent. Nothing, in any genre, comes from nothing, and this must apply to all of the inventions of man. Also we see that all things, in spite of subsequent changes, have conserved, always visibly, always in a way that is evident to feeling and reason, this elementary principle, which is like a sort of nucleus about which are collected, and to which are coordinated in time, the developments and variations of forms to which the object is susceptible."[4]

In this definition, in which Quatremère de Quincy wants to impress that an abstraction is at issue, three aspects of "type" assume prominence:

Quatremère sets "type" against "model"; type is emphatically conceived as the result of a long tradition ("Everything must have an antecedent"); a type is able to change. While this may apply to formal variations when developing a design, the type can itself be fundamentally modified and evolved further ("the developments and variations of forms to which the object is susceptible").

In Quatrèmere's definition, type is defined as "more or less vague." Taking the type as basis "each (artist) can conceive works of art that may have no resemblance." According to the Italian art historian G.C. Argan, who revived Quatrèmere's text in the 1960s, it is the *internal form-structure* that unites works based on the same type.[5] A thorough analysis of this internal form-structure would then reveal the similarities between the two objects.

The primary aim of Quatremère de Quincy's definition was to draw up an analytical system of classification but it can also be interpreted as a generative typology.

Durand

In contrast with Quatremère de Quincy's encyclopaedic concern the French architect J.N.L. Durand (1760–1834) developed in that same period a system of classification that addresses the production of architecture. As a teacher at the Ecole Polytechnique, the counterpart of the Ecole des Beaux-Arts, he wrote two complementary books, both intended as generative typology.[6] In the first, the so-called *Grand Durand*, he presents an exhaustive typologically arranged overview of buildings influential at that time. In the second book, the *Précis des Leçons d'Architecture données à l'école polytechnique*, Durand shows a series of building components presented as standard solutions for numerous design problems that might occur. The remainder of the book consists of directions on how to reinterpret these forms. Durand drew all the building components on the same grid, thus producing a design manual in a building-block typology.

We can regard Durand's typology as a catalogue of "empty forms," forms that do not refer to a specific use or program but are open to every potential content. This made his work an ideal tool for the engineers of the Polytechnique, enabling them to design at speed the buildings required by the new regime. Prefectures, prisons, markets— whatever Bonapartian centralization and national

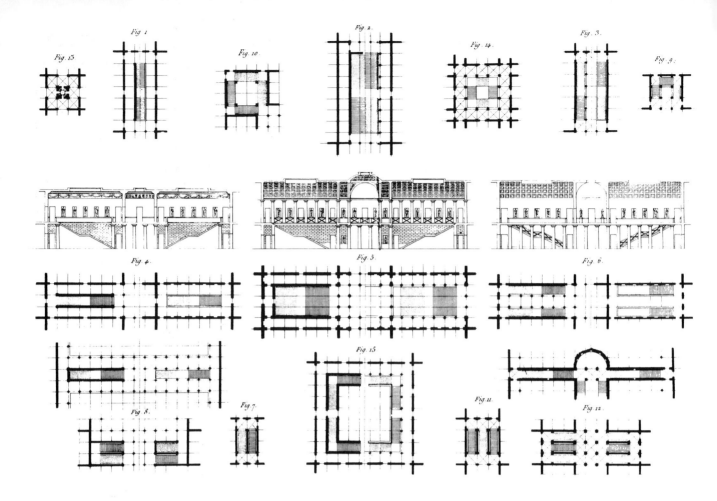

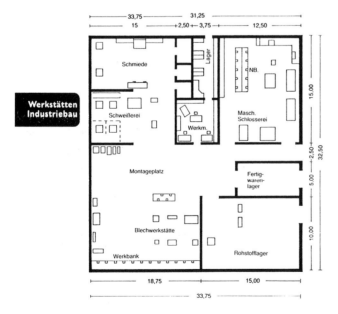

WERKSTÄTTEN

→ 📖

Auskunft: Landesgewerbeamt Stuttgart

In größerer Werkstatt **Arbeitsstätten** getrennt in: → ① .
Autogenschweißerei, Anschlägerei, Bau- und Reparaturwerkstatt,
Kunstschmiede, Konstruktions- und Maschinenschlosserei, vom
Büroraum leicht übersehbar. Fußboden aus Beton, besser Holzpfla-
ster auf Betonunterlage. Die Werkstätte erhält am besten Oberlicht.
Ausreichende Platzbeleuchtung, Einzelantrieb der Maschinen (Ka-
belkästen im Fußboden).

Schweiß- und Schmiederaum sollten auch bei mittleren Werkstät-
ten durch **Stahltüren** abgeschlossen sein. Gute **Lüftung**, Schweiß-
tisch mit Schamottesteinen belegt. Für Gußeisen- und Metall-
schweißungen Holzkohlenbecken zum Vorwärmen, darüber kleine
Esse, auch zum Bronzelöten, Schmieden und Härten geeignet. Da-
neben Wasser- und Ölbehälter zum Härten.

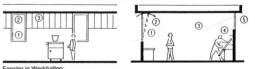

Fenster in Werkhallen:
① Arbstättv (freie Durchsicht), niedrige Brüstungshöhe ② Lüftung (Hochreichende Flü-
gel) ③ Genügend Tageslicht zur Hallenmitte (Hohe Fenster) ④ Arbeitssicherheit (Hantie-
ren von Glasflächen gefährlich) ⑤ Lästige Sommersonne ist an der Südseite einfach abzu-
schirmen.

Page from Durand's *Précis des Leçons
d'Architecture données à l'école Polytechnique*

Page from Neufert's *Bauentwurfslehre*

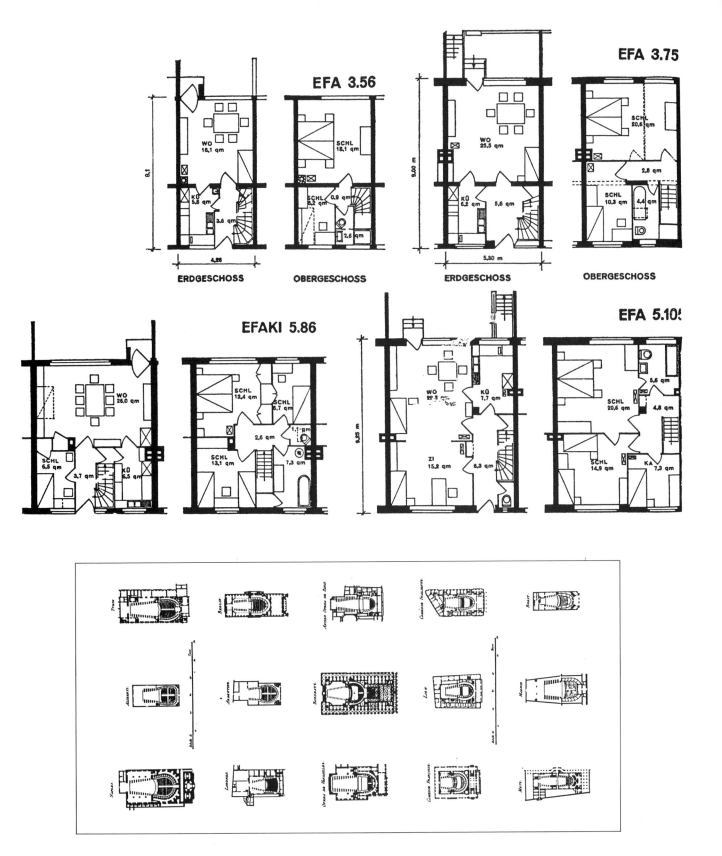

Prototypes of plans for housing projects in
Frankfurt

Page from Pevsner's *A History of Building Types*

Analyses after Muratori of the fabric of the
San Bartolomio quarter, Venice

Aldo Rossi, design for student accommodation,
Chiete, 1976

economic reorganization needed simply flew off the drafting table. In practice the examples were often copied exactly, the type being used as model for the designs.

Unlike Quatremère, Durand conceived the type as a fixed example, and based his typology on the formal features of buildings or components. Design using Durand's typologies is a matter of compiling components of fixed form. This radically alters the relation between a building's formal characteristics and its content. If type according to Quatremère is inseparable from its historic and cultural conditions, Durand, on the other hand, used his typology in independence of this original context.

The functionalists

For the functionalists of the 1920s and 1930s, typologies played a fundamentally different role. These designers approached their designs from a functional rather than a typological angle, in which primacy of form gave way to primacy of program. Here "type" was used in two ways: first, to classify buildings according to function and second, in its capacity as model.

Neufert's *Bauentwurfslehre* and Pevsner's *A History of Building Types* are examples of the first category.[7] Both books are divided according to building programs; hotels, prisons, rail stations, offices, etc. Pevsner's gives an ordered overview of major buildings, taking no account of the spatial composition of the examples. Neufert's buildings, on the other hand, are stripped of their formal and spatial characteristics and reduced to function-organizing diagrams giving the specific solution to a functional problem. At first sight this function-based approach provides a handy division to the book. If you want to design a theater, for example, you open the book at theaters, for a school you turn to the chapter on schools, and so forth.

Besides these functional typologies, the functionalists used the type as a standard or model.[8] The break with the past that they advocated meant rejecting every form of historical example. Therefore, they regarded the type not as the outcome of a historical development but as a standard solution to a standard problem. In the discourse on the "minimum dwelling" they spoke of standard types, dwellings that needed to be developed for a standard family. These designs formed the proto-

type for a new solution to be repeated in series. The model-based role these "type plans" fulfilled in the mass production of dwellings brings to mind that played by Durand's typologies in the nineteenth century.

Typology and morphology

General dissatisfaction with what functionalism produced in architecture and planning gave a new thrust in the fifties to discussions on typology. Part of the criticism levelled at functionalism concerned the functionalists" lack of a valid theory of form. These critics saw typology as a major element for such a theory.

Particularly in Italy, where the break with the past in the architectural debate had been less drastic than among Northern and Western European modernists, a form-based typology reemerged in the spotlight. The most important protagonists of the new discourse were Saverio Muratori, Carlo Aymonino and Aldo Rossi. They focused their research on the existing city and historical continuity, using typological studies as an instrument to analyze existing urban fabrics. This places them diametrically opposite the functionalist approach in which the type was viewed as a new discovery, with no ties with the past, on which to found a new series.

A milestone in this development is Muratori's *Studi per una operante storia urbana di Venezia*.[9] Together with professors and students of the Istituto Universitario di Architettura, Muratori evolved a method of analyzing the form of the city in relation to the typology of its buildings, later to become known as morphological and typological research into urban form. This he did by examining parts of Venice in terms of its urban form on the one hand and of regularly occurring elements there such as dwellings on the other.

The most important conclusions of this study were as follows:
- the type develops its specific features in a concrete situation only, that is, within the built fabric;
- the urban fabric develops its specific features only within the urban structure or in a greater urban context;
- the whole of the urban organism can only be understood in its historical perspective.[10]

Muratori used this research to develop new methods of architectural and urban design by analyzing the historical city. The subsequent progress of this research was largely carried by practicing architects.[11] The architect Carlo Aymonino, for instance, refined the notions of city-form, type and development processes introduced by Muratori by applying them to other European metropolises.[12] Though the typological analysis by the architect Aldo Rossi embroiders on Aymonino and Muratori's investigations, it does not focus primarily on the relation between building typology and city morphology. Rossi carried typological research further in the direction of architectural design. His investigations concern the distilling of architectural types from the urban fabric. The types thus acquired he defines as historically immutable, irreducible primary elements of architecture.[13] In Rossi's eyes these examples are deeply rooted in man, eternally valid types allied to the notion of archetype employed by the psychoanalist Carl Gustav Jung.[14] In addition, Rossi credits the type with a cultural dimension: a specific type represents not only the abstraction of a certain built configuration but is simultaneously a bearer of cultural meaning. These "distilled" types—elementary house-form, tower, arcade—keep returning in Rossi's own designs.

The main similarity between the work of Muratori, Aymonino and Rossi is in the significance all ascribe to the type. It is for them a means of guaranteeing historical continuity in the evolution of architecture and planning. The crucial difference between them lies in their opinion of how changes in the urban fabric can take place. In the ideas of Muratori and Aymonino, the typological characteristics of buildings in the city are persistent factors in the urban fabric, characteristics whose development is influenced by historical and cultural conditions. Access, façade composition, internal organization as well as plot layout are constantly recurring elements in the city. Changes in these structures are effected either by changes in the conditions under which a type is applied, or by specific design interventions in the typological characteristics of the built environment.

For Rossi, by contrast, the types distilled from the existing city (archetypes) are historical constants. In his approach, changes in the urban fabric are triggered off by changes in the order of these fixed elements (types) in a new context.[15] An example of this approach is Rossi's design for the city hall in Trieste of 1974. In it, he welds recognizable forms from the past, including their cultural charge (the original meaning of the typological elements carried over to the present) into a new complex of buildings whose elements together take on new meaning.

In the earlier-named article by Argan, in which he calls for renewed attention to the 150-year old definition by Quatremère de Quincy, he interprets typology in the light of the ongoing discourse. If Quatremère is concerned with an abstraction, a reduction of the built object, in Argan's view the type is the abstraction of a *series of buildings* and is derived from their common structural features. "In the process of comparing and formulating individual forms to determine the type, the specific properties of the individual building are eliminated and all those elements that make up the unity of the series are retained, and those elements alone. The type is thus expressed as a diagram, arrived at through a process of reduction, of the totality of formal variations on a common basic form. If type is the result of this regressive process, the basic form yielded cannot be conceived of as a purely structural framework, though it can as an internal form-structure or as a principle that carries within itself the potential of endless formal variations and even of further structural modification of the type itself."[16]

In this text, which can be conceived as a polemic against the functionalist understanding of type, Argan firmly reestablishes type in relation to experience and tradition. In it the design-related aspects of typology prevail, aspects which in Quatremère de Quincy's analysis-based definition are only implicitly present. Thus, Argan stresses the distinction between two moments in architectural design: the moment of the process of type formation, and the moment of form specification.

The process of formation, the phase in which the type is specified and developed further, Argan describes as a "process of comparison and addition." Here the basic form common to a series of buildings is derived by reducing that series, and is rendered as a *typological diagram*. This basic principle, the internal form-structure, contains the possibility of endless variations in form and even of structural modification. Once chosen as the foundation for a design, according to Argan, the typological diagram loses its historically determined meaning to become available for the further development and form specification of that design.[17]

In the second moment, form specification or *invention*, the design transcends the typological diagram and with it all solutions credited to the historical type. This invention of form is the designer's answer to the specific demands made of the design, as well as his statement about the formal idiom of its architecture. This, Argan contends, is why implicit typological aspects are attached to this second design phase. In Argan's approach the typological moment represents the relation of the design to the past, and the moment of invention represents its relationship to the present and future.

Influenced by the Italian contributions, the seventies ushered in a typology discourse on a world-wide scale.[18] In Europe it was the so-called Rationalists, taking their cue from Aldo Rossi, who persistently dominated the discussion.[19]

The main subjects of the discourse were the interaction between typology of buildings and morphology of urban space, and the role of typology in determining architectural form.

In their practical application in research and design, typologies are used in three different though complementary ways. First, they are used as an instrument for systematic architectural and planning research; second, as a means of investigating the divergent aspects of architecture and planning as mutually related. Finally, typologies are exploited as a design tool.

5.3 Typology and design

After this historical overview we shall examine the relationship between the concept "type" and the design. In the context of this book the most relevant question is how designers can turn their knowledge of examples to practical use. For this purpose we will look more closely at three aspects in the relation of typology to design using Argan's approach as a basis. Three analyses of designs help illuminate these aspects and the way they relate.

Concept and type

The first aspect concerns the degrees of abstraction in each step of the design process. As explained in Chapter 1, the design process can be conceived of as a cyclic or repeating process deepened further by the choices designers make during their work. The process described there reaching from concept to final form is further subdivided in Argan's text into what he calls a "moment of typology" and a "moment of form-invention.'

Even though the theory places the ideas of concept, type and design in opposition, in practice there is a graduated series. Together the three above ideas trace a scale from abstract (concept) through schematic and reduced (type) to concrete (design).

This difference in abstraction between the design stages is essential to designing on the basis of typologies, in that the degree of abstraction is a means of measuring the degree of freedom when taking the next design decision. Thus, the concept of an apartment building free-standing in the landscape is general enough to offer an unlimited number of possibilities for further development; once the building type has been fixed, say in a fan-shaped typological diagram, some variation is still possible though the choice is now more limited; only when the final form has been chosen does the design exhibit its own characteristic features.

Typological levels

A second important aspect when designing from typologies is the relationship between design decisions. This brings us to the question of typological levels. A typological level can be regarded as a scale of planning in which the design decisions present a unified system of choices. The number of typological levels (or layers) in a design is not

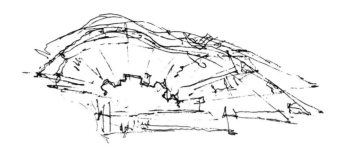

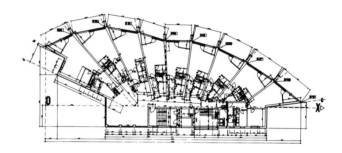

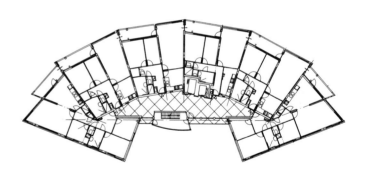

Alvar Aalto, design sketch for Neue Vahr apartment building, Bremen, 1958–1962

Plan of Neue Vahr

Mecanoo, Hillekop housing, Rotterdam, 1985–1989. Floor plan

dictated beforehand but can be specified according to the complexity of the object and the modus operandi of the designer. Argan, for example, distinguishes three such levels in a building: the configuration of the whole building, the major elements of construction and the decorative elements.

These levels are not enough, however, if we wish to describe a large and complex apartment building. We then lack terms to designate the system of spaces between the level of individual dwelling units and that of the entire configuration. In such cases we might, for instance, distinguish the following five typological levels: the configuration of blocks and urban spaces; that of the apartment building including access, the linking and stacking of dwelling units; the level of the dwelling itself; the major construction elements; and decorative elements such as cladding panels. A comparable division into typological levels is equally possible in urban design. For instance, the design for a city district can involve the level of the building, the configuration of the urban blocks and spaces, the level of the neighborhood, that of the district and the relation of district to city. But we can also point to urban areas where the typology of the urban plan is no less than the sum of typologies of the buildings.

If design decisions pertaining to a single typological level of a plan exhibit a powerful unity, then those involving several such levels produce a unity that is much more complex. The way the various levels in a design relate forms the subject of absorbing design discussions.

For instance, a large apartment building can be designed with an elevation that expresses the small-scale individual units as component parts of the whole. Or it could be an elevation whose composition emphasizes the total building and renders individual dwellings illegible. These two cases could easily share the same dwelling type.

Yet the question of how independent of—or how dependent on—each other are different typological levels, is not exclusively a question of personal ideas but as much one of use, of technical possibilities, of convention and so on. Thus, the various imaginable typological levels of a design will not invariably present designers with the same range of choices or interpretations.

Processing a type

The third aspect in the relationship between typology and design concerns the way an existing type can be employed in a new design. Based on Argan, the metamorphosis of type into design can be divided into two phases. In practice, these phases intermesh.

In the first (type-formation), the typological diagram acquired through reduction is variously processed. The processing of a typological diagram can result in a new variant of the existing type, in which case *deformation* (distortion) of the type can be said to have taken place; forms of deformation include rotations, shifts, added differences in level, mirror images and the like. When such changes occur to the type that the diagram is altered structurally, the existing type has transformed into a new one. This phase may occur several times when typological levels are treated individually.

In the second phase, the moment of form-invention, the processed diagram is subjected on all typological levels to the architectural system chosen by the designer. The type is "draped" with an architectural expression or style. Once it has been slotted into an architectural system, the final composition emerges and the processing of its form takes place. The design then acquires its own characteristic properties.

In the typological analyses given below of three paradigmatic schemes, we will concentrate on the unity of the relationships outlined above between typology and design.

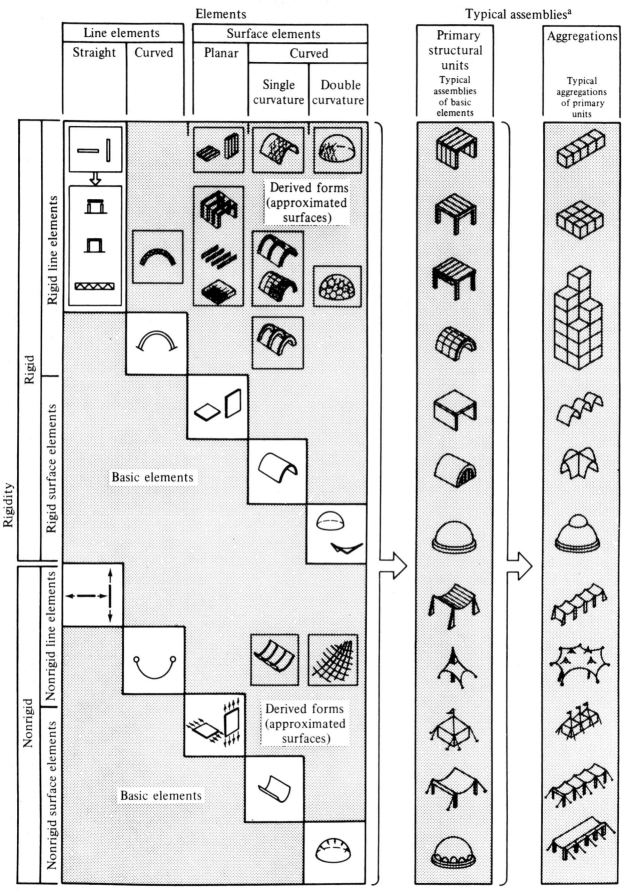

IJ-Plein

An example of deliberately manipulating and transforming an existing type into a new one is the urban design for the western part of the IJ-plein development in Amsterdam-Noord by OMA, Rem Koolhaas's office. High-rises were rejected as a solution during the initial phase, and the designers looked for another layout form in which to realize their original point of departure (a view out across the waters of the IJ for everyone). Their choice fell on a type based on a design by the Luckhardt brothers for a residential sector in Berlin. This unrealized design of 1927, "Stadt ohne Höfe," is configured as a pair of repetitive units, a long slab flanked by a sequence of urban villas. This well-defined layout type enfolds a communal green space with access on the outer side of each layout unit.[20]

An analysis of OMA's initial sketches can help us reach a hypothesis about how transforming the Berlin type has led to the composition of the western part of IJ-plein. In this process we can see transformations as much at block configuration level as at that of street and access.

At block configuration level the Berlin design can be broken down into two series of cube-shaped blocks with a slab to either side. The internal structure of the form here can be rendered in the typological diagram of eight cubes and two beams. The first transformation this diagram undergoes is to be rotated to fit the site, which means dropping two of the square blocks. Then comes an important step; the two halves of the configuration of blocks are slid away from each other, freely siting the urban villas. This is what we call a transformation of type —a new type has been generated, a string of urban villas set before a slab. In the new type the slab functions as a stage set against which the urban villas stand out as discrete objects.

The following imaginary step is to lengthen the right-hand slab and add two sequences of three discrete blocks to the outside of this elongated slab. By siting the urban villas opposite the large open spaces, the spatial impact of the villas in front of the slab is exploited to the full.

At street and access level a complex process begins. Essentially this entails that the original access typology—a cluster of slab and four urban villas organized as an open urban block—has been dropped by OMA and supplanted by an access made subordinate to the architectural detailing of the western part of the plan. Where the Berlin scheme proposed a systematic alternation of street-block-(open) central court-block-street, OMA treat these components as self-sufficient elements in a composition configured in strips. The arrangement of elements is dictated less by the need to provide public (street) and semi-public (inner court) zones than by the will to generate a montage of zones of varying ambiences at street level (see also Chapter 2). In this new arrangement the street intercedes between the long block and the row of urban villas, inverting the original layout and thereby the access type to generate a new relationship between public and private at ground level.

La Tourette

Using an existing type does not necessarily lead to its transformation but can result in its mutation and a new interpretation of the type. Le Corbusier's monastery of La Tourette near Lyons is an illuminating example of such an approach. Built between 1953 and 1960 in the French village of Eveux-sur-Arbresle, this complex can be regarded as a latter-day interpretation of the traditional monastery type built around a cloister. In the traditional monastery is a building type that has changed little over the centuries, one crystallizing the idea that a monastic community should offer as much space for prayer as for the activities its members are obliged to undertake.[21] The Western European monastery type reaches back to Roman and Byzantine castle complexes and consists of a quadrangle surrounded by arcaded walks. Around this cloister are arranged the church, the study areas and other communal spaces for the monks or nuns, and the individual bedrooms, usually located upstairs.

Le Corbusier took this traditional monastery type as his model. However, the main feature of the monastery principle, the walled quadrangle surrounded by arcades, is so radically altered in Le Corbusier's scheme as to amount to a complete revamping: whereas in historical monastery architecture the courtyard is surrounded and protected by the remaining masses, in La Tourette these volumes are lifted up. The arcade containing individual cells now sits on the third floor. This leaves the church, held at arm's length and scarcely taller than the rest of the monastery, in a less dominant

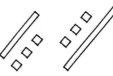

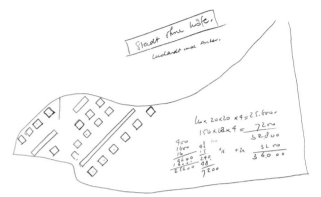

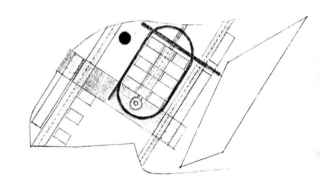

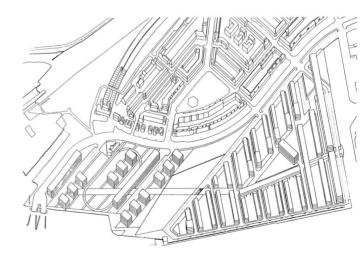

OMA, design sketch showing 'Stadt ohne Höfe' in context of IJ-plein

OMA, design sketch for western sector of IJ-plein

Luckhardt brothers, 'Stadt ohne Höfe.' Model, Berlin, 1927

Typological transformation of 'Stadt ohne Höfe' into IJ-plein

OMA, planometric drawing of final IJ-plein scheme, Amsterdam, 1980–1989

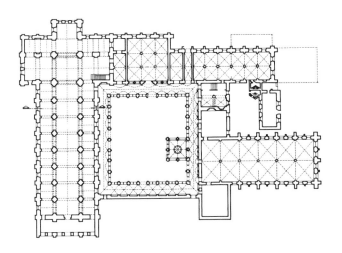

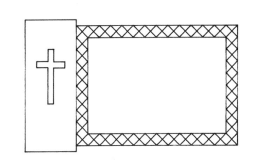

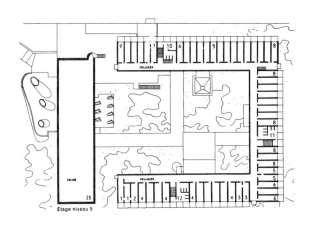

Etage niveau 5

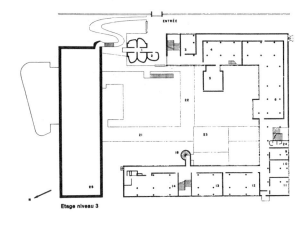

Etage niveau 3

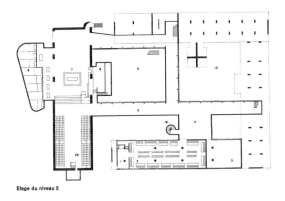

Etage du niveau 2

Fontenay monastery, twelfth century

Le Corbusier, La Tourette Friary,
Eveux-sur-Arbresle, 1957

Typological diagram of monastic church and
cloisters

Plans of La Tourette Friary

position in the complex as a whole. The living area includes numerous communal spaces, including the library and the dining hall, interconnected by footbridges. This new response to the original type is largely a result of the steeply graded site of La Tourette and the elevated volumes. As the building is raised on pilotis, the slope runs through the courtyard of the monastery. The original meaning of the monastery courtyard is changed utterly as a result: instead of a space screened off and protected against hostile nature, that very nature is brought into the courtyard. Indeed, in the twentieth century nature has lost its hostile nature; more than that, it has become a place of sanctuary. The "unspoiled nature" penetrating deep into the courtyard underlines the meditative impact of the new monastery. Yet these reinterpretations do not affect the essence of the traditional type; the changes take place at typological levels that prove inessential to the "monastery-ness" of La Tourette. Imitating the traditional type at the level of the configuration of the type's quintessential components (quadrangle and roofed passages) in La Tourette's case evidently generated more than just the freedom to radically process other major components of the building. For at the level of architectural detailing, too, it allowed every literal reference to existing examples to be cast aside without this requiring that the original type be transformed into something new.[22]

Typological experiments in Frankfurt

A good example of an urban design in which the various typological levels of the urban plan are lucidly drawn together is the Römerstadt district in Frankfurt.

The district belongs to the Nidda Valley project, one of the large housing projects in the 1920s that gave the avant-garde the opportunity to put into practice all the aims of functionalism on a large scale. The project was one big experiment on all levels of planning: with "Siedlungen" or new forms of expansive urbanization at the urban level, with layout forms at the level of the Siedlungen, and with housing types at the level of the development.

Together with other famous urban experiments such as the English garden city and the School of Amsterdam, the Frankfurter Siedlungen are often regarded as major steps in the gradual transition from the traditional nineteenth-century city of perimeter blocks to the twentieth-century city of modern, open row layouts.[23]

Römerstadt, built in 1927–1928, occupies a key position in the series of Siedlungen. The urban plan and its architectural detailing can be considered as an attempt to sytetize the qualities of the traditional city with the functionalist demands on housing (see Chapter 2.7).

Römerstadt nestles between the through road "In der Römerstadt" and the River Nidda. Its basic arrangement is simplicity itself: a number of residential streets running parallel to the Nidda are bisected by an access road. This arrangement was modified to accommodate the qualities of the site and its surroundings (see Chapter 6).

Ernst May and the design team set out to create legible urban spaces with the design resources and vocabulary of modern architecture.[24] They responded to the functionalist demands of light, air and space for each dwelling unit and a differentiated use of specific housing types. Typology played a three-tiered role in creating the required urban space.

At the level of the district as a whole there is a differentiation in block types to create a composition of blocks. By introducing differences into the layout forms the designers stressed the hierarchy of the scheme's components while distinguishing between public, semi-public and private realms.

At the northern edge, for instance, the through road is marked by taller development shielding the district from the road; the dwelling types in the taller blocks are oriented to the sun. Similarly, the access road to the district, in its winding descent through the hilly terrain, is pointed up by a pair of taller blocks.

At the level of the building blocks the open row development is deformed at a number of places to accommodate the blocks in the composition of the district. As opposed to the western part, the streets in the east curve with the underlying landscape, giving it a different character. Where the residential streets meet the access road, the heads of the blocks are rotated and set square to this road. This kink in the heads spatially marks off the central courts between the open rows and gives the residential streets in the design a high degree of intimacy. On the side of the winding access road these rotated heads give the latter extra emphasis.

In the neighborhoods the open rows are separated from one another by informal footpaths, which are equally a link between the neighborhoods and the belvederes on the southern rim of the district. Here, for the benefit of the view, the open blocks are replaced by a single row in which taller blocks set at right angles mark the vantage points to the landscape.

At the level of the house and its immediate vicinity the residential streets exhibit a relationship essentially comparable to that enjoyed by the open rows. The houses have a public street-oriented front and an informal garden-oriented rear.

Although sunlight had no decisive effect on the composition of the district, the relation of house to sun was very much a focal point at the house-type level. Dwellings on the north side of the street have their kitchens at the rear (the cold side) and a second large room set on the sun-oriented façade. At the same time these houses have a capacious front garden, though this is mainly for ornamental purposes in view of the open siting.

The houses on the south side are organized differently. In these narrower units the kitchen is located alongside the front door. There being no front garden, this door has only a front step to separate it from the street. To lessen the possible lack of privacy ensuing from this proximity, the entrances to the south side houses are screened off by a wall. Here dwelling is concentrated entirely onto the private garden side. This distinction between dwelling types on the north and south sides of the street throws up an asymmetrical street profile.

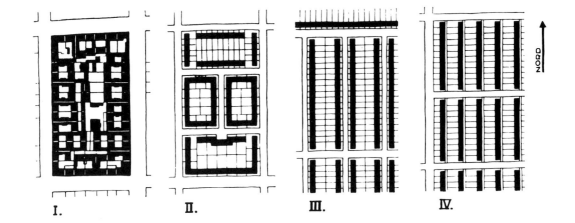

Ernst May, diagram showing the development
from perimeter block to open row layout
(*Zeilenbau*)

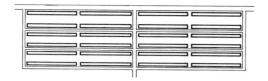

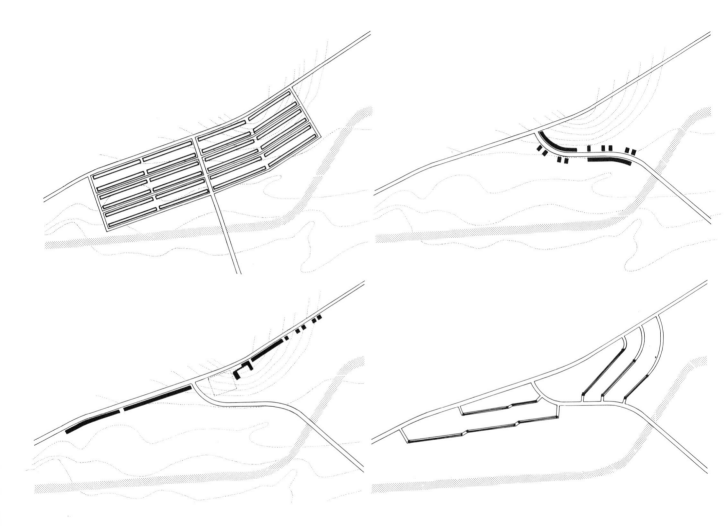

Römerstadt, typological processing
a typological diagram of the Römerstadt plan
  type
b the plan type projected onto the site
c marking the through road
d marking the access to the district
e intimate character of the residential streets

Schematic section through Römerstadt

5.4 Typology and landscape

In landscape architecture, there has been little of a
well-defined debate on typology. It is only during
the last ten years that books on typology relating to
the compositional system in landscape architecture
have begun to appear.

In the seventeenth and eighteenth centuries rules
did exist about the place, size, shape and material of
(green) elements from which gardens and courtyards
are composed. This visual system, a component of
the landscape-architectural composition, consists of
a series of elements of (arche)type that individually
and united are a representation of nature. The
French garden cultivated in the seventeenth century
contained a variety of planting forms (lawn, wood)
and water elements (spring, cascade, ornamental
pond, rivulet). These elements all had a prescribed
size, scale, place and material.

In the second half of the nineteenth century, at
the time of the large-scale restructuring of Paris
under Haussmann, the need arose for a typology
of green elements geared to production. So-called
model books were compiled of the countless elements
determining the design of urban space. J.C. Alphand,
Haussmann's garden architect, published in the
period 1967–1873 *Les promenades de Paris*, a book
cataloguing models of promenades, squares, parks
and street furniture—a Durand for urban space.

Typology of the cultivated landscape

There is a long tradition in agricultural engineering
techniques of reclaiming and exploiting the landscape. This is particularly true in the Netherlands
where one finds a typology of drainage models that
reaches back to the method of reclamation as
practiced in late medieval times. This method
produced a layout of long thin parallel strips of land
and ditches. In the sixteenth and seventeenth centuries, this schema was given a rational approach
and transformed into a reclamation typology with a
square or rectangular grid pattern. These schemas
gained broad acceptance in land reclamation projects
in and out of the Netherlands on the strength of
tracts issued by the Leiden Surveyors School.

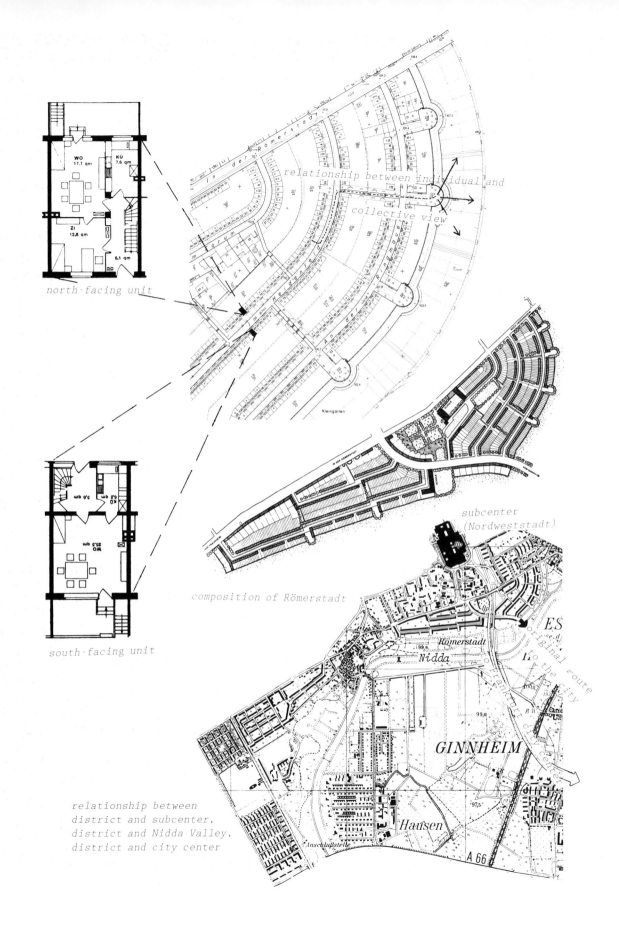

north-facing unit

south-facing unit

relationship between individual and
collective view

composition of Römerstadt

subcenter
(Nordweststadt)

relationship between
district and subcenter,
district and Nidda Valley,
district and city center

Römerstadt, cross-scale analysis

6
Design and context

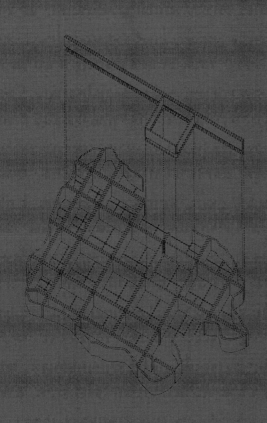

6.1 Introduction

Designing is not done in a vacuum. Designs are made for a specific place in a specific environment imbued with its own history. These characteristics, the constraints of the site, comprise the context in which a design is set.

The idea of context has played a particular role in architecture and planning. While it would seem perfectly logical to the layman that the site and its surroundings should influence the design, for planners it is not as simple as that. The main problem stems from the fact that "context" is no clearly defined phenomenon but different each time.

Context is not tied to a particular physical or temporal scale. The most tangible data—topography, existing buildings, existing functional links—as well as indirect factors—the origin, history and current significance of the place—can likewise make their mark on the design.

Thus the question of how the features of the site impinge upon a design has no cut and dried answer. This is something that designers themselves decide, and is contingent on their ideas and on the site in question. Whether an intervention in a large-scale landscape or the conversion of an existing building, a short operation or the onset of a long-term transformation process, all these approaches require that designers choose a stance on the context of their design.

And because context is never the same, it is important how they interpret a particular site.[1] Therefore, knowledge of and insight into the site are essential. The designers" interpretation of the context enables them to fix their own design premises. In addition, this insight can help pinpoint the problems of a site and subsequently formulate the design task. Finally, awareness of the planning constraints means that a proposed intervention can be made intelligible to others and so open to discussion.

We shall now examine the role the context of landscape or city can play in a design and the resources used to address the relation of design to context. Our analyses will focus on the relation between the site, the design response, the means employed and the design ultimately produced. These analyses are hypothetical in character and each time may be regarded as an interpretation of a design and the role context plays in it.

The examples given below are divided into two series: interventions in the landscape (6.2–6.5) and interventions in urban areas (6.6–6.9). In each series the complexity of the context is gradually stepped up; this is because the successive stages of development in landscape and city are conceived as separate "layers" that become superimposed over time. The more layers the greater the complexity of the context, i.e. the number and nature of factors influencing the design. Together the separate layers constitute the context. Any subsequent design operation adds a fresh layer that combines with the existing ones to determine the context for future interventions.

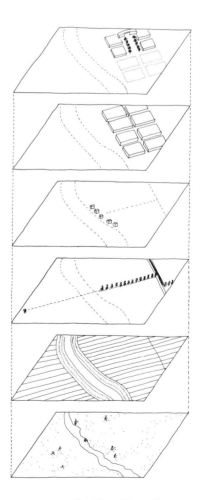

Stacking of 'layers'
- transformation
- the designed structure
- spontaneous growth
- architectural landscape
- cultivated landscape
- natural landscape

6.2 The landscape

Time is a crucial factor in what is often a continuous
process of landscape formation and development.
The growth rate of trees and the gradual build-up
and breakdown of inorganic matter by, say, erosion
are slow processes when compared with building a
house. All the same, these so-called natural processes
can be subject to sudden change as a result of natural
phenomena such as flooding. They can equally be
influenced by man's activities—for instance the
restructuring of large areas through reclamation.

Layers

Landscapes can be regarded as a stacking of horizontal layers over time; one layer provides the spatial
context for the next, and so on. This composition
can be determined by a natural system, such as the
deposit of layers of clay over peatland. The upper-
most layers can likewise be regarded as the context
for deliberate interventions by man, such as the
close-knit system of dikes, settlements, farmlands
and drainage ditches in a polder. Hallmarks of the
lower-lying layers of the landscape filter through
this pattern of visible spatial elements. To take one
example, the Spanish Steps in Rome recall the
underlying relief lines of the city.

We may conceive the composition of the landscape as an active processing of the preexisting
layers through the interaction of three systems
— natural, cultivated and architectural.

Nature, cultivation and architecture

The *natural landscape* is the result of the effects of
organic (living) nature on inorganic matter, such as
plants on sand and clay.

The *cultivated landscape* is the result of the effects
of a cultivation system (e.g. water management or
agricultural exploitation) on the preexisting natural
system.[2]

The *architectural landscape* is the result of a
conscious architectural processing of the natural
and cultivated landscape into a formal, architectural
composition.[3]

The following sections of this chapter examine
these three landscape types. The cultivated landscape
is examined using a Dutch "polder" as example.
The architectural landscape uses six examples:
a polder, two villas, two gardens and a park.

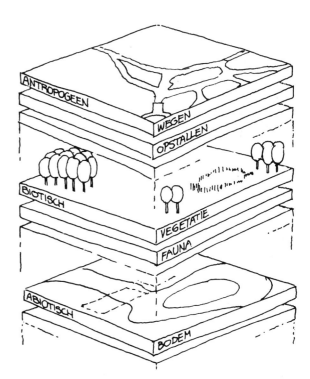

Isometric of landscape of superimposed layers

6.3 The natural landscape

The expansive systems of mountains, gorges, plains, forests and seas we call landscape came about naturally (i.e. unaided by man) over an immense period of time. This natural landscape is the product of exchanges between a physical system (inorganic matter such as sand, clay and peat) and a biotic system (the life forms of plants and animals). The natural development and dynamics of, say, erosion or tidal movement through wind and water currents govern the shape of that landscape to this day.[4]

This original structure, what we might call the *Ur-context*, is the basis on which man's interventions take place. In rock landscapes such factors as a solid ground on which to build and a safe altitude are reasons not to intervene unduly. In a river delta such as that of the Netherlands, by contrast, it is necessary to continually regulate the landscape and modify the terrain to sustain human life. In the Netherlands not a single square meter of land has been left unturned, so the Dutch situation is a good illustration of how natural landscape can be developed into a cultivated landscape.

The geology of the Netherlands is largely made up of clay, peat and sand, and in most cases has been reclaimed and worked since medieval times.

Sand and clay are composed of tiny grains; sand particles are larger, providing a sturdy foundation as well as possessing great porosity.[5]

The sandy areas in the Netherlands form such a stable basis, what we call a "geographical skeleton" with clay deposits and peat growth in and alongside it. This skeleton is comprised of the sand beds of the East and South Netherlands, the shingly and sandy midstream beds of the rivers, and the elongated sand banks and barrier bars. The latter lie in a north–south direction behind the present coastline.

The dynamics of the delta are most conspicuous in the area between the barrier bars of West Netherlands and the sand bed of East Netherlands. There an unbroken succession of erosion and accretion of land has created a lagoon-like area of islands built up of clay and peat.

In their natural state the peatlands consist of living peat moss which overran the lagoon at a time when the area was free of sea-flooding. They are in effect great wet sponges ("peat cushions") of com-

pressed plant organisms, laid out in an undulating pattern intersected by a network of peat rivers. Peat is able grow alongside and over clay and sand, and during flooding can be washed away or covered with clay. Taken vertically, a lagoon piles up alternating strata of clay and peat like a layer cake.

The clay region is largely the result of sea-flooding through coastal inlets carved out in the barrier bars by the river mouths. The clay polders of Groningen, Friesland, Holland and Zeeland provinces are in effect dried-up lagoons with taller banks of clay or salt marshes. This landscape type is the product of two movements: a fairly even influx of clay deposited by the sea, and a network of drainage systems or ebb creeks. The clay and peat areas express the geological composition of the West Netherlands landscape in a stratification reinforced by the land development system which regulates its dynamics.

The geology of the Netherlands:
sand, clay and peat

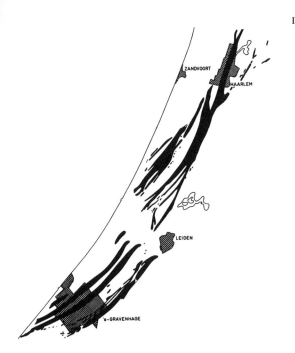

6.4 The cultivated landscape

When it comes to managing the landscape, Holland has its own tradition.[6] The "lowland technique" of drainage, discharge and coastal defense arose out of the need to regulate and fix the dynamics of the water movements in the delta area. Modifications and technical innovations are constantly required to deal with soil settlement and sea-level rise. It is a culture of survival, with a weather eye to the future and with hydraulic engineering dictating how the landscape is cultivated. The Dutch tradition of land management reaches back to late medieval times and especially to the seventeenth century, when the landscape was transformed in its entirety and dominated by reclamation and impoldering. This readying of the underlying structure for human activity involves specially preparing the ground, draining and opening it up, parcelling it and developing it.

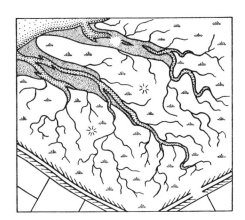

Peat and clay polders

To make a polder habitable and cultivate the claylands and more especially the peatlands, the one overriding concern is to regulate the water.[7] The situation from which work proceeded was the large and expansive peat bog of lakes and peatlands of living moss between the sands in East Netherlands and the coast. From the twelfth century on, this natural landscape has been methodically drained and cultivated by digging a taut mesh of ditches.

Narrow strips of land then emerged at right angles to the twisting course of the peat rivers, projecting long fan-shaped structures onto the natural peat landscape with building development on one bank only. Development, drainage and opening up —together these present a close-knit land management system. As a result of continual drainage the peat dried out, shrank and oxidized, causing the originally rolling peat surface to subside still further. It came to rest as a taut, even expanse of grass or peat meadowland, which, criss-crossed by countless drainage ditches and hemmed in by dikes, is still today the hallmark of the Dutch landscape. The water level is regulated artificially by channels and mills or pumping stations; this landscape unit we call a "polder."

The reclamation of the claylands was bound up with the process of diking in, draining and tilling the higher-lying parts of the shallow coastal waters

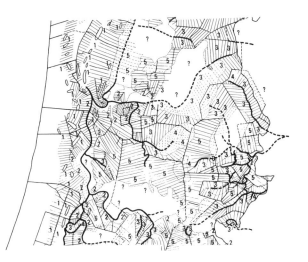

Barrier bars of Zuid-Holland province; the Old Rhine breaks through the narrow bars of sand level with Leiden

Salt marshes in the natural clay region

Cultivation of the peatlands in Noord-Holland province

or salt marshes. In the irregular shape of the dike alignments and the remaining channels we may still feel today something of the dynamics of the old lagoon. Smaller polders were assembled into a larger whole of a wafer-like structure. Opening up and developing as a rule follows the dike alignments, whereas the drainage process in the form of creeks does not. This landscape structure can be best seen in the southwest Netherlands, where diking has been a steady process since the late Middle Ages. Proceeding from a core area (such as the sands of West-Brabant or the ancient land of Zuid-Beveland) the adjoining salt pastures were diked in.[8]

The development of the impoldering technique encouraged the practice of emptying and cultivating lakes formed in the west of the country by peat-digging. A good example of such a reclaimed lake is the Beemster polder in Noord-Holland province.

The Beemster, a reclaimed lake

A polder of some five by eight kilometers set in the peatlands north of Amsterdam, the Beemster was originally a lake in a natural peat bog. The subsoil consists of fertile clay eminently suitable for exploiting agriculturally.[9] Many peat lakes have been pumped dry and cultivated in this way since the mid sixteenth century. Every such reclaimed lake is encircled by a canal into which pumping stations discharge the excess water from the lower-lying clay ground.[10]

The outer edge of this canal is defined by the former bank of the lake and locks into the surrounding peat meadowland, while the inner edge is part of the enfolding dike whose gentle slope provides an irregular border to the lower-lying clay polder.

The design of the Beemster takes its cue from the long tradition of cultivating the clay regions of the West Netherlands. The pattern of drainage is other than the usual procedure in peatlands, which kept the drainage system distinct from the pattern

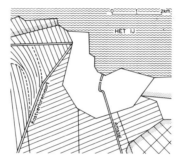

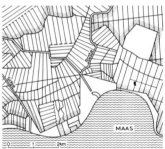

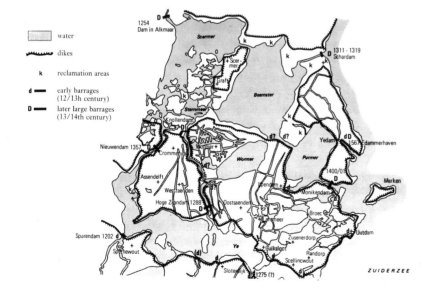

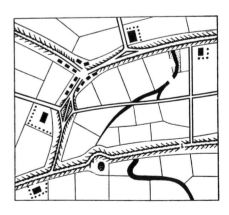

Topographical fixation by diking in the cultivated peatlands in Noord-Holland province. Ring-shaped dikes mark land needing protection from tidal waters

The cultivated peatland around Rotterdam and Amsterdam

The diked-in agricultural landscape on the coastal plains in the southwest Netherlands

of building development. From the end of the sixteenth century Dutch agricultural engineers became acquainted with Italian treatises on architecture and fortified cities built to geometric grids. In the Netherlands, knowledge on this subject had its focus at the Leiden Surveyors School (founded in 1600), where agricultural engineering, urban planning and fortress construction were all taught.[11]

The grid, such as that discussed in Chapter 2 in connection with Miletus in Greece, was developed further by the Romans and laid over the landscape as a framework for agricultural colonization. Such neutral grids were responsible for projecting the image of harmonious order typifying the Classical cultivated landscape onto the Dutch polderland.

The Beemster was pumped dry in 1612 under the direction of the hydraulic engineer and builder of mills, Jan Adriaanszoon Leeghwater (1575–1650 —his surname literally translates as "empty water"!). He was charged with the commission by a number of well-heeled Amsterdam merchants, who wished to invest their business capital in land reclamation. Two surveyors, Jan Pieterszoon Dou and Lucas Janszoon Sink, designed the parcelling using two systems of drainage ditches and roads set out of alignment but sharing a square grid of 1300 by 1300 meters. This pattern was projected onto the natural shape of the drained lake so that the principal direction of the grid corresponded as much as possible to that of the polder. The direction of the grid in general runs parallel to the former bank, to keep down the number of cut-offs. Yet at polder's edge a change occurs in the relative positions of the two patterns, encouraged by the convolutions of the polder's circumference. It is a shift dictated by practical considerations, the object being to leave a residual area with dimensions adequate to accept agricultural activity. For the polder as a whole, the pattern of squares is confronted with deviations deriving from the site. As a consequence, the hierarchically branched and irregular drainage network imposes a civil

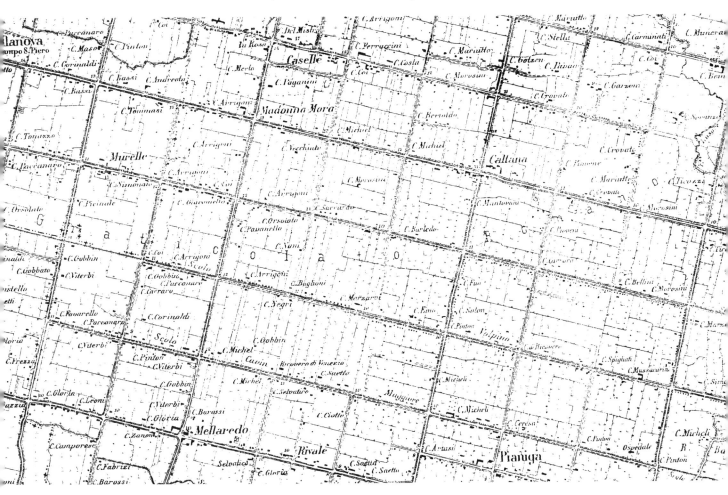

Grid of agricultural colonization in the Bassa Padana

engineering order on the squared layout.

The polder ground level sloping gently to the
northeast necessitates concentrating most pumping
stations on that side. Moreover, the predominating
southwest wind drives the greatest amount of water
there. Given the increasing depth of the polder, the
hierarchically organized drainage system of creeks
and parcelling ditches is subdivided into four polder
levels. This drainage system has been largely instrumental in fixing the positions of the farms on the
roadside of the plots, generating concentrated clusters
of buildings round the square access pattern.

These farms with their square plan and pyramidal
roof proved extremely well suited to the rapid
colonization of new areas due to the limited number
of building components and the efficient system of
assembly. Formwise a modular unit deriving from a
grid, this farm type had a bearing structure of a
mere four pillars, causing great central loads, something which sturdy clay ground could accept. Here
too a functional order, this time of agricultural
industry, was projected in squares. Densifying the
pattern of ditches in the most northeastern polder
area and siting smaller horticultural plots in the
southwestern part were moves prompted by the
context. The crosswise links through the polder had
to be squeezed into the square road pattern, which
itself failed to mate up consistently with the roads of
the surrounding area—hence the resulting modifications to the old land and the variety of road
widths.

For its first twenty years the layout of the
Beemster was fixed by the agricultural system alone.
Thenceforth the arrival of plantations, avenues and
settlements turned the polder into a rural resort.

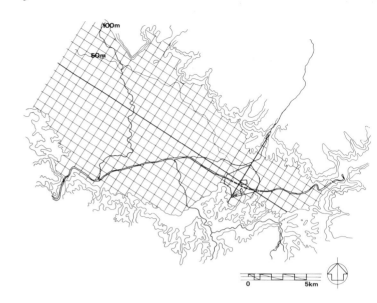

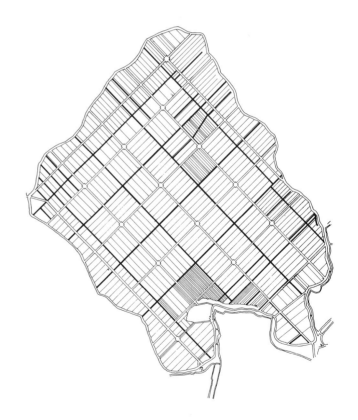

Arno Valley, alignment of Roman land division
runs parallel to the valley borders

Beemster reclamation area; engineers' diagram
showing drainage and agricultural production

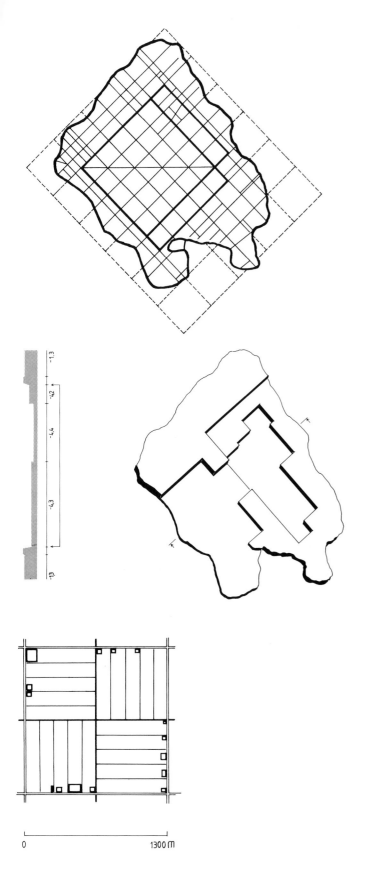

6.5 The architectural landscape

The transformation of the Beemster into a leisure landscape is a good example of architectural processing largely contingent on the cultivated ground pattern. Besides the Beemster, this section analyzes the Villa Rotonda, the garden of Versailles and the garden of Stourhead (see Chapter 2). These three designs are representatives in landscape architecture of staging in the rational, formal and picturesque modes respectively. In analyzing the garden designs in Chapter 2 the planning instruments used were three systems, geometric, spatial and pictorial. These tools prove equally applicable to analyzing designs in relation to their spatial context.

During the course of the seventeenth century the land development scheme of the Beemster took on an architectural dimension. This expresses the way the Dutch urban elite of those days came to terms with the landscape, relating as they did the arcadian ideal to agricultural exploitation.[12] They viewed land reclamation as a useful and profitable business that required ideological legitimacy and an architectural form. The Dutch countryside was then regarded as a technological arcadia, with the entire surface populated and worked.[13]

This Dutch landscape with its flatness, its straight lines, its unobtrusive coulisses and chiaroscuro effects generates a great sense of depth and an abstract idea of space. Changes in the weather and the light lend it a dramatic charge. The effect of depth created by a succession of objects receding into misty surroundings brings to it an atmospheric perspective, one that is enhanced when the polder is observed from higher-lying edges such as river banks and dikes.

Beemster reclamation area; shift in the diagram at the edge

Beemster; four polder levels

Beemster; concentration of clusters of development owing to the drainage system

Processing the cultivated landscape

In the Po Valley, as in the late sixteenth-century Italian villa farms, the Arcadian ideal was translated into the landscape of agricultural production.[14] The neutral land development grid of the valley is stepped up at Villa Emo in Fanzolo using a system of coordinates. In the central section of the villa, two axes intersect at the point where the house is raised above the wings. One axis (the transverse) organizes the agricultural program by means of a long colonnade, while the other "stages" the view over the cultivated landscape with a subdued poplar-lined avenue. The two together express the status of the landowner. In the Beemster this order is "democratized" and spread neutrally across the polder, though the engineer's schema was overlaid with a system of long tree-lined avenues along the access roads and country houses.[15] In the painting *The Avenue, Middleharnis* (1685) by Meindert Hobbema can be seen the essence of the avenue as compositional element, with the view from the road of the cultivated landscape framed by a tunnel of elms.

The avenues present a neutral pattern of square landscape compartments stretching across the entire polder. At the center of the polder the compartments are surrounded by four walls of trees, and the avenues linked to the horizon by a tunnel perspective. The effect is that of a tug-of-war between the horizon in the avenues, dissolving in an atmospheric perspective, and the limitedness of the compartments.

Processing the natural boundary

At the rim of the polder the grid underlying the cultivated landscape contorts, altering the character of the compartments and avenues. Here the tunnel perspective is governed by the slope of the dike, suggesting a strengthened perspective. The compartments are bordered on one side by the dike, which is kept free of planting. The grass of the meadows continues on up the dike slope, which gives the impression that the crown of the dike is the horizon. These circumstances derived from the context serve to optically lengthen the actual space. At the edge the spatial impression of the middle of the polder with its contained compartments and endless tunnel perspective is reversed. Here we see a direct confrontation between compartments and horizon. Rows of watermills originally lined the dike to give monumental expression to the encircling canal.

Philips Koninck, *Extensive Landscape with a Road by a Ruin* (1655). This painting shows the plain dominated by long rows of planting in between which lie towns, roads and rivers on equal footing. The human dimension of bridges, dikes and orchards is here pitted against the endless horizon

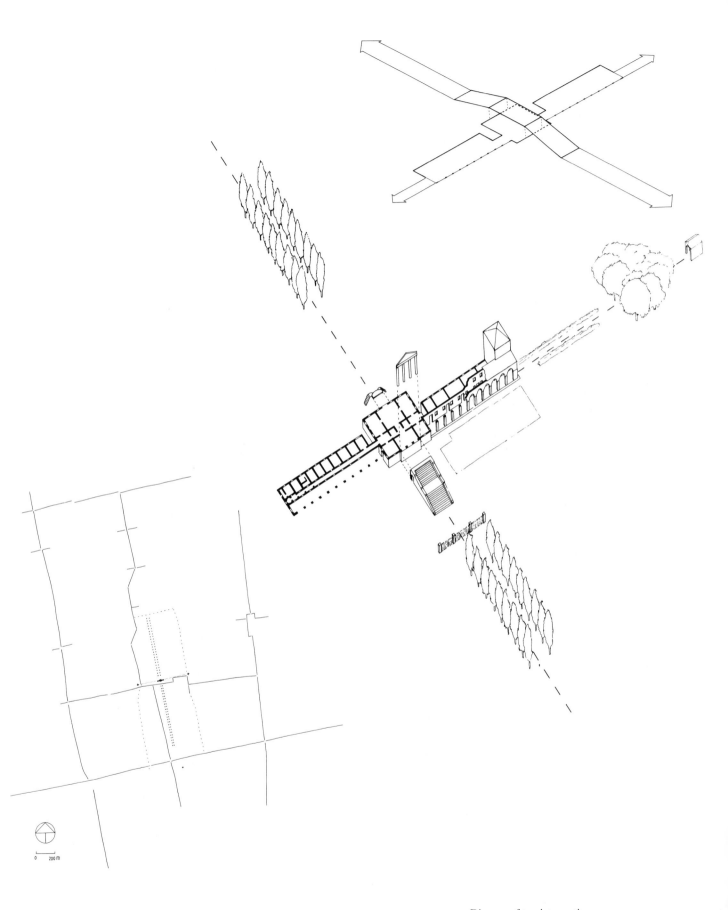

A. Palladio, Villa Emo, Fanzolo (1560).
Position of the villa complex in the agricultural
landscape

Diagram of two intersecting axes

A. Palladio, Villa Emo. Isometric showing the
two axes

0   200 m

Meindert Hobbema, *The Avenue, Middelharnis*
(1685)

Avenue of trees in the Beemster looking towards
the polder's edge

Country estates

The cultivated landscape of the polder was expressed architecturally at plot level too. The dotted rhythm of the pyramidal farmhouse roofs added subtlety to the taut, omni-sided image of the landscape compartments, the triangle of the roof standing out starkly against the delicate tracery of the elms. Sometimes a flush façade was set against the pyramid, recalling the Amsterdam canal houses—country life expressed architecturally by the urbanite. In a few cases the farmhouse as dairy farm was suppressed entirely by the plantation as urban arcadia.

Spatially these plantations, together with the house and grounds, reflected the restraint and utility of the polder. Vredenburgh, built in 1640 by the architect Pieter Post, is a good example.[16] At the beginning of the nineteenth century there were no less than 52 such country estates in the polder. All have since fallen into disuse and not one is left standing today.

Vredenburgh, like the Italian Villa Emo at Fanzolo in the Po Valley, was built up of elements of function and production. In the Beemster country estates there were orchards, vegetable gardens, avenues, canal-like water features and the house itself, all sited in a non-hierarchical relationship. By this means, the country estates reflected the natural, neutral character of the polder. The settlement of Midden-Beemster reflects this neutral character too. There is nothing to accentuate the place where its two avenues cross. All planes of development including the church and the open spaces are arranged unassertively round this intersection. Architecturally, the cultivated landscape in the Beemster is informed by the rational mode of staging, whose optical effects in turn exhibit formal features. This holds in equal measure for our next example, the Villa Rotunda.

The autonomous siting of the Villa Rotonda

When siting the Villa Rotonda, Palladio sought a relation between the villa and the surroundings on two distinct levels. At the level of the surrounding landscape, the villa is precisely positioned though without forfeiting its autonomous form. At the level of the immediate environment Palladio used the terrace as a link between the villa and the encompassing landscape. He describes the existing situation as follows: "The site is as pleasant and as delightful as can be found; because it is upon a small hill, of very easy access, and watered on one side by the Bacchiglione, a navigable river; and on the other it is encompassed with most pleasant risings, which look like a very great theater, and all are cultivated, and abound with most excellent fruits, and most exquisite vines: and therefore, as it enjoys from every part most beautiful views, some of which are limited, some more extended, and others that terminate with the horizon; there are loggias made in all the four fronts."[17]

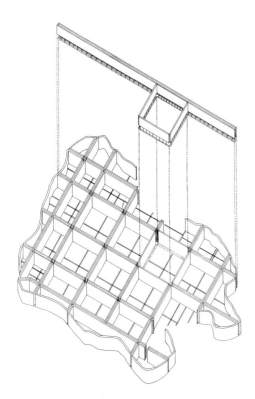

The Beemster as plantation; architectural division into avenues and landscape compartments

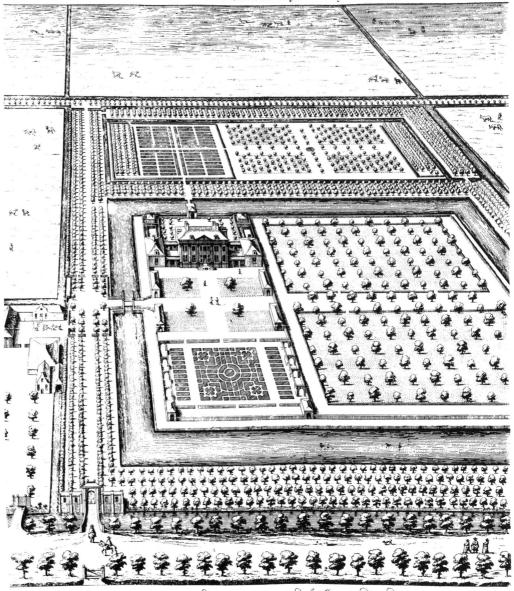

Pieter Post, Vredenburgh country estate (1640)

Positioning of the villa

On the map the villa's dome forms a pointed element on the center line of a ridge running parallel to the river Bacchiglione. By placing the house on this axis the differences in the surrounding landscape are exploited to a maximum in the panoramic views to be had from the porticos. Similarly, in positioning the villa on the hill the house is rotated 45 degrees, so that all façades receive several hours of sun a day. Seen from outside, the dome is an autonomous sign in the landscape, standing out against the irregular morphology of the surroundings. With the villa raised and projecting from the ridge, the porticos dramatically overlook the surroundings.

The southwest portico is linked to the tallest mountaintop in the vicinity, Monte Bella Guardia (129 meters), whereas the northwest portico relates to a chapel in the direction of Vicenza.

The northeast portico overlooks the cultivated landscape around Vicenza; the southeast portico, in turn, faces onto the river valley to the south of the villa. The contrast between cultivation and nature is brought into perspective by these alternating panoramas of natural and cultivated landscapes. Seen from a distance the quadrilateral, symmetrical composition of the porticos is every bit a stage-set in a landscape theater.

Assimilating the immediate surroundings

The hilltop occupied by the villa has been flattened out into a trapeziform plateau and bordered with four low retaining walls. The terrace thus created provides a link between the villa and the landscape.[18]

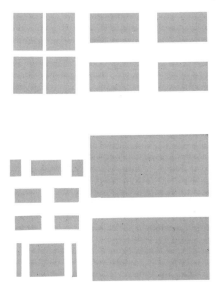

The villa stands in the center of this terrace. In order to relate the villa's symmetrical composition to the surrounding landscape types, the terrace's outward development proceeds differently in different directions. Visual elements in the surroundings are reflected in abstract terms in the terrace's layout using trimmed grass and fine gravel. The form and residual form of this division express the position of the villa on the plateau, thus rendering within the confines of the terrace the transition from stone to vegetation.

The geometric system determines the directions of the terrace walls and calls upon elements of the surrounding topography. The southwest boundary runs parallel to the line joining villa and chapel, establishing a connection with the buildings of Vicenza on the ridge. The southeast boundary assumes the direction of the grid of agricultural plots across the Bacchiglione. The northeast boundary follows the foot of the elongated ridge on which the villa stands.

Spatially, too, the terrace plays its part in "staging" the villa. The southwest side of the terrace wall is somewhat underdeveloped, its negligible depth seeming to consign the villa to the woods on this side. On the southeast side there is a slight rotation, shifting the panorama more towards the river valley. On the northeast side can be seen the first stage of a formal axis running between two sculptures placed symmetrically at the edge of the terrace. Finally, the northwest side provides a vista created by reducing the dimensions of the terrace and by its transition to the drive. The drive itself is wedged between two walls crowned with sculptures. On the south side the autonomy of the sculptural terrace block with retaining walls is given a touch of subtlety in the shape of indentations at the corners of these walls, providing a counterform to the villa block. Although the latter stands an autonomous object in the cultivated landscape, the land encompassing the villa contain elements relating to the villa's geometric system. An agricultural access road and a dike embankment once serving as a way through from the river are set on the northeast-southwest axis, thus anchoring the villa in the surrounding cultivated landscape.

Diagram showing composition of Vredenburgh country estate

A. Palladio, Villa Rotonda, Vicenza.
Views from the four porticos

Geometry of the terrace

The villa's position between the Bacchiglione
valley and the hills round Vicenza

Its decentralized position on the asymmetrical
plateau

0   25 m

0   400 m

Giving form to the landscape of Versailles

André le Nôtre deployed the architectural tool of optical manipulation in Versailles (i.e. in the formal garden design discussed in Chapter 2) not just to control the garden's internal composition. It also served him as a way of anchoring the garden in the landscape of a large, flat expanse of valley and the cultivated surroundings.[19] This valley is set at the head of a southward meander in the Seine, a basin-shaped marshy area in origin of two by one and a half kilometers. Using the optically manipulated principal axis mentioned earlier, Le Nôtre shortened the immense length of the plain. Designed as a vista, this axis combines a parterre (on the eastern hill), a descending walk (the eastern rim of the basin), a canal (the plain) and a rising grass track (the western rim). By having the axis mount the hill, Le Nôtre not only achieved unity within the garden, he anchored it in the great space of the valley, capitalizing on the flat expanse to bring the horizon into the garden. The principal axis of the vista is set asymmetrically in the valley, a condition Le Nôtre masked by giving the axis symmetrical form.

Preparing the ground

At the canal and the terrace the two cross axes are produced in a southerly direction, stressing the position of the main axis in relation to the edges of the plain. This effect is further enhanced by the different modes of terminating the cross axes; here are the only visible references to irregularities in the underlying morphology. A series of water features in the gardens eloquently allude to the relief, fountains and pools set on the axes marking the higher and lower points. The forms and positions of the parterres, steps and water features play down the mirror symmetry and pull together the garden composition and the irregular morphology of the ground. Where the formal garden touches the rim of the valley, there is confrontation between the geometric system of the plan and the natural form of the area. Differences in height on the edge of the valley are camouflaged with forest containing the garden's leisure program. The wooded edge of the domain isolates the garden from the surrounding cultivated landscape. Even so, avenues slice through the fringe of the wood and fan out across the plain,

anchoring the garden in the cultivated landscape and forging a perspectival link between the formal staging of the garden and the surroundings.

Stourhead and the picturesque staging of nature

In Chapter 2 we examined the English landscape garden of Stourhead as an autonomous architectural composition held together by a series of picturesque scenes. However, the morphology of the underlying and surrounding landscape also figures prominently in the garden's composition. This spatial context is worked into the design in three ways: by dramatizing the natural ground, by architecturally developing the slopes of the chalk plateau, and through the agency of a number of architectural objects placed outside the garden in the surrounding cultivated landscape.[20]

Stourhead is set against the steep western edge of Salisbury Plain, a vast stretch of chalk uplands gently sloping off in the east. Springs at the foot of the plateau have spawned many rivulets eroding the steep edge into a lobed form.[21] The sources of the River Stour lie in the long narrow valley of Six Wells Bottom; the garden of Stourhead is set in a much shorter and smaller valley at the place formally

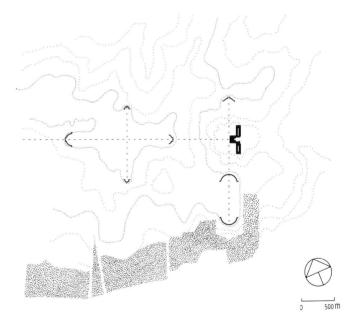

Garden of Versailles, ends of main and transverse axes. The irregularity of the underlying morphology, with differences in height camouflaged by woods

occupied by Stourton village green. Certain interventions have reinforced or dramatized elements of the natural ground. For example, damming the main valley revised the natural asymmetry of main and secondary valleys, generating a reservoir in the shape of an equilateral triangle. The ends of the reservoir have been masked by enlarging the pre-existing vegetation. In addition, the horizontal expanse of water hides the descending floor of the valley and centers the three rising plateau walls around a smooth reflecting lake, creating what is in effect a natural theater.

Architectural injection

The slopes of Salisbury Plain evoke a Mediterranean mountain landscape like those in the paintings of Claude. This picture of Classical Arcadia drenched in clear southern light is projected in a northern, English landscape hung with mist. The atmospheric perspective combines with the curving planted ends of the lake and the receding hills beyond in an evocation of depth and infinite distance. The various picturesque scenes are arranged around the lake and against the slopes. Most are centered on architectural objects alluding to classical antiquity; they are so placed as to bring out particularities in the underlying morphology.[22]

These objects in the landscape are set at various levels of the incline; some, such as the Grotto, the Palladian Bridge, the Temple of Flora and the Paradise Well, are reflected in the surface of the lake. Halfway up the incline is a mound on which sits a reduction of the Pantheon; at the top an imitation Temple of Apollo announces the edge of the plateau.

The positioning of indigenous and foreign vegetation on the slope is partly governed by the orientation to the sun. Acting as coulisses, these plantings draw attention to the built features. Finally, the theatrical effect of the architectural injection on the slopes is heightened by linking the objects along lines of vision (see diagram).

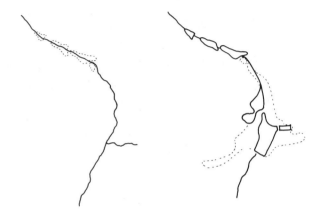

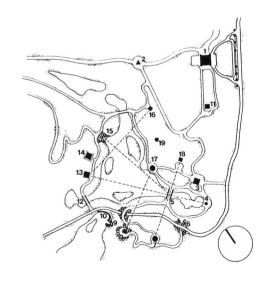

Stourhead garden; original state of upper reaches of the Stour

Stourhead; the course of the Stour regulated by fishponds and reservoirs

Relationship between objects around the lake

1   Stourhead House
2   Obelisk
3   Gardeners Building
4   Bristol Cross
5   Palladian Bridge
6   Rocks
7   Temple of Apollo
8   Seat
9   Waterfall
10 Dam
11 Apollo Belvedere
12 Iron Bridge
13 Pantheon
14 Hermitage
15 Grotto
16 Seat
17 Temple of Flora
18 Orangerie
19 Chinese Alcove

0   200 m

Stourhead; objects around the lake, prospect
across Palladian Bridge to Pantheon

Position on the edge of Salisbury Plain

The objects on the plateau

If the relation of the surrounding cultivated land-scape at Versailles is effected with systems of avenues, in Stourhead this is done by placing a number of objects at some distance from the garden. One of these is an obelisk marking the boundary of the chalk uplands.[23] This classical reference is joined by requisites illustrating the history of the English cultivated landscape, such as a Gothic roadside cross. Just visible from the garden is Alfred's Tower, a triangular tower 48 meters tall built as a memorial to the victory there by that Anglo-Saxon king against Danish invaders. This stand-out point marks the westernmost end of Salisbury Plain, and subtly draws the topography of the regional landscape into the composition.

This section closes with two further examples from more recent history. The first is a Dutch villa in a dune landscape, whose designer, unlike Palladio and the Villa Rotonda, allowed the form of the building to be heavily influenced by the spatial context. The second example is a city park whose setting is urban though the design itself has a rural disposition. It looks ahead to the following sections on urban context.

Villa Looijen, a contextual design

Built at Aerdenhout near Haarlem in 1950 to a design by Bernard Bijvoet, the erstwhile partner of both Johannes Duiker and Pierre Chareau, Villa Looijen melds chameleon-like into the landscape. Object and context seem to melt into one another. The house is set on the ridge of a dune incline facing northwest. The plot on which it stands is fixed by two parallel borderlines linking the ridge with the road below. Bijvoet anchored the house into its setting in two ways. The most important of these is the rotated angle; the other is the influence of context on the house's material.

Angle of rotation

The best way to analyze the relation between the composition of the villa and the shape of the site is by following three imaginary steps. A factor crucial to our analysis is the angle of rotation between the two blocks constituting the villa's composition.[24] In the first step we may regard the villa as two autonomous blocks set on a rectangular site; the bedroom wing and sun lounge, and the living wing. In this

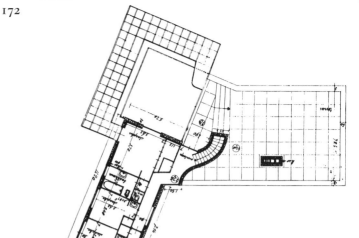

Bernard Bijvoet, Villa Looijen, Aerdenhout.
Plan

Villa Looijen, Aerdenhout. View from north
of entry zone

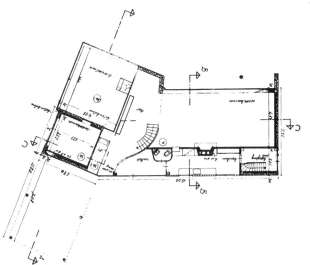

step the two blocks are set at right angles, parallel to the property boundary and grouped around a forecourt.

The second step we should regard as a modification of the composition to comply with a border following the line of the dune. This involves rotating the bedroom/sun lounge wing 23 degrees away from the living wing. The effect indoors is to make space for a free-form hall with a stair arcing up elegantly to the bedrooms. From the hinge of the rotated angle the visitor has a magnificent view diagonally through the living room to the dunelands beyond. Gently angled at both front and back, the two masses enfold an external space on both sides. At the front the blocks are joined by a garage to define a forecourt, at the rear the villa marks out the upper edge of a lawn ascending the dune.

The third step of the analysis sees the villa finally anchored in the site. Turning the entire ensemble clockwise gives the living room and sun lounge a more westerly orientation. Furthermore, the villa locks in to the morphology of the dunescape by engaging the slope diagonally from a position fixed with a surveyor's precision. A pair of imaginary lines between which the villa is wedged define the ultimate direction it will take. One of the lines is the building limit, 20 meters in from the north side of the site, the other is determined by two small angles in the plot boundary.

The drive to the villa winds along the sandy incline at whose highest point it reaches the forecourt. From here the view of the lower-lying dunelands is screened off by the all but blank wall of the living wing. The garage dug into the dune marks the slope on the east of the site; the bedroom wing is raised up on pilotis, generating an informal route running beneath it to the living room terrace and garden at the back. Diagonal paving on part of the route reiterates the angle between the blocks. There is a second route running from the hall up the stair to the roof garden. From here one can enjoy a view out over the dunes towards the sea. This route has a sequel across a kind of balcony attached to the steel pergola of the sun lounge. Here we find a major point of convergence: from this balcony, where internal and external routes cross at different levels, garden, dunes and sea melt into one great panorama.

Villa Looijen, pergola at rear

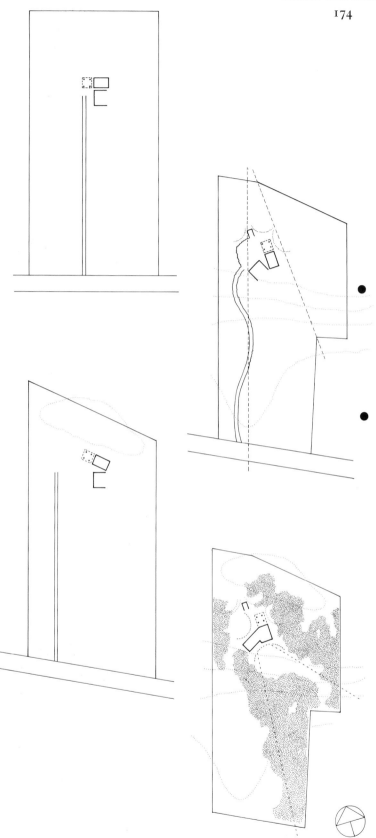

Material

Our chameleon metaphor can be extended to include the material. The untreated concrete and rubble clad walls of the villa allude to the gray-brown of the sandy surroundings, whereas the tenuous glass-and-steel sun lounge reflects the area's spatial limitlessness and continuity. These references to the character of the surroundings are cast into bolder relief by the various directional lines and shapes of roof, which take their cue from the undulations of the dune landscape.

Parc del Clot, the dramatizing of the urban topography

After the foregoing examples which proceed from the context of the natural and cultural landscape, we turn the situation round to examine a rural intervention in an urban setting.

In the city, the park preeminently expresses how urban culture is bound to nature. City parks are a product of nineteenth-century urban culture: the expanding metropolis developed a new way of expressing its relationship with the landscape, originally employing to this end the eighteenth-century picturesque landscape design (see Stourhead).[25] In early city parks the composition of the landscaped garden was turned inside-out, placing nature in the center of the park and built development on its edge.

The winding route through such parks was coupled to a sequence of scenes in which the surrounding development was confronted with the inward-facing natural layout. From the turn of the century this programmatically empty container of the picturesque design was increasingly adapted to fit the expansion in leisure facilities of the modern urbanite.

In some cases this led to the park being split into an urban and a rural section, with the picturesque composition more and more hollowed out into a template amidst the park's programmatic features.

In today's city park, traditional and modern formal means are quoted at will in a free composition of elements. The literal stratification of the site has its roots in an extensive urban program; Spain and France head the field in this development.[26] In Spain in recent years squares and parks have become major building blocks in a planning strategy aimed at improving the city as a whole. The issues each

Schematic positioning of the villa components on the plot

Final anchoring of the villa in the terrain

The villa's organization adapted to suit the morphology of the dunelands

Spatial position in the morphology of the planted dunelands

time are to clarify the park's place in the urban structure, carve out space in the compact metropolis and make accessible amorphous areas in the city. The continuity of the urban fabric is improved as a result, there being fewer barriers. Barcelona is a good example of a city where this planning strategy has been applied many times.

The park

The Parc del Clot is set in the grounds of a former Spanish rail works yard, wedged between the ancient village of El Clot with narrow streets densely built-up and the suburb of San Marti with its characteristic composition of large perimeter blocks, the so-called Cerdà grid. The natural topography follows a gentle southeastern incline to the sea. Slowly ascending this slope is the northeastern exit road from old Barcelona on which lies the village of El Clot. The railway track and rectangular plan of the works yard is located southeast of the village.[27]

The Cerdà grid, projected as it is on the natural site, follows broadly the contour lines of the slope and meets the exit road and railway lines at an angle. The grid is further intersected by avenues running diagonally which directly link the nodes in the urban fabric. A number of the perimeter blocks in the grid have been replaced by tall residential tower blocks, with the taut rectangular confines of the former railway yard standing out as well-defined urban elements in these piecemeal surroundings. Two dead-straight axes slice through the park, locking into the surrounding urban topography by way of the clearly defined borders. The park is built up of two sharply separated areas, one urban (a promenade and a square), the other landscape (a bare hill and a wooded area).[28]

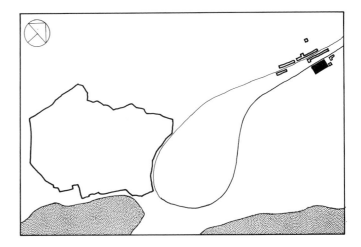

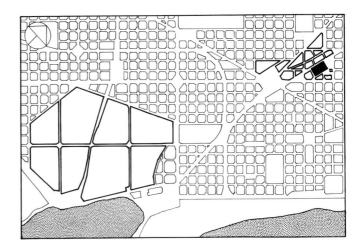

Parc del Clot, Barcelona; position in the natural topography

Position of Parc del Clot and the railway track in the first half of the nineteenth century

Position of the railway yard in the Cerdà grid

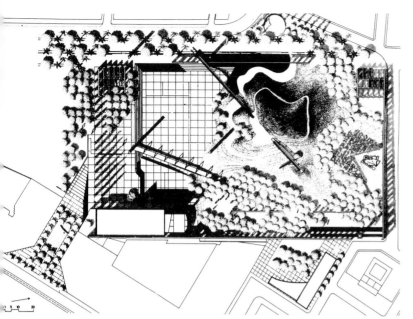

Directions in confrontation

Carved out of the capriciously shaped landscape section are various geometric elements including a maze.

The directional lines of the surroundings, usually deriving from the Cerdà grid, clash with the linear strip of the former factory walls and the newly laid-out water features, steps and vegetation enclosing the park. This confrontation is continued in the park itself by pitting the tracks of the two axes deriving from the surroundings and the shape of the maze against the rectangle of the site. This culminates in a point where one axis punctures the western edge of the site in a cluster of directional lines, thereby expressing the park's position as part of a node in the local urban topography. The tensionality between natural topography and overlaid geometric schema is intensified by these confrontations and references and played out in the park design. Four tall light masts stationed in the square similarly allude to the module of the Cerdà grid. The direction of the grid is taken up by two pedestrian axes where it clashes with the direction followed by the hard-surfaced square and the steps.

The sunken square; an urban theater

The major spatial elements in the park are a sunken square and a raised bare hill. The resulting differences in height are exploited in the spatial staging. Such components as the stage, the stands and the landscape decor are pulled together by an umbrella element, the "director's box," which binds all components together in two routes that literally overarch the stage. These axial routes, aimed at a former chimney in the eastern corner of the site, mate up with the splintered structure of desire lines in the surroundings. The material treatment of the park is expressive and sculptural. Remnants of the railway yard double as long colonnades on the edges of the park to mark the site's limits and to pick out various spatial forms. Existing elements such as the factory walls combine with the strikingly designed light masts, water features and footbridges as expressive nodes amalgamating past and present. Selectively regulating the use of the intermediary zone between park and city, they link up with three areas beyond the park whose lines derive from the Cerdà grid but whose material presence is fixed by the park. They differentiate the park boundary as well as express the reciprocal involvement of park and surrounding urban topography.

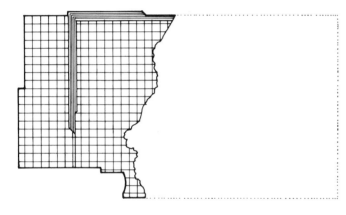

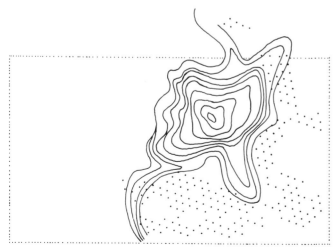

Parc del Clot, plan

Parc del Clot; urban and rural parts

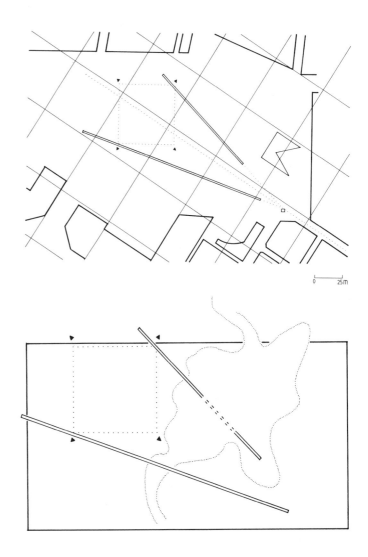

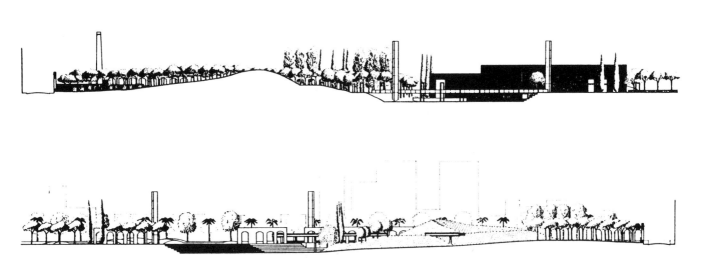

Cerdà grid worked into park design

Confrontation of directions in the park periphery

Sections through the park

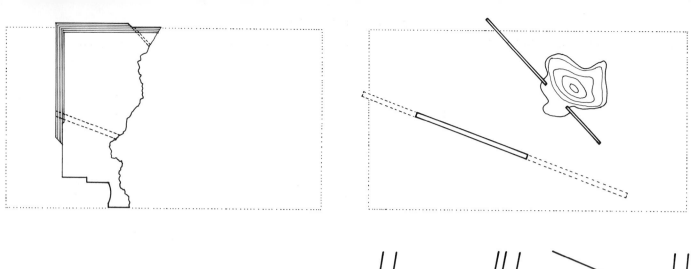

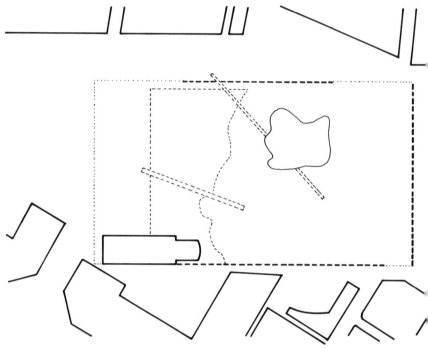

Node of elements: light mast, factory wall, pool
and footbridge

Spatial composition in three levels; the sunken
square, the hill with raised bridges and the
ground level of the urban surroundings

6.6 The development of city form

If the foregoing sections focused on the relationship between context and design in a rural setting, the following concentrate on the urban area as design context.

It is not only technical, economic, political and social circumstances that influence the way the city adapts to the requirements of time; prevailing ideas in architecture and planning are also a major factor. Accordingly, the relation of context to design has varied enormously over time.

One example of a far-reaching tabula rasa approach—i.e. treating the site as a blank page— is Le Corbusier's celebrated Plan Voisin of 1925. In this project the Haussmannian city has to clear the field on the right bank of the Seine for a crisp pattern of cruciform tower blocks. Only selected monuments from the old city are spared and as-similated in the scheme. The only relationship between the context and the design is in the align-ment of the point grid of the towers, into which is worked the existing westward axis of the Louvre.

The other extreme can be exemplified by the response by the French architect Bernard Huet, whose design study stresses the historical develop-ment of the site. In his interpretation of the histo-rical context Huet even goes further that the actual history. Thus, in his 1986 plan for the Bassin de la Villette in Paris he projects a "patte-d'oie" onto the area for redeveloping, Ledoux's Rotonde and sur-roundings. Huet brings a "perfecting" symmetry to the originally asymmetrical urban node by adding an imitation canal. Aspiring to a historical ideal, this solution merely relieves the site of its specific features in its efforts to "repair" the urban fabric.

In the final decades of the twentieth century we see context figuring heavily in many prevailing ideas on design. One of the prime issues of research designers and historians consider in the develop-ment of city form is which factors determine this development. In such research the city is treated emphatically as a spatial phenomenon and not, as in other periods, as a socio-economic system.

This concern with the relationship between context and design gathered particular momentum in the fifties and sixties when Team Ten and the Tendenza group around Ernesto Rogers offered a scathing criticism of the design ideas of function-alism and its tabula rasa tendencies.[29] Saverio Muratori and Carlo Aymonino's research into the developing of new design methodologies, done in Venice in the fifties, forged a link between the morphology of the city and the typology of built development. Their aim was to discover which were the constant and which the variable factors in the city's evolution.[30] In the sixties, when the Italian research took a great leap forward with the work of Aldo Rossi and others, the issue of research into urban form began steadily to impress itself on other countries too.[31]

Thus, in Barcelona the accent came to be on combining research into the form of the city and research into the meaning of that form in everyday life, with the use of urban space conceived as an expression of urban culture.[32] In this approach, dominated as it is by the reciprocal relationship between form and use, the link is made between city form and morphological research into functions of urban space. A fine example is the restructuring of the Barcelona district of El Raval, in which intro-ducing a new sequence of public spaces brought about changes in the urban structure.

In other studies mainly done by historians, the development of the city form is seen rather as a relatively autonomous process that largely eschews big interventions. In the historical theories of the French Annales School, whose chief representative is Fernand Braudel, a distinction is made between different processes in history operating at different "speeds," each with their own "dynamics" and their own spatial "patterns."[33] According to these theories processes of change in, say, day-to-day life are much slower than changes in politics, economics and pro-duction (where they are marked by "events" such as revolutions, shifts in trade routes and technological discoveries). The patterns of the various processes slide by each other as historical "strata"; it is their interrelationships that determine the structure of city and landscape.[34] In the light of these theories the history of city form can indeed be seen as a comparatively autonomous process with its own speed and its own dynamics.

In his research into the history of the Parisian inner city, the French architect Bruno Fortier con-cludes that the form of the city is not fixed only by large urban operations, but just as much by developments independent of such interventions.[35] These are often informal structures of use closely bound up with daily life in the city. One of his discoveries is the apparently autonomous birth of nineteenth-century arcades in the shelter of Haussmann's boulevards, with a major part to play in the commercial and cultural life of Paris.

As we can see from the wide range of approaches, studies and research, the quest for the development of the city's form is still in full swing. The overriding issue remains that of which factors fix the physical appearance of the city and what role design can play there.[36] Does the form of the city have its own life history or can it be understood only in the light of developments undergone by other factors? In the first interpretation the evolution of the city is treated as a relatively autonomous process with its own speed, dynamics and spatial patterns. In the second, city and landscape are looked upon as the products of growth and transformation processes lasting centuries, in which changes in one historical stratum are able to generate changes in other strata and in the structure as a whole.

Le Corbusier, Plan Voisin (1925).
Model viewed from the northeast

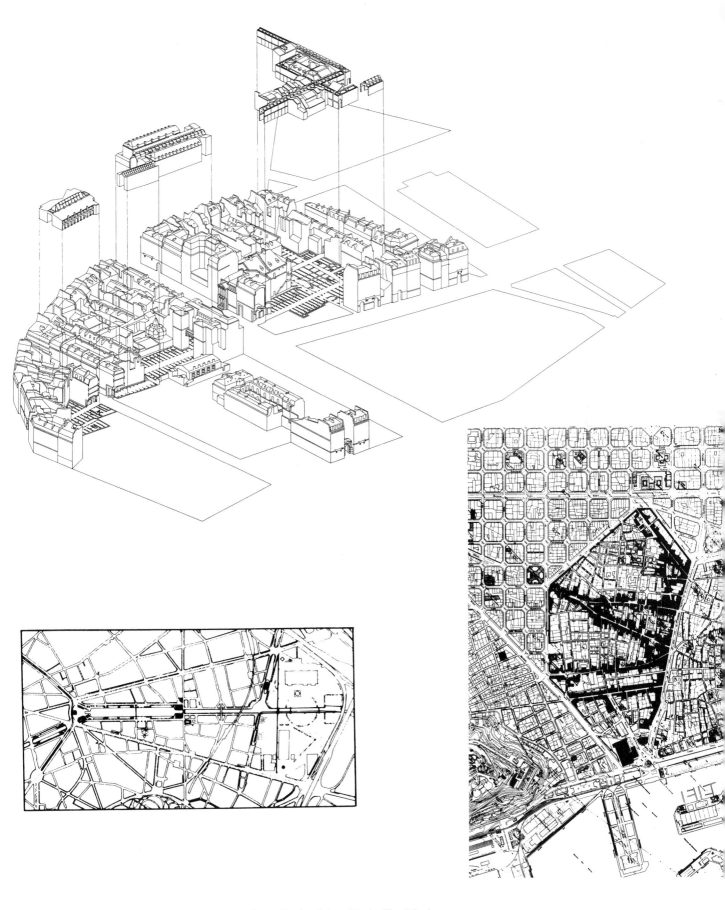

Bernard Huet, design for the Bassin de la Villette (1986), design drawing with Place Stalingrad (center) and Ledoux's Rotonde

Bruno Fortier, Atlas of Paris. The Atlas is a thorough investigation with precisely drawn indications of changes in the urban fabric; here is the nineteenth-century arcade between the Rue du Faubourg Montmartre and the Rue du Quatre Septembre

Barcelona, El Raval. Changes in the city's structure brought on by introducing a new series of public spaces; analytical drawing of the existing situation

6.7 Growth of the urban fabric

Settlements are the outcome of one of two processes. First, they can be a natural or spontaneous development at places where conditions are favorable to human subsistence—high, dry places, on routes across land or water, at crossroads, at a natural harbor or mooring place. Second, they can be founded, meaning that they are designed and built at a single stroke, usually by governmental decree; we shall be looking at the founding of cities in section 6.8 (the designed structure).

In the case of natural growth, towns are not in fact "designed"; the developments occur without a preconceived idea of what the result will be. Designing, by contrast, is a conscious, creative act with a preconceived plan.

This absence of design can be read in the outward appearance of such settlements. Structure, form and image derive from the close collaboration between natural givens and human needs. They are determined exclusively by the geomorphological ground, by received experience and by the prevailing technology, available materials and so on. There is no conscious manipulation of natural givens. Thus, the disparate appearances of, say, a Swiss mountain village or slums in Mexico City are the result of differences in natural givens, social conditions and available technology.[37]

This doesn't mean that there is no form of design whatsoever in such phases of development. What conscious, preconceived interventions there are remain limited, though, to the individual components of the whole and to practical considerations. Analogous to the step-by-step development from agrarian to urban area, changes that occur within this entity are gradual ones. The inducement for such change may come from adjustments in the needs of its inhabitants, advances in civil engineering or shifts on the social or political plane. This type of urban development satisfies certain forms of human society, mostly at a low level of development. In Europe, for instance, the natural growth of settlements has seldom occured since the end of the Middle Ages and the rise of the highly developed civic town. A perfect example of a settlement whose structure is governed by the interplay of geomorphological data and human needs is medieval Amsterdam. The influence of the sophisticated system of draining the peatlands on the settlement pattern has here produced a unique urban structure.

The geological foundation

In the fourteenth century, the peatlands of Holland were almost exclusively cultivated, with a network of peat rivers large and small at right angles to which were long slivers of reclaimed land.[38] In Amsterdam, where the River Amstel—one of the large peat rivers—flows into the IJ, the landscape consisted of relatively large slabs of peat whose pattern was fixed by the rational system of drainage: long strips of peat in a comb configuration square to the river. A sea dike parallel to the IJ protected the reclaimed land (the settling peat) from the water beyond.

Level with the Amstel the dike billowed inland to dam the river from the open waters of the IJ. This dam across the Amstel created an artificial hydraulic engineering entity, Amstelland. It also advanced the technical state of the river from a natural harbor basin to a reservoir with a discharge into the IJ. The direct link with the open water now took the form of two new canals parallel to the river, linking the Amstel to the IJ through sluices in the dike.[39]

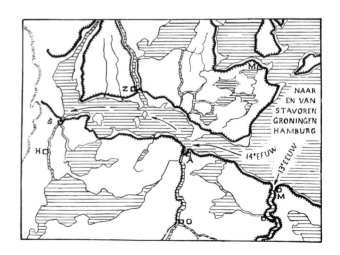

Medieval diking-in round the IJ

The urbanization pattern

The most important factors determining the form of the first settlement were the meandering course of the Amstel and the mode of entering the IJ. The first buildings were set on either side of the inward-curving dike.

The further urbanization of the agrarian area took place as a step-by-step infill of the space between the first built development and the newly dug water courses. Existing drainage ditches and paths of the peatlands were incorporated into the structure of the settlement; they would fix the course taken by streets and alleys. The center of the burgeoning town grew around the Dam, which would also play a major part in the ingenious water system. Around it arose the market, town hall, church and exchange.[40]

City of water

During the Middle Ages Amsterdam developed on either side of the Amstel in equal measure. Each expansion took place according to the same principle; new water courses were dug at a short distance from and more or less parallel to the existing ones and plugged into the sophisticated water management system. The existing pattern of avenues, paths and polder ditches were assimilated in the built development which enfolded the older parts like a new skin. There thus emerged a system of secondary side and back streets more or less square to the primary water network. This secondary system combined radial land links with the main routes to and from the city.

The water was the most essential component of medieval Amsterdam, governing its spatial structure and functional composition alike. The water network provided the main transportation structure of city and harbour; it likewise served to carry off refuse and fecal matter.

There were fundamental differences between the (primary) water system and the (secondary) road system. The position and dimensions of the waters were fixed by civil engineering and shipping requirements. By contrast the position, direction and size of the back and side streets were predicated upon geological data.

There were differences of function too. The waterside development served trade, transport and storage, whereas the secondary traffic network was given over to houses, suppliers and specialized crafts.

An air of hydraulic engineering permeated the entire urban fabric. Each expansion of the urban area meant an expansion of the water network; the new water courses were each time the new borders to the growing town. This principle of the water-based city would prevail throughout all medieval urban expansions of Amsterdam up until the seventeenth century.

The areas outside the medieval town were not subject to this pattern of urbanization. Consequently from the fifteenth century on, ropewalks, wharfs and allied crafts clustered at random in the IJ-side area beyond the dike.

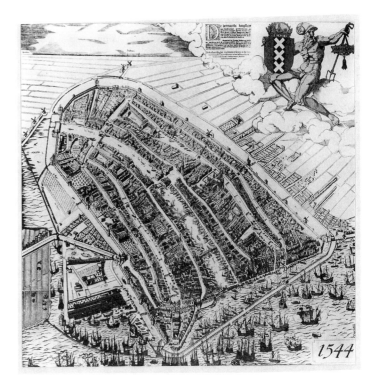

Amsterdam in the Middle Ages

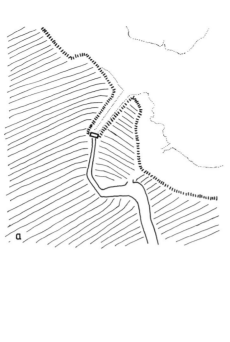

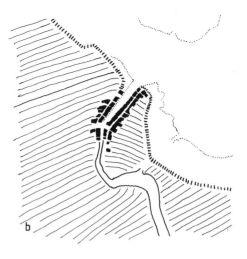

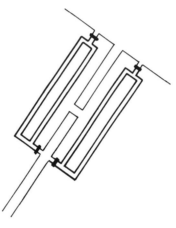

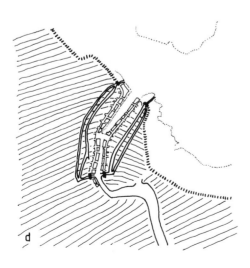

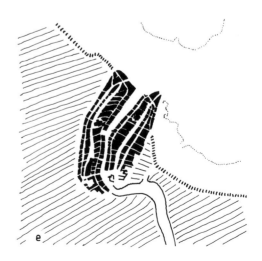

Amsterdam in the Middle Ages, reduction drawings
a the peat landscape after diking in
b the first built development either side of the sea dike
c diagram of the drainage system
d the drainage system on site
e the development structure

6.8 The designed structure

The need for a rational approach to the development of the city came at a time when ideas were taking shape regarding the city as habitat for a particular form of society.[41] In the broadest sense this has obtained since the grid city models of the Greeks functioned as a spatial translation of the concepts "polis" (city) and "democracy," up to and including the urban expansions of our time.[42] If spontaneous growth can be conceived as a palpable reflection of a society—that of Europe in the Middle Ages, for example—then city design can be regarded as an attempt to create the ideal spatial conditions for a society worth striving for.

With the emergence of planning came a rational approach to urban development. From that moment on, city form could undeniably boast a design; formal ordering principles made their appearance and with them the possibility to interpret and manipulate the context.

The most important stimulus for this development came from the diagrams of ideal cities in the ascendant in Italy since the fifteenth century. Such plans were developed with the rise of the Renaissance and satisfied in their formal composition the humanist demand for total correspondence between the perfect socio-political arrangement and the perfect architectural form for the city.[43] The "città ideale" was designed according to the new insights and the laws of perspective. The ordering principles applied—geometric figures such as grids, circular forms containing a concentric or radial configuration and regular polygons—were tuned to the laws of symmetry and proportion.[44]

With the advent of perspective and the attendant increase in scale the spatial composition and form of a city could be deployed as a symbol of the latter's function and meaning. In later times and particularly among the absolute monarchs the city form was systematically used as a means of expressing power.

In the further spatial development of the city the ideal city designs of the Renaissance would function as types, in the sense of concept, type and model.[45] In the first instance, the ideal city diagrams were mostly employed for the founding of new cities. In addition, the abstract diagrams served as models which were copied literally and projected onto a new context. There was nothing here of a specific relationship between context and design. The "ideal" fortified town of Palma Nova was just such a standardized export product, as can be surmised from the Dutch fortified town of Coevorden.

In the further development of the ideal city attention shifted in the design from unity of form to applicability in practice. To this end applications were sought for programmatically exceptional city types (such as ports, fortresses, garrison towns and court capitals) but also for possibilities of applying the ideal city diagrams in the expansion operations of existing cities. The latter took place at a great scale in the European urban expansion schemes of the sixteenth and seventeenth centuries. In this context the abstract and ostensibly rigid schemas demonstrated such a degree of flexibility that they could be modified to suit every contingency. These "site-specific" corrections often gave rise to structures in which geological conditions played a major role, much as they had done in evolved cities.

In a design, other than in natural growth, the relationship between context and plan is the result of deliberate decisions.

Given the application of design to the city form, one of the key points in the design process is the question of whether an intervention responds to the context and if so, how. Often it is the very manner of dealing with the site that produces a particular design or gives rise to the features and identity of a city or district.

Amsterdam in the Golden Age[46]

If medieval Amsterdam is a good example of how natural givens and human needs interact, then its expansion in the seventeenth century is a perfect demonstration of the modifications the formal ordering principles of the ideal city diagrams could undergo when applied in practice.

Formal ordering principles

The concentric rings of canals in Amsterdam incorporate two ideal city diagrams: Daniel Speckle's fortified city and Simon Stevin's commercial city.[47]

The affinity with the fortress—a perfected war machine in which form and structure were determined exclusively by military aspects—can be discovered in the formal composition of the canal rings: a polygonal fortification with a radial structure. Likewise, similarities with Stevin's model, designed

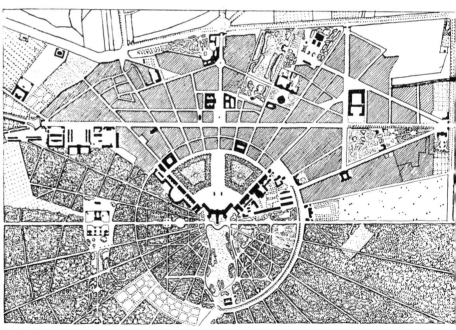

The Dutch fortified town of Coevorden. Founded in 1597, its plan is based on that of Palma Nova

The ideal city as concept: Antonio Averlino *filarete*, conceptual drawing of the ideal city of Sforzinda (from *filarete*'s architectural treatise, completed circa 1464). This schema is still based on the tradition of the medieval representation of the globe and the principles then prevailing in surveying and cartography. Only later would it transpire that the star-shape possessed clear military advantages

The shape of the city as a means of expressing power: the residential city of Karlsruhe

The ideal city as model; Palma Nova, Italy. Built to protect Venice in 1593 to a plan by Vincenzo Scamozzi, the city is a perfect example of a fortified city "ex novo." A particularly exacting aspect of the task was inserting the hexagonal Place d'Armes in the nine-sided bastioned fort

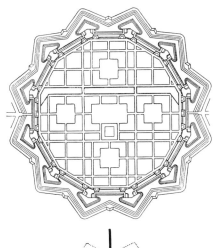

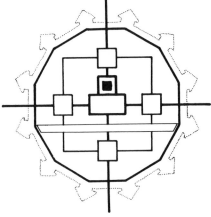

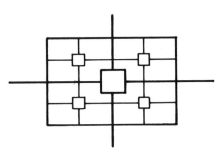

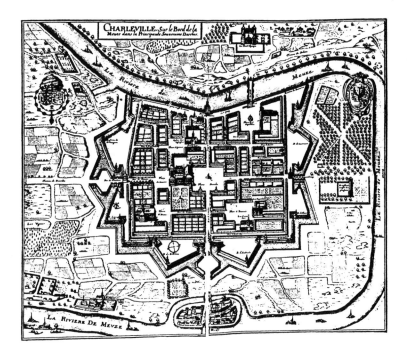

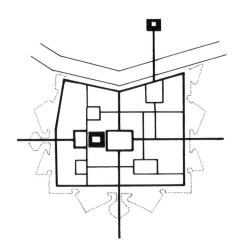

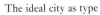

The ideal city as type
a Vincenzo Scamozzi, ideal city design from
  circa 1600
b reduction drawing of Scamozzi's ideal city
c the typological diagram: plan with four
  quarters
d reduction drawing of Charleville

Charleville, founded in 1608

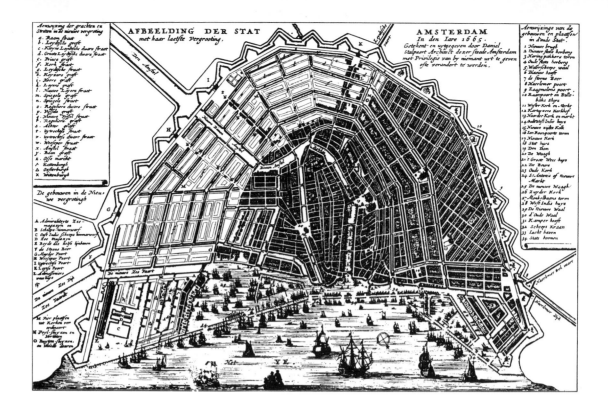

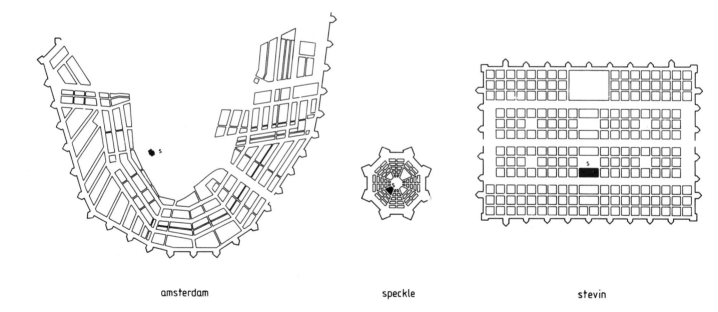

amsterdam   speckle   stevin

Plan of Amsterdam dating from 1665 showing
seventeenth-century city layout. The western
part of the ring of canals and the Jordaan area
are complete, the plans for the southern and
eastern parts of the expansion are still at the
design stage. In old plans of Amsterdam the IJ
is at the foot of the city, with North below

The ring of canals compared with Speckle's and
Stevin's ideal city diagrams: the three plans are
drawn to the same scale

with regard to optimum use of the plot layout and in which military aspects were subordinate to flexibility and efficiency of the commercial town,[48] can be read in the linear organization of those rings and the size and scale of the building plots. Just how much these canals were a "projection" of the abstract diagrams on the preexisting landscape, or a sensitive insertion of a specific design in a specific context, can be discovered by analyzing the seventeeth-century city.

Adapting to existing situations

For the purpose of comparing this part of Amsterdam with Speckle's plan, the canal ring has been modified into a regular polygon. From this it transpires that the expansion plan is less regular than might be assumed at first sight. The ring of canals is, admittedly, "kinked" in some segments, yet the radials intersect quite at random. Their positions are more governed by their inclusion in the medieval town and by existing land routes than by a formal composition.

For comparison with Stevin's scheme the canal ring has been straightened out and drawn as a linear strip. It shows most clearly the differences between components of the plan. All three parts (the western part with the canal ring of 1611 and the Jordaan district, the southern part of 1657 between the Jordaan and the River Amstel, and the part east of the medieval town of 1682) show to perfection just how wide-ranging the contextual interpretations of a design can be.

Thus, in the canal ring (comprising Herengracht, Keizersgracht and Prinsengracht) the treatment of the context varies per "stratum" of the plan. Seen in terms of the spatial and functional organization of parallel canals separated by generous, deep urban blocks, the canal ring is a continuation of the medieval Dutch town on the water. In its formal composition, by contrast, it is a projection of the "città ideale" onto the polder—a rationally designed segment of city built at a stroke and taking no account of the underlying ground.

The Jordaan, on the other hand, is a direct translation of the existing cultivated landscape into an urbanized area. Its spatial structure is a consequence of retaining the old ditches and paths; the intervening meadows would be primed (possibly raised) for building. This difference in approach coincides

with the differences in function and use of the two areas. Whereas the canal ring is a representative part of town for lavish houses for the well-to-do, the Jordaan contains services and businesses plus housing for the lower classes.

The southern part of the expansion follows broadly the composition of the canal ring; the new structure is laid over the agricultural pattern of the polder. The irregularities at the edge of the plan —at the borders of the medieval town and the new bastioned fortress—are neutralized in shallow, irregularly shaped building blocks. These housed the services for the representative canal ring.

The eastern portion, finally, consists of two quite distinct parts. If the southern part remains a continuation of the canal rings with its main structure parallel to the moat, in the northern part the plan's principal alignment is rotated 90 degrees and set square to the moat. In one fell swoop, the landscape to the east of the city is turned on its head: the new extension is laid diagonally over the ground pattern. At the same time the thirteenth-century sea wall is lost in a largely orthogonal grid.

On another level to that of the ground pattern, this component of the plan does enjoy a firm relationship with the surroundings. It matches up with the structure of the island archipelago east of the medieval town which had meanwhile developed from a place beyond the dike for fringe activities into a series of islands for living and working.[49] This elaboration of the eastern component heightened the differences visible in Amsterdam since the Middle Ages. The work sector of the city became concentrated in the eastern part whereas the canal ring grew into the representative part of the city. As to the link—if there is one—between a form of snobbery among the seventeeth-century bourgeoisie and the deviations from the radial ideal city diagrams in the Jordaan, the irregular blocks in the southern part and those in the northern section of the eastern part, it is not our concern here.

From our analysis, it transpires that formal considerations in the design of the seventeenth-century city extension are less decisive than it seems at first sight.

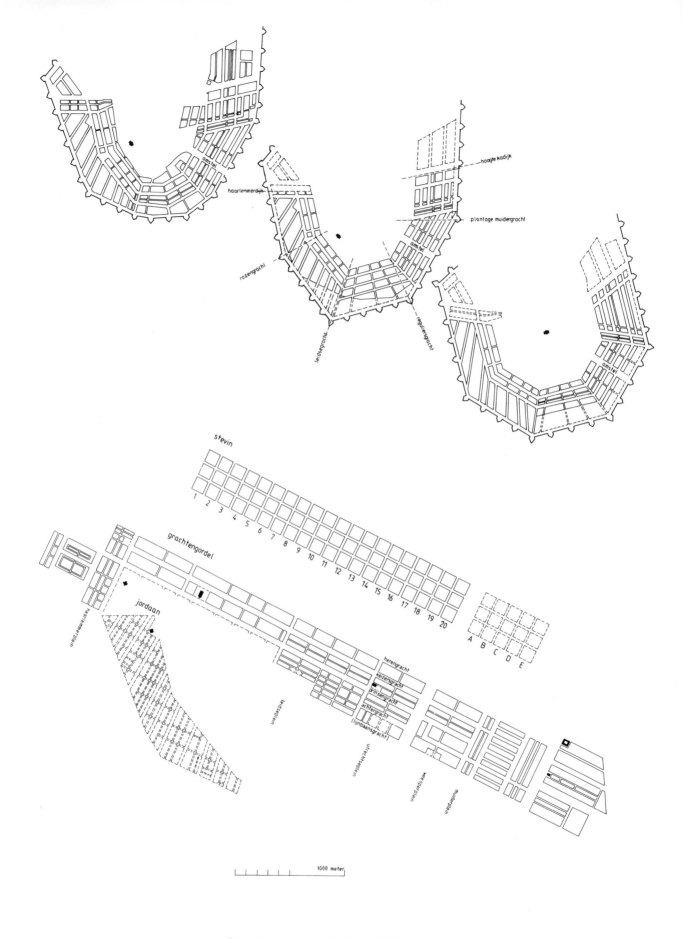

Amsterdam ring of canals schematized as
a regular polygon

The ring of canals straightened into a linear belt

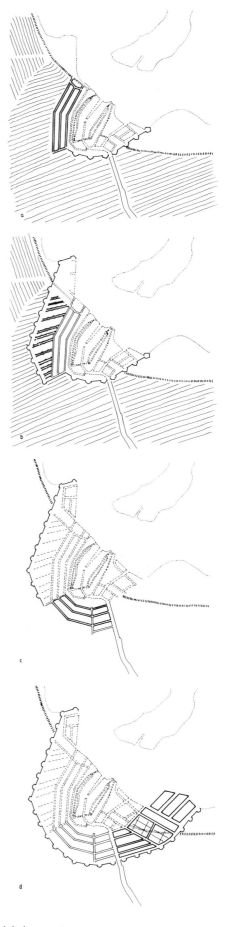

The stylized emblem of Amsterdam

Reduction drawings of the ring of canals
a the canal ring, a latterday variant on the old drainage system
b The Jordaan, urbanized peat landscape
c the southern part, a continuation of the canal ring
d the eastern part, terminating the canal ring and continuing the island archipelago

The Frankfurt experiment

A design that demonstrates a powerful interaction of
scheme and context instead of a unilateral influence
of context on scheme is the Frankfurt district of
Römerstadt. Part of a satellite town devised for that
city in the twenties by Ernst May, it was to transmute
the concentric expansion of Frankfurt into a dispersed development of satellites or "Siedlungen." In the
satellite concept, city and landscape are conceived as
a single urban conglomeration whose form is sup-
ported by the green structure—"landscape formation
through urbanization," we might call it these days.[50]

Römerstadt was designed proceeding from the
two principal elements of the satellite concept:
the green structure as structuring element in the
urbanizing process, and a coherent landscape system
given shape by the new settlements. In our analysis
of Römerstadt, then, we are most concerned with
the interplay between the landscape features of the
Nidda Valley and the design.

The Siedlung forms part of a large cohesive
development area on the northern rim of the Nidda,
where a whole string of "satellites" (Westhausen,
Praunheim, Römerstadt, Heddernheim) serve to
safeguard the uninterrupted landscape system from
undesired urbanization, also in the long term. This
urban strategy can clearly be seen in Römerstadt:
stretching 1.5 km along the slope of the valley,
the Siedlung is a magnificently designed boundary
between the river and the upland area scheduled
for urbanizing.[51]

The design, which resolutely seizes on features
of the surrounding landscape, breaks down into two
parts held together by taller development along the
central access road. This road snakes up the hill in
an analogy with the contour lines on the valley. The
residential streets on each side of the winding road
run parallel to the valley so that the development
steps down in a series of terraces to the river.

Each of the neighborhoods enjoys its own relationship with the landscape. The western part of
residential streets following a straight if unbroken
course keeps in the main to the contour lines of the
valley. While this part is given form as a gentle
accompaniment to the Nidda the eastern portion
with its continuous curved streets rears its expressive head to the landscape, resembling more than
anything else a front-line bastion guarding the
course of the (channelled) river.

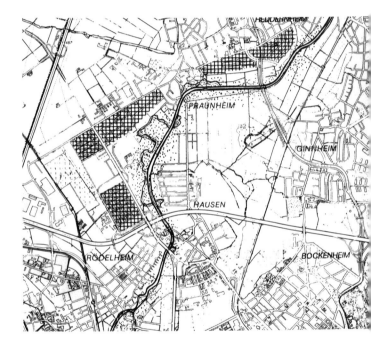

Frankfurt am Main, topographical map
superimposed on which is the series of
Siedlungen on the northern rim of the
Nidda Valley

The design principles of the satellite town model are applied the most explicitly in the periphery of the settlement. Marking off the Siedlung to the river is a long curved retaining wall which, punctuated by taller development, is interrupted at regular intervals by jutting "bastions," observation posts looking out over the cultivated river landscape. Planted with linden trees and fronted by an avenue, the wall sharply divides the landscape and the urbanized area. In the expressive form given its periphery Römerstadt seems to be defining the landscape's contours. At the same time, the Siedlung faces the distant city as an island cut off in that same landscape. The image of the autonomous enclave gives the impression of a "dispersed" urbanization. Historically speaking the imagery of retaining wall and bastions allude to the city wall of the past — a twentieth-century rampart.

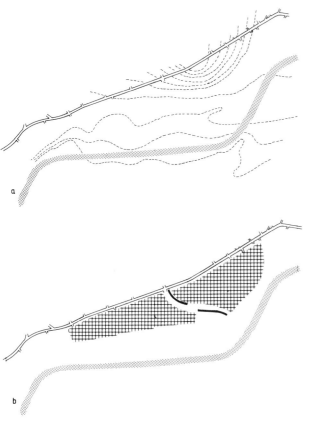

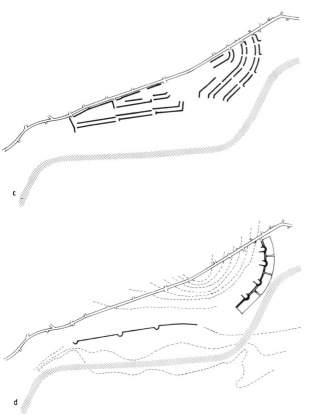

Reduction drawings of Römerstadt
  a on-site planning constraints: height lines, the channelled river, the through road
     ("In der Römerstadt")
  b insertion in the terrain: residential neighborhoods parallel to the valley, the main access square
     to the slope
  c the differences between the eastern and western parts
  d "twentieth-century rampart" marking off the Siedlung

Römerstadt in 1930, seen from the northeast

6.9 Transforming the urban fabric

The transformation of the urban fabric is distinguished from the other, generally earlier phases particularly by the fact that the context for intervention is different structurally. Transformation refers to interventions that take place in an urbanized area and not in a natural or cultivated landscape, as in the case of evolved or designed structures. Here, urbanized also means areas not urbanized by development yet within the city's sphere of influence. Each time the urban fabric undergoes transformation every factor that might be of influence on a design is involved: existing development, spatial and functional contexts, aspects of use and the area's history. Because of the many possible influences and their mutual relationships a transformation almost always admits to a complex relationship between context and design.

The concept of transformation is certainly not applicable to every refurbishing operation in the city. Only if the situation changes radically as a result of the intervention can the word transformation be used. You could hardly describe replacing a nineteenth-century block of jerry-building with a twentieth-century urban regeneration block as a transformation. You would, though, in replacing such a block with other buildings or housing types and adapting the shape, use or meaning of the urban space.

The transformation of a segment of city can be spatial or functional by nature, can relate to the use and meaning of a place in the city or affect several aspects of it. In fact, because a transformation involves an existing urban situation with a past of its own, aspects of use and (historical) meaning are often of the most crucial importance.

Likewise, the demand described in section 6.6 for cohesion between the development of the city form and of other elements in the urban arena — social, cultural, economic—plays a seminal role in the event of a transformation. Indeed, it could create the possibilities of a change in the physical structure of the city triggering off changes in other "strata." This "catalysing" impact plays a part in design tasks relating to transforming derelict urban areas, such as the structuring of railway shunting yards, abandoned dockyards and dilapidated indus-

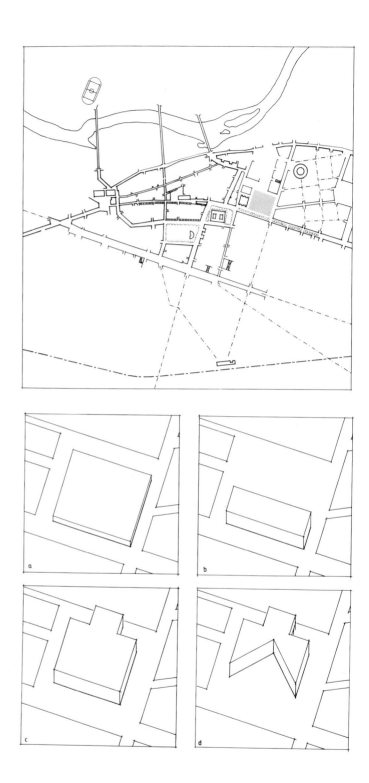

Reduction drawing of Logroño, the planning site in the urban context

Processing of volumes and urban space
a the program projected in a single layer on the site
b the program stacked
c the program blown up to double size
d excision of the square

trial areas. Much the same holds for design tasks in the urban periphery. Such tasks raise the question of whether the city can still be considered a spatial entity or should be conceived as an assemblage of fragments whose functions link them to a wide diversity of planning scales, such as a region or national or even international networks.[52]

In the examples treated below, which extend scalewise from a single building and a structuring element to the transformation of a rundown area in the urban periphery, it is less a (one-sided) influence of the context on the design that is at issue than a give-and-take between context and design; that is, the consequences design interventions in the urban fabric can have for strata other that the purely formal.

Logroño

Built in 1981, the city hall of Logroño in the Spanish province of La Rioja is one design in which the impact of the building plays a decisive role in its setting. The city hall is an intriguing example of the notion harbored by the Spanish architect Rafael Moneo, that public buildings in the city acquire their meaning from the way they relate to the surroundings.[53]

The site was eminently suitable for creating far-reaching effects in the surroundings using the city hall as strategic instrument. At the transition from historic center to nineteenth-century districts this public facility is a programmatic move to upgrade the dilapidated nineteenth-century city. Situated at the edge of a chaotic riverside area, the city hall further serves as a key project in strengthening the city-river relationship.[54]

The spatial cohesion of building and surroundings is crucial to realizing such potential. Moneo resorts to a whole range of design resources which, though of a purely spatial nature, can forge relations on other levels too, in functional terms through everyday use, through image and meaning of the building.

Moneo derived these means from architectural elements characteristic of the old city, where arcades, passages and green squares govern the appearance and character of urban space. There, arcades are situated primarily at places with a public character, such as city squares and busy routes. The passages serve as informal short-cuts.

These characteristic elements Moneo exploits in various ways. First, these elements spatially define the relations between the building, its immediate environment and the city. Secondly, he uses the elements to inform the architectural image of the building itself. And thirdly, using these means he places the city hall in its setting so that it acquires meaning in the workaday use of the city.

Several aspects were instrumental in siting the building at that particular place. In view of the size

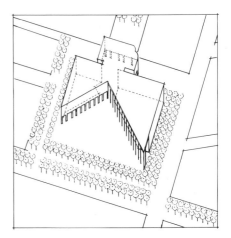

Rafael Moneo, Logroño city hall (1980). Axonometric

Logroño city hall, the tall colonnade on the east side of the square

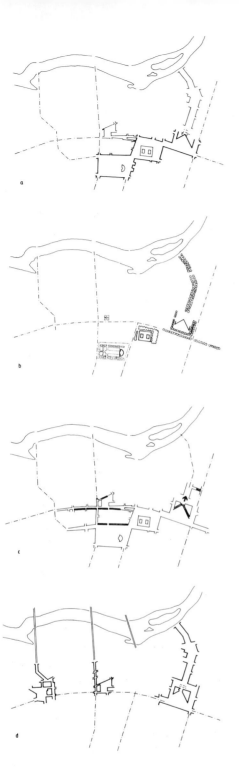

of the location, the program's requirements are quite modest.[55] This is important for the relationship between the city hall and the city boulevard, in other words how the civic building appears from the main road. Its position also has a bearing upon the use and the meaning of the public space in which it stands. This can vary from a ceremonial city hall square to an urban square geared to collective, daily use. Finally, the building's relations with the immediate environment, historic city and river are dictated by how it is sited.

In slotting the city hall into the site Moneo has succeeded in combining the widely divergent and at times contradictory interests of the various aspects by adopting a highly inventive design approach. In it the building's limited program was subjected to a cunning maneuver. First the volume was expanded to more than double size. It was then brought back to the required dimensions by cutting, hollowing out and raising up. This act of reducing the volume generates explicit urban spaces around which are the various programmatic components.

The two voluminous components—public functions and officialdom—are accommodated in a pair of triangular volumes of unequal size. The third component, the main hall, is isolated on stilts beyond the triangles. The latter, their inner corners overlapping, generate a square opening to the boulevard and point diagonally towards the historic city. Where the volumes intersect there is a passage, created by lifting up the main hall, to the area beyond. Hence the building works as an oversized funnel. The new square collects the movements between historic and nineteenth-century parts of the city and channels the movements between city and river.

The building's image takes its cue from the various functions of the square. Moneo's differentiated use of the city's architectural vocabulary has spawned well-defined spaces and stresses the difference in function between the two wings. Before the eastern, public wing is a tall narrow open gallery on slender steel posts. Facing the sun, it is a popular place where townspeople like to linger. The jutting end of the gallery serves as a gateway between the city hall square and the neighboring district.

By contrast, the arcade on the west, official wing is a broad contained space. Carved out of the building, it is intensively used as a covered pedestrian

a   the building in its urban context
b   reduction drawing of the sequence of squares: a classically designed city park, a tree-lined square,
    the city hall plaza, the esplanade to the river
c   the system of colonnades and arcades
d   the relationship between city and river

route between city areas. The two arcades intersect at a tall roofed lobby forming the festive entrance to all components of the city hall as well as a noteworthy start to the esplanade leading to the river.

These design methods have endowed the tree-lined triangle with both the character of a ceremonial city hall plaza and the qualities of a square geared to everyday use.

At an urban level the building works as a catalyst for upgrading the adjoining parts of the city. The city hall itself, the developments in the surrounding districts and those on the river are effortlessly drawn together. Finally, its relationship with the historic center is effected by a sequence of green spaces terminating in the city hall square.

In their references to the city's vocabulary the major elements of the design clearly derive from the typical urban spaces of Logroño. In fact, the city hall seems more like an unbuilt public space than a built volume, particularly in the use of different types of public space as prime elements. This is what makes the building such a splendid symbol of a public institution.

Nancy

The famous series of squares in Nancy is an example of a design in which new elements slotted perfectly into an existing situation generated a spatial unity that has not only operated as a structuring element on the scale of Nancy and its surroundings; in the course of time it has itself come to symbolize that city.

Before the squares were laid out in 1752, Nancy consisted of two relatively autonomous towns, the medieval Ville Vieille and the seventeenth-century Ville Neuve, whose autonomy was largely due to the defense works that encircled each. Commissioned by Stanislas Leszczynski, ex-king of Poland and Duke of Lotharingen, to design a Place Royale as a "worthy setting" for the statue of his son-in-law Louis XV, and for a new town hall and ducal palace, the architect Emmanuel Héré de Corny saw his way clear to transforming the double town into a single entity.[56]

The new programs were set in the context in such a way that together the components of the intervention provided a structuring element in the city, a "trait d'union" for the double town.

Héré situated the new, almost square Place Royale —now Place Stanislas—in the open space in front of the moat, directly opposite the medieval city gates; the site is tuned to the grid pattern of the new city. The design constructs the square as an architectural whole in a style deriving from the existing Hôtel de Craon. On its long side is the town hall flanked by civic buildings; the open corners of the square are closed off with the famous gold railings and fountains of Jean Lamour. Another component of the design was the link-up with the medieval town. A tall triumphal arch opposite the town hall flanked by low colonnades effects a subtle transition from the Place Royale to the entrance square of the old town.

In the square Place the statue of Louis XV marks the point where two major routes intersect: the existing north–south route linking the old and new towns and the new east–west route drawing together the city and the surrounding country.[57] Triumphal arches at the edges of the city mark the transition to the landscape.

The laying of the east–west route changed the relationship between city and surroundings dramatically; the landscape was then enticed into the city as far as the Place Royale by the perspectival view along the dead-straight route.

In the medieval town there emerged a worthy counterpart to the Place Royale: an oval concourse set at right angles to it, the Hémicycle, on which stood the new ducal palace. Breadthwise the oval colonnades afford a magnificent entrance to the palace; lengthwise it is the link between the medieval town and the promenade along the rampart.

To link the Place Royale and the Hémicycle, the elogated space of the medieval tournament arena was transformed into the Place de la Carrière. This new square was treated as an autonomous spatial element; the taller development of the existing Hôtel de Craon plus three copies of it mark its corners. The intervening development, on the rampart and on the side of the city, was accorded a new uniform frontage whose architecture was likewise inspired by the preexisting building. The free space of the Place de la Carrière was planted with a charming avenue of linden trees; the promenade in its turn was framed by a series of lanterns and gold railings.[58]

In terms of the double town the Place de la Carrière is the key component of the spatial composition of squares. What had already a long and narrow space was then developed in such a way that its length-breadth ratio was manipulated further, so as to emphasize the perspective when looking along it. At the focal points of the perspective it seems as though the might of the citizenry and the official authority of Nancy—the town hall and the ducal palace—are observing each other at a safe distance.

In terms of the city, on the other hand, the Place Royale is the key component, serving as a pivot between the landscape and the components of the city.

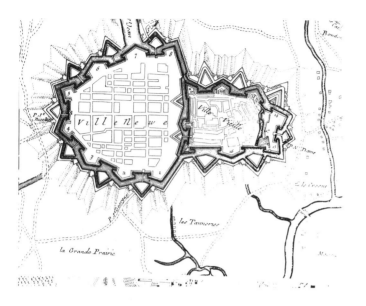

Nancy, plan dating from before 1750. Following the tradition, Nancy is drawn laid "flat"; North is to the right

Nancy, the sequence of squares seen from the northeast, circa 1985. From foreground to background: Place Stanislas, Place de la Carrière and Hémicycle, with the city park at the rear (right)

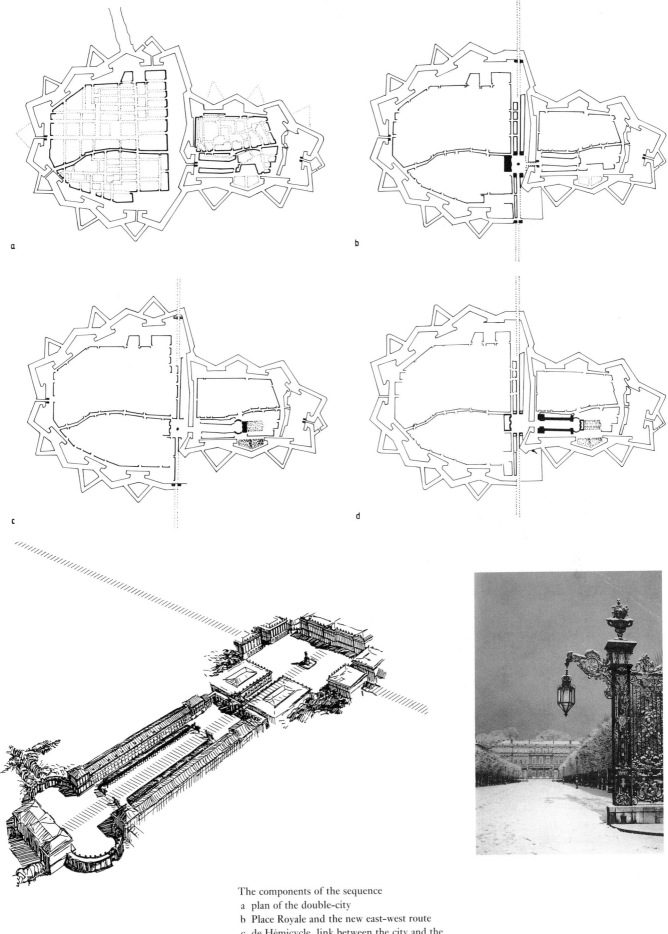

The components of the sequence
a plan of the double-city
b Place Royale and the new east-west route
c de Hémicycle, link between the city and the
   walk along the city wall
d Place de la Carrière mounted in the context

Nancy, bird's-eye view of the sequence of
squares

Nancy, Place de la Carrière looking towards the
ducal palace

Lille

Unlike the other designs discussed here the Euralille project of the Rotterdam firm of OMA is a project in progress. True, implementation of the scheme has begun, but construction is at such an early stage that the work is far from ready for "testing in practice." It will be examined here exclusively in terms of design drawings. Commentary on the relationship between context and design is thus very much hypothetical.

And yet the design in its drawn state is sufficient inducement to include it in our discussion of transformations of the urban area. The reasons for doing so lie in the nature of the project (a large-scale transformation to satisfy a complex building task), in the nature of the setting (the urban periphery) and finally in the design itself and the way it treats the context.[59]

For the French provincial town of Lille the construction of the Channel Tunnel and the arrival of the Train à Grande Vitesse (TGV) signify a dramatic change of status in the infrastructural network of Northwest Europe. Lille has advanced from quite an outsider position in the economic arena to a central place.[60] On the strength of this change the city itself has taken steps to ensure that the expected positive effect on the economic and functional front could work positively on the urban front as well. Arguably the most important step was the decision not to develop the new TGV station as an autonomous project away from the city. Siting it a mere stone's throw from the old center was a deliberate choice, one that makes Lille's attitude towards the TGV quite unequivocal: the high-speed train is quite simply a chance in a million. Siting the station thus not only maximizes the economic impact of the TGV on the historic center, it paves the way for radically transforming the urban periphery.

The station site is a two-kilometer long, 500-meter wide strip where the fortifications used to be, between the threadbare fringes of the historic center and the suburbs south of Lille. It exhibits all the hallmarks of a fringe area. Large-scale infrastructure with the inevitable spaghetti of sliproads slices through the area, throwing up invincible barriers between the fragments of periphery. The impressive collection of fragments is itself a comprehensive list of spatial and programmatic details: the central rail station, an ancient cemetery, an abandoned barracks, office towers, a city park, car parks and bundles of railway lines. The area has long served as a dumping ground for plans that though necessary were unwelcome inside the city itself.

OMA's design in fact is configured as two distinct operations. On one side it thoroughly revises the local infrastructure.[61] The new TGV station is used in the design as the element organizing the flows in the area. The ring road, metro stops and parking garages are set parallel to the station and partially underground. The link between city, station and suburbs is set square to the station and bisects it.

Secondly, the planned programs are spread across the site.[62] In spatial terms the design shows the features of a collage. It projects new fragments throughout the site whose location, programmatic infill and spatial-functional organization are fine-tuned to each other. The station, set as it is on a long "plinth" which resolutely partitions off the station zone from the suburbs to the south, serves as a structuring element for the other components of the plan.

The tall towers atop the station visually impact at the scale of the city where they have a landmark function. The triangular Forum, a shopping mall directly opposite the station, is the link both spatially and programmatically between station and city. Set at the eastern extremity of the plinth, the park is at once a connection through to the city and a buffer to the large-scale infrastructure. The "Congrexpo," a congress and exhibition building at the western end of the plinth, pulls together the components of the second phase of implementation and the station.

Of great importance when fleshing out the station and surroundings is that the city is made to feel the presence of the TGV. An inventive use of differences in level in the area has generated a multiplicity of visual relations between the high-speed train and its environment. Thus, looking from the station forecourt, the access road and the Forum the TGV can actually be seen inside the station, opened up as this is to the city. Likewise, the towers of the business center refer in their architectural design to the TGV's presence in the "plinth.'

Using the plinth as a structuring element in the design, the program components are gathered up functionally and spatially and linked together. With the Forum acting as the key link between city and station, and the towers as link at a higher scale,

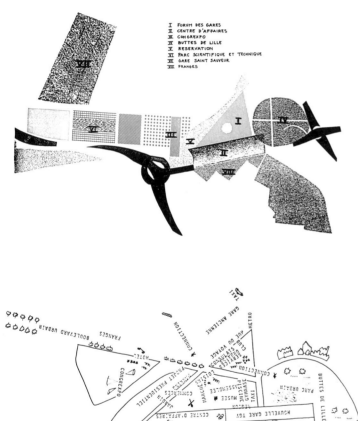

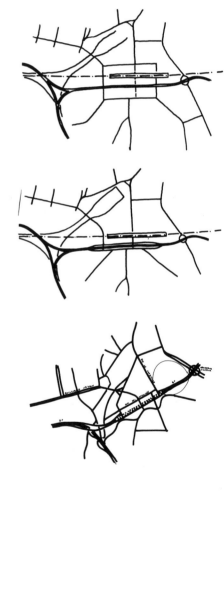

Euralille, division of the program over the site,
a collage of fragments

Spatial disposition of programs

OMA/Rem Koolhaas, Euralille (1990).
The design mounted in the context

Euralille, diagrams of the unravelling of the
infrastructure; below, the old situation

a powerful unity emerges in the collage of fragments. This imbues the scheme with a relative indifference towards eventual modification at the construction stage. This means that, for example, the Congrexpo, initially planned as a long "bridge" between the station and the second-phase development, could be effortlessly exchanged at a later stage for an ovoid design without forfeiting the cohesion between the individual planning components.

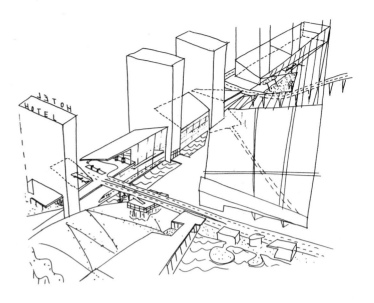

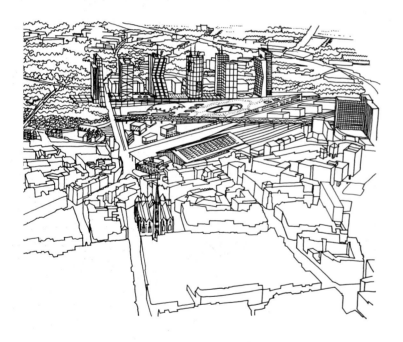

Euralille, visual relations between the TGV and the surroundings

Euralille, the station as organizing element in the periphery of Lille

Euralille, the new TGV station as a landmark

Appendix
Drawing techniques
to aid analysis

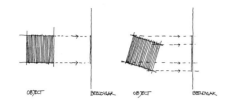

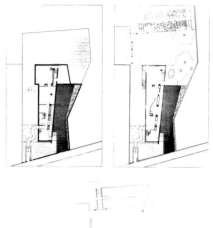

1.0   The basic projections

Drawings give only a limited picture of what they represent; they are an abstraction of reality. Each analysis begs its own method of drawing. Before examining the various types of analytical drawings, this section offers an overview of the different drawing methods and modes of projection used in the practice of architecture, urban design and landscape architecture. There are two main groups, *paraline projections*, also known as axonometrics, and *converging line projections* or perspectives.

1.1   Paraline projections (axonometrics)

The principal feature of paraline projection is that the object or area is projected onto the picture plane using parallel lines. Types of paraline projection can be classified as follows:
1. *Orthographic projections*, subdivisible into *metric* or flat projections such as elevations, plans, sections and topographical maps (fig. 2) and proportional projections amongst which *isometrics*, *dimetrics* and *trimetrics*. (fig. 3)
2. *Oblique projections* such as *planometric*, *cavalier* and *cabinet*. In these views, one face of the object is drawn as a flat plane and the remaining "distorted" faces at an angle. (fig. 4)

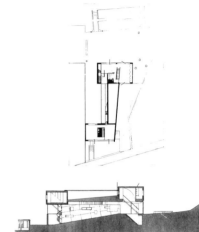

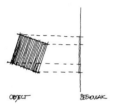

1.1.1   Orthographic projections

Metric projection

In metric or flat projection an object or area is relieved of its volume and drawn as if one were looking at it centrally from infinity. This projection formula is used for topographical charts, profile views (urban or landscape sections), plans, sections, elevations and building façades. In drawing a section or plan one is cutting away part of the building either vertically or horizontally, and viewing it centrally from infinity. The parts cut away may be indicated with a thicker line, hatched or colored in. Those parts visible from the chosen viewpoint are marked with a thinner line. As the object is shown devoid of form (i.e. flat) this common mode of projection is ideal for working drawings and contractual drawings but also for other scale drawings disseminating information for various ends.

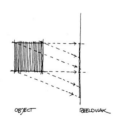

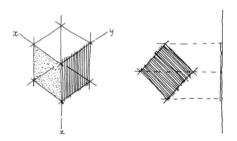

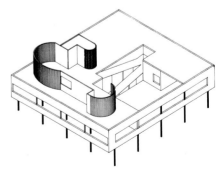

1   Paraline projections seen from above

2   Metric projection seen from above

3   Proportional projection (e.g. isometric, dimetric or trimetric) seen from above

4   Oblique projection (e.g. planometric, cavalier and cabinet) seen from above. One plane is projected truly, the rest are distorted

5   Plan and section of Villa dall'Ava, OMA/ Rem Koolhaas

6   Proportional projection: isometric (in the case of a cube the ribs x, y and z are of equal length)

7   Isometric of Villa Savoye, Le Corbusier

However, the observer faced with these drawings has to mentally fill in the three-dimensional element himself. (fig. 5)

Proportional projections

This category includes isometrics, dimetrics and trimetrics. The object is projected at an angle, giving an impression of three dimensions.

1.1.2   Oblique projections

To the category of oblique projections belong the planometric, cavalier and cabinet. In these types the object is projected in two directions simultaneously. Though only one of the planes is projected truly and the rest are distorted, the result is a spatial image nonetheless.

Planometric

This projection is often erroneously described as axonometric. The latter term however is the collective name for paraline projections. (fig. 9) Planometric projection is an exceedingly common and easy-to-execute mode. The ground plane (or top face) is set up truly at a chosen angle (say 30 or 60 degrees); the verticals, which may be shortened, are drawn straight up. Planometric drawings are used to explain the relationship between plan and elevations.

Cavalier and cabinet

The method these two obliques share involves setting up one of the side planes truly, with all other planes, which again may be shortened, distorted. These drawings focus on the relation between section and elevation.

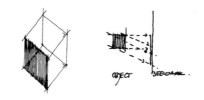

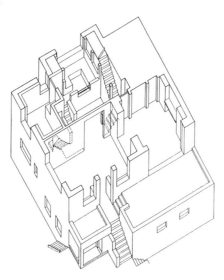

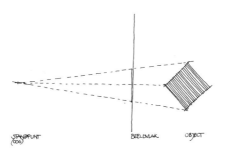

1.2   Converging line projections (perspectives)

The hallmark of converging line projection is that the object is projected along the visual rays of the observing eye. (fig. 11) In general, perspective drawings are able to give a three-dimensional picture of an object that largely corresponds with the image the observer might get in reality given a fixed viewpoint. Perspectives can be divided into three groups, depending on the projection mode and the number of Vanishing Points: *one-point* or *central perspective*, *two-point perspective* and *three-point perspective*. Which of these is chosen depends on the aim of the analysis. A series of central perspectives might, for instance, be perfect for illustrating a route through an English landscape park. The perspectives can further be classified according to the height of the observer's eye. Two extremes in this respect are the *bird's-eye* or *aerial view* and the *worm's-eye* or *ground view*.

1.2.1   One-point or central perspective

When drawing a one-point perspective one chooses a viewpoint looking straight at or into the object. For instance, a section or elevation drawn to scale can serve as the premise for a one-point perspective, with only the shortening of the depth measurements needing to be estimated or calculated. In a one-point aerial perspective the viewpoint is high in relation to the object or landscape. In a one-point ground view the viewpoint might be made to equal the height of a standing person.

8   Oblique projections: planometric

9   Planometric projection: Adolf Loos, Moller House

10   Oblique projections: cabinet

11   Converging line projection (perspective), seen from above to best show the projection method

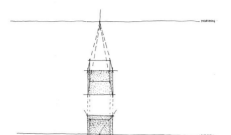

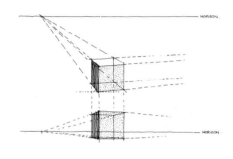

1.2.2 Two- and three-point perspectives

In two-point perspective the viewer observes the object at an angle. Here too it holds that the viewpoint in a two-point aerial perspective is high in relation to the object or landscape and at eye-level in a two-point ground view. The advantage of two-point perspective is that it gives the observer a realistic three-dimensional rendering. Their disadvantage is that the foreshortening of the sides has to be estimated or calculated. This foreshortening bears a direct relation to the angle at which a plane is shown (e.g. in fig. 13 a large angle at the left gives a strong foreshortening of the relevant side).

In order to show the relationship between the two perspective types (aerial view and ground view) these are drawn one above the other (see figs. 12 and 13). In both cases the verticals are of equal length and are extensions of the same line. When drawing such views freehand it is advisable to make an aerial perspective first. The information this provides, such as the position of the vanishing points and the position and shortening of the verticals can be a great aid in drawing perspectives with a lower viewpoint.

2.0 Processing the drawing

There are three modes of processing a drawing when making an analysis of a design, *reduction*, *addition* and *démontage*.

2.1 Reduction

This is the most elementary way of processing a map or drawing. Its purpose is to visualize the structure of a design.
A commonly used technique in design analysis, reduction consists essentially of omitting all irrelevant data from a design drawing so that only information essential to the study remains. The art in making such an analytical drawing is in deciding what is to be drawn and what left out. Experience has taught that the tendency is to include too much detail in an analytical drawing rather than too little. An analytical drawing should make sense at a glance and be self-explanatory rather that requiring explanation. Often a series of drawings with a limited quantity of data is easier to

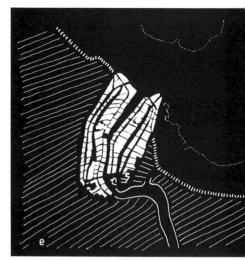

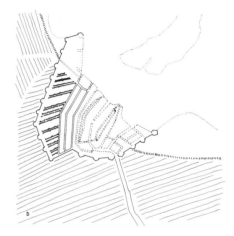

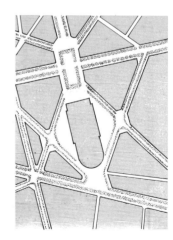

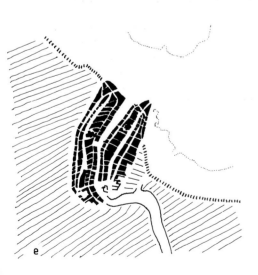

12 Bird's-eye and worm's-eye central perspective

13 Bird's-eye and worm's-eye two-point perspectives

14 Amsterdam, spatial structure of the medieval town. Morphological reduction

15 Amsterdam, spatial structure of the medieval town. Morphological reduction in negative

16 Amsterdam, changes in the spatial structure in the seventeenth century. Morphological line reduction

17 Paris, part of the system of Haussmann boulevards, circa 1870. Morphological reduction, space versus green

read than just one containing a great deal of information. There are two fundamentally different modes of reduction: morphological reduction and typological reduction.

Morphological reduction

Morphological reduction is a means of uncovering and explaining the spatial structure of an object. The purpose of the analytical drawings is to visualize the spatial characteristics of a building, city or area. To do so, they make a distinction between built (i.e. mass) and unbuilt (space or void); usually the mass is drawn and the space left out. Depending on the object and the scale at which processing takes place there may be further differentiation within the mass and space. For example, buildings and green elements such as avenues and parks, can be rendered differently. There can also be a distinction made between, say, streets, alleys and squares, or canals and meadows.

The usual codes in a morphological reduction are planes (uniform, hatched or halftone) and lines (continuous or dotted, single or double). Which drawing technique is used depends on the scale of the object and the aspect to be examined. Pen thicknesses are another useful means when making analytical drawings. The technique most applied is the "ordinary" black-and-white drawing in which black areas and lines are used to indicate the mass and white areas and lines the space. Such drawings are suitable for analyzing the spatial composition or the nature of the built development (perimeter blocks or open rows). In a "negative drawing," the space is given in black and the mass in white; this technique focuses on the unbuilt parts of the scheme. Different aspects of a drawing can be emphasized using a drawing technique involving only unbroken and dotted lines and points.

The basis or "ground" can in principle be any map drawn to scale, particularly topographical maps (not tourist maps, as these tend to distort towards the edges). Analysis is done by partly drawing over the underlying map; the latter's scale is governed by the nature of the analysis and the scale of the object. Thus topographical maps at a scale of 1:50,000 can be used to draw landscape patterns or give the posi-

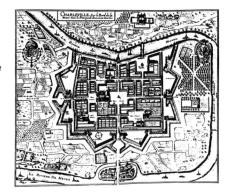

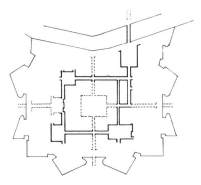

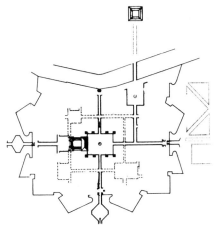

tion of settlements in relation to large-scale elements such as highways, high-voltage cables, railway lines and waterways. Then again, the scale of 1:25,000 is eminently suitable for drawing the main structure of a city (the structuring elements) and the position of key buildings in it, or for the spatial structure governing different parts of a city. At a scale of 1:10,000 we can distinguish individual buildings and routes and differentiate between the nature of one mass or void and another. Scale 1:5,000 or larger is better suited to examining the spatial features of a single urban fragment than to analysing the relationship between fragments.

It may be necessary to use both current and historical maps. Because the latter are usually not entirely to scale it is advisable to "graft" the information from a historical map onto a more accurate up-to-date example.

This processing of cartographic material can focus on a whole range of aspects of a design's spatial structure. Drawing the structuring elements of a city or city area, for instance, can tell us how the urban space there is experienced. Key elements in such analytical drawings are intensively used routes, major squares, landmark buildings and green space. Such morphological drawings can also be used to bring into view the cohesion (or lack of it) between parts of a city. The development of the urban structure can be rendered in the form of a historical atlas, with successive maps (identical in scale, size and location) illustrating the changes undergone over time. By this means, the relation can be charted between specific events in the city (such as the laying of a railway line) and their consequences for the spatial structure.

18 Charleville 1608
a plan
b morphological reduction of spatial structure
c morphological reduction of structuring
   elements

Typological reduction

This mode of reduction can serve two distinct ends.

Firstly, stripping a design to its essentials leaves a diagram of the underlying structure. This may correspond with similar diagrams of other schemes, in which case we use the term "typological diagram." Such a diagram can be said to contain the essence of a given type.

Secondly, by comparing the diagram of a design obtained by reduction with the typological diagram of a type from which that design probably derives, we can get an idea of the changes the design has undergone with respect to the original type.

This tells us whether a design is a variation on an existing type (i.e. a deformation) or represents a new one (i.e. a transformation).

The drawing codes and methods normally used to make a typological reduction are allied to those pertaining to morphological reduction. Once again, topographical maps are well-qualified as a "ground." In general, design or presentation drawings are better suited than contractual drawings for making typological analyses of buildings. Compared to morphological reduction, the typological version goes a step further. The design is stripped of all irrelevancies and made more diagrammatic. The processings in a typological analysis concentrate on the typological aspects of a design, on the resemblances to and deviations from the original type and the way the various elements relate (i.e. the typological levels). Thus, comparing a regular pattern and a variant upon it can serve to bring out the features of the original type as well as the way these features are applied in the design under analysis. That same process can be employed to discover how deformations of the original type are employed for specific design solutions in a given situation.

Among the processes used to alter existing types we can distinguish rotation, mirroring, doubling, additions and mixing with other existing types.

2.2 Addition

Another possibility when making analytical drawings is to add information that is either non-visual or non-architectural. It may be

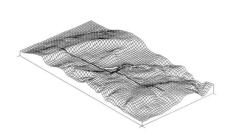

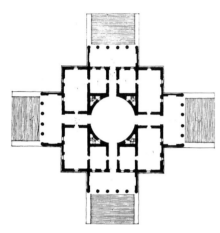

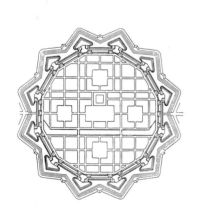

19 Morphology of the grounds of Castle Howard. The drawing shown here is a 'mesh' drawing, in which a network is laid over the topographical map with the aid of a computer. Each node of this network is then brought to the correct height. In this example the scale is distorted; the vertical direction is exaggerated with respect to the horizontals. (In the original the scale of the x and y axes was 1:65,000 and of the z axis 1:8000)

20 Plan of the Villa Rotonda. This drawing can be considered a morphological reduction showing only material (solid) against space

21 Vincenzo Scamozzi, ideal city, ca. 1600. Plan

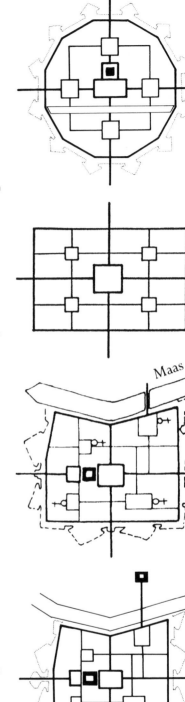

22 Typological diagram of Scamozzi's ideal city

23 In this radical reduction the typological diagram has been stripped of the features peculiar to Scamozzi's city. The result is a typological diagram of a city with literally four quarters

24 Charleville 1608. Plan

25 Typological reduction of Charleville

information about function or use, or that tells us something about the underlying geometric system. It is advisable to add information only once the drawing has been stripped of superfluous and distracting data. The morphological reduction drawing described above is a good departure-point for such analyses.

- Possible additions include the following:
  geometry of the spatial and material
- systems, axes, zones, and so on
  indications of function or use by means
- of colour, halftones or pictograms
- lines of vision and movement
  lines of force

Geometric system

In order to explore the geometric system of a design we can introduce into the drawing the material and spatial axes, zones and grid lines. The illustration of Palladio's Villa Emo in Fanzolo (1560) shows clearly how the various components are organized along an axis. If the built mass fails to directly indicate how the axis organizes the composition, one can always render the building in cutaway, as here in the central villa block.

An axis in external space can be marked by drawing just the minimum of spatial elements, in this case the flight of steps and the entrance gate. A tree-lined avenue might be drawn as an elongated mass to underscore the open space.

In the following illustration of the Villa Medici the geometric system, the house and the garden are distinguished by different thicknesses of line and degrees of abstraction. The house is the central portion from which the diagram derives and is therefore shown in horizontal section with the material thicknesses inked in. The garden is drawn in fainter lines. The thickness of line of the geometric system is halfway between those of house and garden. As its components consist of squares, these invariably contain a diagonal to prove that the sides are indeed equal. The suggestion of an axis in the garden is indicated by a dotted line the same thickness as that of the geometric grid system.

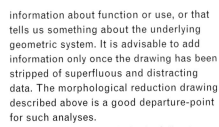

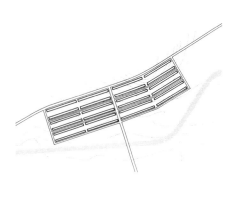

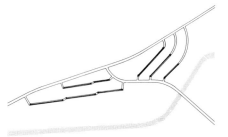

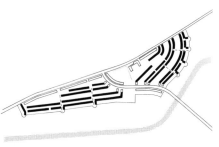

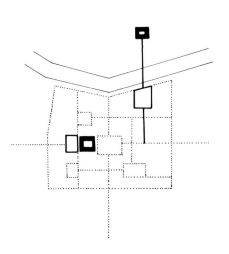

26 Deviations in Charleville from the typological diagram of the four-quarter city

27 Frankfurt Römerstadt, layout type

28 The type projected on site

29 Processing the type: undulation and heads

30 Fleshing out the type: the design as built

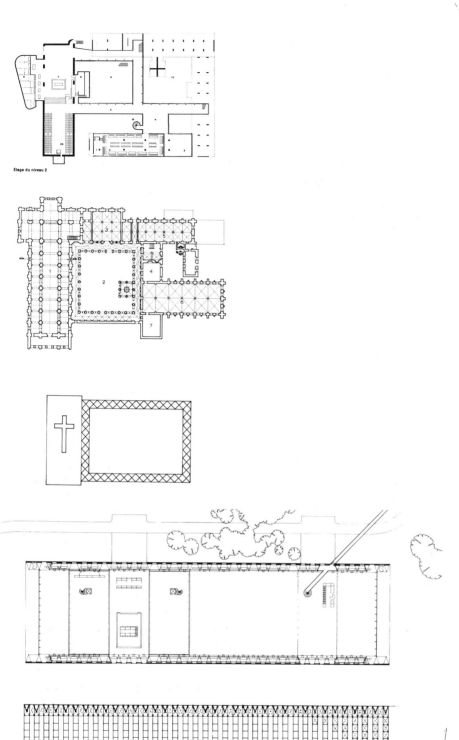

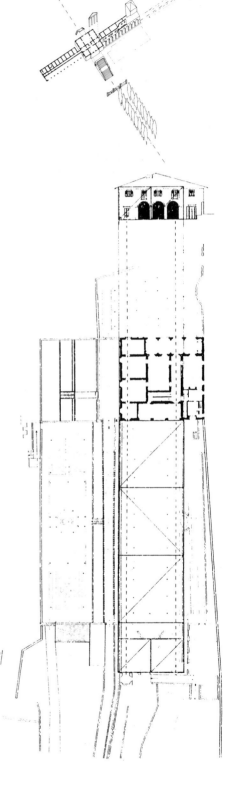

31 La Tourette

32 Medieval monastery

33 Typological diagram of monastery

34 Sainsbury Centre for the Visual Arts,
reduction drawing of the structure. The
positioning of the lattice trusses brings
modular structure into view

35 Villa Emo, Fanzolo. Axis joining house and
landscape

36 Villa Medici, geometric system regulating
the composition of house and garden

Function and use

Colored pencils or halftone tranfers are a simple aid towards mapping out the use of a building, a part of a city or a park. In most cases ground-plans are eminently suitable for such drawings; sometimes a section so treated can make for added clarity.

To avoid using too many colors or halftones it is advisable to first critically ascertain which aspect of the scheme's use needs examining. In the case of a large public building, one might choose to relate the position of the principal function to those of the secondary functions. In a house the emphasis will usually be on the distinction between living areas and circulation/facilities.

All codings and color applications are dependent on the aspects to be analyzed. In order to be able to compare analyses, a generally applicable color code can be applied as follows:

For a house:
living: red edging
cooking etc: orange fill
sleeping: dark blue
internal circulation: bright yellow
external circulation (stairs, gallery, doorstep, porch): pale yellow
storage, garage: brown edging
wet cells: light blue fill
drying area: blue dots
work area (e.g. office or practice attached to house, studio): orange edging
shop space: purple fill
hobby area/workshop: black edging
For a larger public building the principal function is given in red or red edging, for the rest (circulation, ablutions) see the color scheme for a house.
For analyzing part of a city the following color codes pertain:
residential: red
shops: purple
cafés, restaurants and hotels: pink
offices: orange
factories/workshops: black
public building: blue plus letter code
slow traffic: yellow
fast traffic: light grey
When analyzing the design for a park or garden the following codes may be used:
public green space: dark green
private green space: light green
water: light blue
playground: yellow ocher

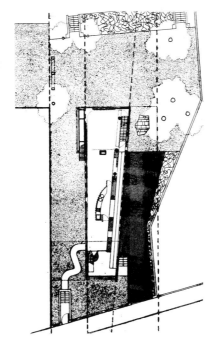

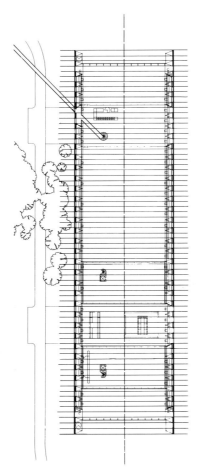

herb garden, ornamental garden, nursery garden: mauve
sportsfields: pale pink

When using halftones it is advisable to start from the lightest tone, using it for the function with the greatest surface area. The smaller the surface area of ancillary functions, the darker the tone. In the analysis of a house shown here the two principal living areas are given at ten percent (in size of dots). The other functions are indicated with a darker screen (30 or 50 percent). Official documents used to fix the use of a city according to function or zone often consist of maps conveying information by means of colors or halftones. Such cases may exhibit a widely differentiated system of activities. To ensure legibility it is necessary to restrict the information in the drawing and illustrate one or more aspects only. This is often done by visualizing just those functions with a public or collective character, such as civic buildings, cultural institutions, shops, night-life establishments and green facilities. As a result, the residential areas become a neutral backdrop against which the map can be easily read.

The method of coding with colors and screens described above reflects the way modernist urban design analyzes the city and divides it into functions. Criticism of this functionalist approach has encouraged urbanists to explore other methods of registering use that simultaneously give a visual impression of an area or a scheme. One such tool for illustrating variation in use is the *pictogram*.

Drawing lines of movement and vision is a way of illustrating how the user would experience the space. As the examples show, that can apply to the plan and section but also in an isometric. When choosing a ground the one important factor is that the drawing should show those elements important for experiencing the space.

Because a drawing often contains too much information, it is advisable to reduce the ground and only incorporate what is really essential to an understanding of the sequence or movement. Small sketches can be an additional aid.

One possible way of analyzing the structure of a building is to render the distribution of forces in that structure. This too is done

37 Villa dall'Ava. Organization into zones

38 Sainsbury Centre for the Visual Arts. Organizing lines and a symmetry axis help to clarify the geometric system of the material, whose position is indicated by linear zones of identical shape

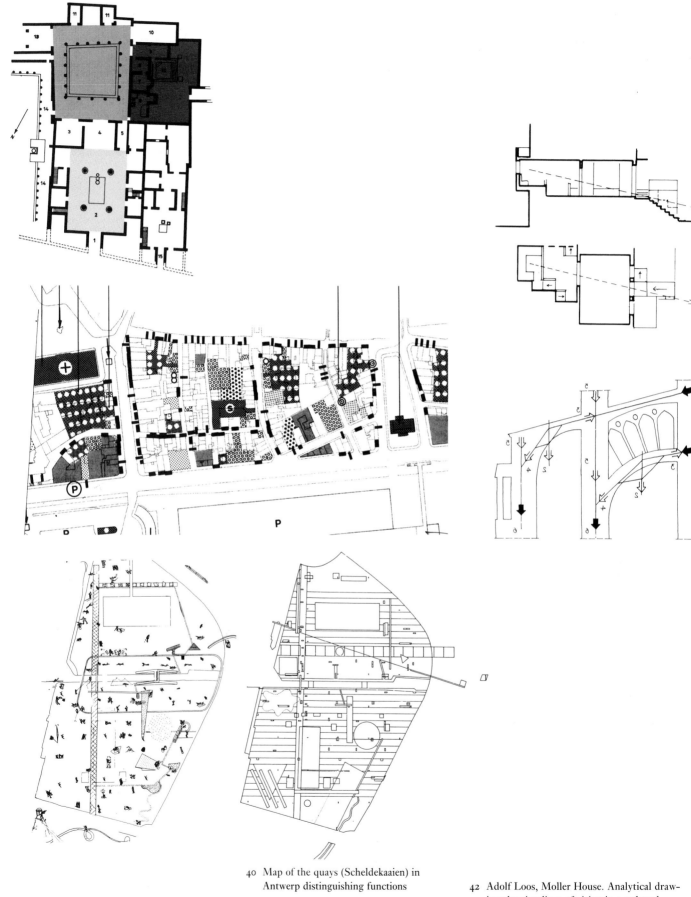

39 Analysis of aspects of use in a Roman house
    atrium (representative)
    peristyle (informal)
    servant and household quarters

40 Map of the quays (Scheldekaaien) in Antwerp distinguishing functions

41 Presentation drawing of OMA's competition entry for Parc de la Villette. The various planned activities are indicated by pictograms

42 Adolf Loos, Moller House. Analytical drawing showing lines of vision in a reduced drawing of the section and plan

43 Section through Gothic cathedral. Arrows mark the distribution of forces

by adding information to an existing drawing. As loads are directed downwards by gravity, sectional drawings are best suited to the purpose. The forces acting on the structure can then be indicated with arrows. Insight into the distribution of forces can provide relevant information about the building's form or the way the various building parts fit together. The section through a Gothic cathedral shown here gives a better understanding of the relation between the built form and the transfer of forces.

2.3 Démontage

A good way to examine the relation between various aspects, systems, elements, phases in time or design and context is to make what is called a démontage drawing or exploded view. Juxtaposing or superimposing drawings giving complementary information can be helpful when examining the relationship between different aspects of a design. These can be different stories of a building of different strata in a design. The following layers are among those that can be superimposed: compositional elements, ground and object, scales, historical layers, stories, conceptual layers, and structure and design.

The démontage or disassembly of a design provides insight into the build-up of the spatial structure of the object under scrutiny. Démontage can be done by unfolding the scheme in various "layers" (e.g. geomorphological, infrastructural, built or green layers, structural or utility layers) or by explicating the various components of the scheme (e.g. the edges, the infill or the binding elements). When analyzing a component of a larger entity it is often necessary to include superfluous information simply to place the object in a broader context, such as by drawing certain points of orientation or the course of a river. An efficient means of giving insight into the relation between the various typological levels is to make a drawing in which these different levels are shown individually. Also, when analyzing the structure of a building, démontage is often an eminently suitable means. In a démontage drawing or exploded view the different components comprising a structure can be drawn individually, shedding light on the method

and order of construction or on the functions fulfilled by individual structural components within a building.

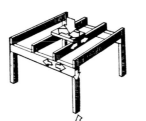

9.3   SLAB ON POST AND BEAM SYSTEM

9.4   ONE-WAY REINFORCED SLAB

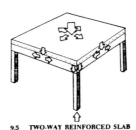

9.5   TWO-WAY REINFORCED SLAB

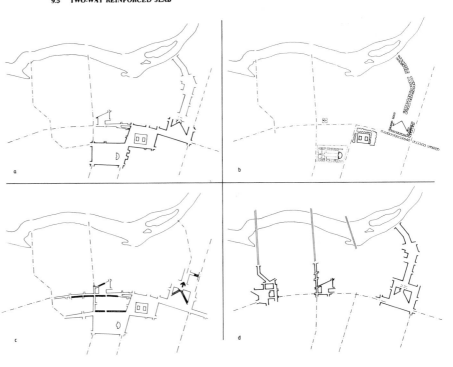

44   Planometric projections of three variants on a supporting structure for a square slab, showing the distribution of forces

45   Logroño, the design in the urban context; démontage in various planning layers
a   the town hall plaza as the next in the series of squares
b   the series of green spaces; a classically designed city park, a tree-lined square, the town hall plaza, the esplanade to the river
c   the system of colonnades and arcades
d   the city's relationship with the river

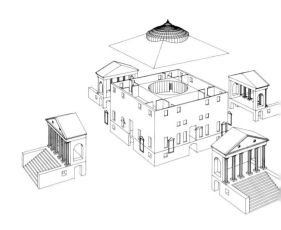

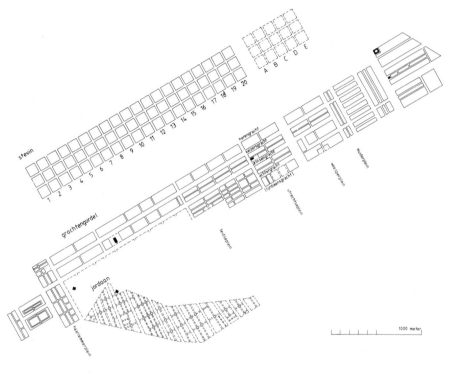

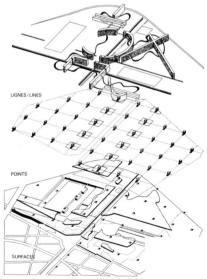

47 Villa Rotonda, exploded view of elements
visualizes composition

48 Tschumi's Parc de la Villette, division into
three conceptual layers

46 Amsterdam, the ring of canals drawn as a
strip; here the design components are placed
in sequence as a new composition

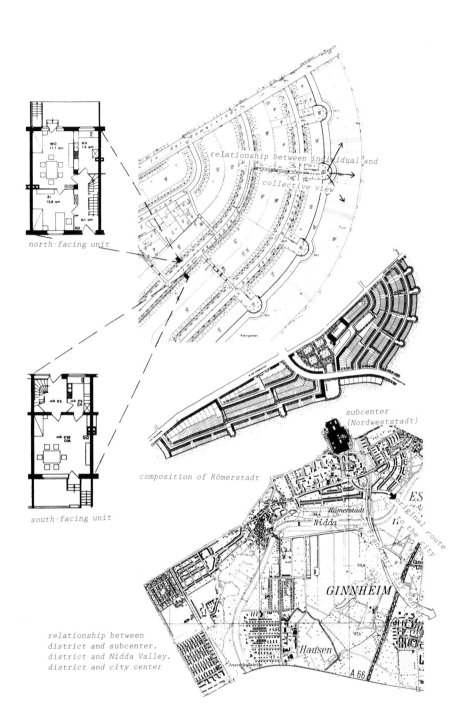

WO
17.1 qm

KU
7.6 qm

ZI
12.8 qm

6.1 qm

north-facing unit

south-facing unit

relationship between individual and collective view

composition of Römerstadt

subcenter
(Nordweststadt)

ES

original route to the city

Römerstadt

Nidda

GINNHEIM

*relationship between
district and subcenter,
district and Nidda Valley,
district and city center*

Hausen

A 66

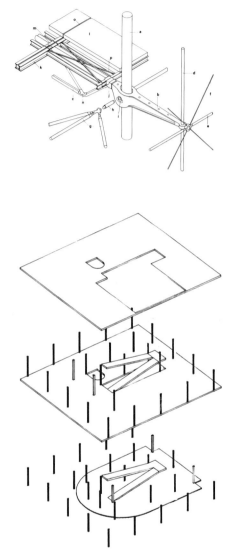

50 Centre Pompidou. Exploded view of the
beam-truss connection. The drawing gives
an accurate picture of the constituent elements

51 Villa Savoye. Exploded view distinguishing
structural functions in the various building
parts

Notes

1 Design and analysis

1 Bernard Leupen, "Een nouvel concept," *de Architect* 12/1989

2 Hubert Tonka, *Opera de Tokyo*, Champ Vallon, Seyssel 1986

3 Ebenezer Howard, *Garden Cities of Tomorrow*, Faber and Faber, London 1946. First published in 1898 as *Tomorrow: A Peaceful Path to Real Reform.*

2 Order and composition

1 Rasmussen, 1951, p. 70

2 Hubert de Boer and Hans van Dijk, "Het park van de 21ste eeuw," *Wonen* TABK 12/1983, p. 24

3 Kaufmann, 1968, p. 75f

4 Mitchell, 1990, p. 131f

5 Benevolo, *The History of the City*, 1980, p. 143

6 Vitruvius, 1960, pp. 13–16

7 Leon Battista Alberti, *On the Art of Building in Ten Books*, trans. Joseph Rykwert, Neil Leash and Robert Tavernor, MIT Press, Cambridge (Mass.)/London 1988, p. 305

8 Tzonis, 1972, p. 21

9 Kaufmann, 1968, p. 79

10 Palladio, 1570, book I, p. 59

11 Steenbergen, 1990, p. 16

12 Reh *et al.*, 1996, pp. 51–56

13 Baroque here refers to the architectural tendency that flourished during the Counter-Reformation in Italy, South Germany and Austria, one which expressed the Roman Catholic Church's flush of victory following the Council of Trent (1545–1563). The Church became the center of life, albeit temporarily. As a result, Baroque architecture is found primarily in churches and monasteries and in areas where the Counter-Reformation was strongest.

14 Kaufmann, 1968, p. 78

15 Castex, 1990, pp. 311–314

16 Note 15, p. 317

17 Marcel Röthlisberger, *Claude Lorrain. L'Album Wildenstein*, Les Beaux-Arts, Ed. d'études et de documents, Paris 1962, pp. 7–8

18 David van Zanten, "Architectural composition at the Ecole des Beaux-Arts from Charles Percier to Charles Garnier," in Arthur Drexler (ed.), *The Architecture of the Ecole des Beaux-Arts*, Secker & Warburg, London 1977, p. 112

19 Note 18, p. 115

20 Note 18, p. 162

21 Adolf Loos, "Ornament und Verbrechen," in Franz Gluck (ed.), *Samtliche Schriften*, vol. 1. Herold, Vienna 1962, p. 276f

22 See also Johan van de Beek, "Adolf Loos — patterns of town houses," in Risselada (ed.), 1988, pp. 27–46

23 Arjan Hebly, "The 5 Points and form," in Risselada (ed.), 1988, pp. 47–53

24 Theo van Doesburg, "Tot een beeldende architectuur," *De Stijl* vol. 6, 1924, no. 6/7, p. 81. Quoted in Frampton 1980/1985, p. 145

25 Clark V. Poling, *Kandinsky—Unterricht am Bauhaus*, Weingarten, Weingarten 1982, p. 107

26 David Harvey, *The Condition of Post-modernity*, Basil Blackwell, Oxford/Cambridge (Mass.) 1980, pp. 63–65

27 Hubert de Boer and Hans van Dijk, "Het park van de 21ste eeuw," *Wonen* TABK 12/1983, pp. 24–29

28 Bernard Leupen and Christoph Grafe, "Een metropolitane villa," *Archis* 1/1992, pp. 12–21

29 Koolhaas, 1978, pp. 127–133

30 Leupen, 1989, pp. 38–40

3 Design and use

1 John Summerson, *Heavenly Mansions*, The Cresset Press, London and Hertford 1949, p. 112

2 Mumford, 1966, p. 247

3 Vitruvius, 1960, p. 181

4 Bentmann and Müller, 1981, pp. 24–38

5 Giedion, 1954, pp. 50–100

6 Mumford, 1966, p. 503

7 E. Taverne, *In 't land van belofte, in de nieue stadt. Ideaal en werkelijkheid van de stadsuitleg in de Republiek 1580-1680*, Gary Schwartz, Maarssen 1978, pp. 40–42

8 Evans, 1983, pp. 3–16

9 S.E. Rasmussen, *London: The Unique City*, MIT Press, Cambridge (Mass.) 1982, pp. 219–235, 292–306

10 Walter Benjamin, "Paris, die Hauptstadt des XIX. Jahrhunderts", in *Passagenwerk*, Suhrkamp, Frankfurt 1983, p. 52 Benjamin describes the changes that took place during the course of the nineteenth century, taking Paris as an example. His remarks are already applicable to London in the second half of the eighteenth century, as can be deduced from Rasmussen's description (see note 9).

11 H.R. Hitchcock, *Architecture: Nineteenth and Twentieth Centuries*, Penguin, Harmondsworth 1977, pp. 353–381

12 Sullivan himself meant something different. His celebrated slogan referred to the relationship between form and an appropriate structure; see Frampton, 1980/1985, p. 56

13 M. Steinmann, "Sigfried Giedion, Die Mechanisierung der Wohnung und die 'machine à habiter'," in S. van Moos and C. Smeenk (eds.), *Avantgarde und Industrie*, DUP, Delft 1983, pp. 135–150

14 Grinberg, 1977, pp. 104–111

15 Alexander, 1964, p. 2

16 A. van Eyck, "De bal kaatst terug," *Forum* 3/ 1958

17 L. Kahn, "Order is," in *What Will Be Always Has Been. The Works of Louis I. Kahn*, Rizzoli, New York 1986, p. 305

18 B. Tschumi, *The Manhattan Transcripts*, St. Martins Press, New York 1981, pp. 7–8

19 M. Küper and I. van Zijl, *Gerrit Th. Rietveld 1881–1964*, Centraal Museum, Utrecht 1992, pp. 99–102

20 N. Habraken, "Aap, Noot, Mies/The three R's voor Housing," *Forum* 1/1966

21 H.W. Kraft, *Geschichte der Architekturtheorie*, C.H. Beck, Munich 1991, p. 509

22 C. Jencks, *Current Architecture*, Academy Editions, London 1982, pp. 98–100

4 Design and structure

1 Viollet-le-Duc, 1978, p. 451

2 Summerson, 1949, p. 149

3 Van Duin *et al.* (ed.), 1991, p. 118

4 Werner Müller and Gunter Vogel, *Atlas zur Baukunst*, Deutscher Taschenbuch Verlag, Munich 1981, p. 497

5 Von Meiss, 1990, p. 168

6 Berlage was taught by Gottfried Semper at the Eidgenössische Technische Hochschule in Zurich.

7 Frampton, 1980/1985, p. 92

8 Adolf Loos, "Ornament und Verbrechen," in Franz Gluck (ed.) *Samtliche Schriften*, vol. 1, Herold, Vienna 1962, p. 276f. Quoted Frampton, 1980/1985, p. 93

9 Tafuri and Dal Co, 1980, p. 103

10 Adolf Loos, *Spoken into the Void*, Oppositions Books, Cambridge (Mass.) 1982, p. 66

11 Le Corbusier, "In the Defence of Architecture," *Oppositions* 4, 1974, pp. 93–108. Quoted Frampton, 1980/1985, p. 160

12 Le Corbusier, 1986, p. 227

13 Since the emergence of skeleton construction terms such as loadbearing and space-defining have entered the language. However, they tend to give the impression that a loadbearing structure simply supports and a space-defining partition merely separates. It requires little architectural expertise to note that in the concrete skeleton of the Villa Savoye the floor slabs double as a space-defining element and the façade construction supports itself if nothing else.

14 Le Corbusier, 1986, p. 18

15 Hans van Dijk, "Een volstrekt Amerikaanse avant-garde," *Archis* 11/1990, p. 41

16 Von Meiss, 1990, pp. 169–170

17 Nervi, 1956, p. 17

18 Nervi, 1956, p. 27

19 Louis Kahn, "I love beginnings," in A. Latour (ed.), *Louis I. Kahn, Writings, Lectures, Interviews*, Rizzoli, New York 1991, p. 288

20 Frampton, 1980/1985, p. 244

21 Jan Dirk Peereboom Voller and Frank Wintermans, "Een geloofwaardige rol voor de architect," *Wonen* TABK 23/1982, p. 26

22 Frampton, 1980/1985, p. 281

23 Adapted from Ad Koedijk, "The art of engineering," interview with Sir Ove Arup, *Forum* 29/4, p. 168. Arup Associates were involved in the construction of the Kunsthal.

5 Design and typology

1 Panerai, 1979

2 Since the invention of printing this word is also used for letter.

3 Carl Linnaeus, *Systema Naturae*, 1735 and *Classes Plantarum*, 1739

4 Quatremère de Quincy, 1788–1825, vol. III, p. 544. English trans. in *Oppositions* 8, 1976, p. 148

5 Argan, 1965

6 J.N.L. Durand, *Recueil et parallèle des édifices de tous genres, anciens et modernes*, Paris 1801 and J.N.L. Durand, *Précis des Leçons d'Architecture données à l'Ecole Polytechnique*, 2 vols., Paris 1802-1809

7 E. Neufert, *Bauentwurfslehre*, Vieweg, Braunschweig 1936 and Pevsner, 1976

8 Panerai, 1979

9 Muratori, 1959

10 V. Lampugniani, "Das Ganze und die Teile, Typologie und Funktionalismus in der Architektur des 19. und 20. Jahrhunderts," in V. Lampugniani (ed.), *Modelle für eine Stadt*, Siedler, Berlin 1984

11 French architects of the young generation, notably Jean Castex and Philippe Panerai, were to take up the typological studies at the end of the 1960s.

12 Aymonino and Rossi, 1965; Aymonino and Rossi, 1970

13 Rossi, 1982

14 Carl G. Jung, *Analytical Psychology: Its Theory and Practice*, Routledge and Kegan Paul, London 1935

15 Vidler, 1976

16 Note 5. It is logical that Argan, a historian researching typology and historical forms, would be the one to revive Quatremère de Quincy's text.

17 Note 5

18 The emergence of Computer Aided Architectural Design (CAAD) has brought to the Anglo-Saxon world design methods proceeding from mathematical processing and verification, from the selecting and combining of classified data. As these methods reject typology as a relic of a craft-based past, they fall outside the scope of this chapter.

19 See also Giorgio Grassi, *La costruzione logica dell'architettura*, Maersilio, Venice 1967

20 Leupen, 1989, p. 27

21 Müller *et al.*, 1981, p. 359

22 Cf. Van Duin *et al.* (ed.), 1991, p. 141

23 Jean Castex *et al.*, *Formes urbaines: de l'ilot à la barre*, Bordas, Paris 1980

24 The urban plan for Römerstadt was designed by Ernst May together with H. Boehm and Bangert. For the architectural fleshing out May was joined by C.H. Rudloff, Blattner, Schaupp and Schufter. *Das Neue Frankfurt*, no. 4/5 1930, pp. 77–84

6 Design and context

1 See also Chapter 1 on interpreting the brief

2 C.M. Steenbergen *et al.*, Plananalyse Prijsvraag Stromend Stadsgewest. Eo Wijersstichting, 1993

3 Reh and Steenbergen, 1996

4 J. Piket, *Nederland in 3 dimensies*, Falkplan, The Hague

5 Verhulst, 1981

6 Lambert, 1971

7 Visscher, 1972

8 Wilderom, 1968

9 A.J. Kolker, *Kroniek van de Beemster*, Canaletto, Alphen a/d Rijn 1981

10 Lambert, 1971, pp. 179–229

11 Taverne, 1978

12 Hunt and de Jong, 1989

13 Lambert, 1971, pp. 212–220

14 Steenbergen, 1990, pp. 86–88

15 W. Reh, G. Smienk and C.M. Steenbergen, *Nederlandse landschapsarchitectuur tussen traditie en experiment*, Thoth/Academie van Bouwkunst, Amsterdam 1993

16 Kuyper, 1980, pp. 159–160

17 S. Polano (ed.), *La Rotonda*. Electa, Milan 1988

18 Steenbergen, 1990, pp. 88–93

19 Steenbergen, 1990

20 Reh and Steenbergen, 1996, pp. 136f

21 A.E. Trueman, *Geology and Scenery in England and Wales*, Pelican Books, 1948

22 J. Appleton, "Some thoughts on the geology of the picturesque," *Journal of Garden History*, vol. 6, 3/1986

23 This obelisk is set in the grounds of nearby Stourhead House.

24 R. Geurtsen, B. Leupen and S. Tjallingi, LAS-*werkboek*, Publikatieburo Bouwkunde, Delft 1982, pp. 1–16

25 Steenbergen (ed.), 1990, pp. 13–20

26 Steenbergen (ed.), 1990, pp. 73–88

27 J. Busquets, *Estudi de l'Eixample de Barcelona*, Ajuntament de Barcelona, 1988

28 R. Makkink, "Parc del Clot," in R. Geurtsen et al., *Barcelona, stadsontwerp en moderne architectuur*, Excursiegids TU Delft, Delft 1988

29 Han Meyer *et al.*, *Stadsontwerp Groningen*, Publikatieburo Bouwkunde, Delft 1991; see also Chapter 3.4, the postwar period

30 Muratori, *Studi per une operante storia urbana di Venezia*, Istituto Poligrafico dello Stato, Rome 1959.
C. Aymonino, *La formazione del concetto di tipologia edilizia*, Istituto Universitario di Architettura di Venezia, Venice 1965.
C. Aymonino *et al.*, *La città di Padova*, Rome 1970; see also Chapter 5, Design and typology

31 Rossi, 1966; see also Chapter 5, Design and typology

32 See the work of, among others, Oriol Bohigas, Joan Busquets, Josep Acebillo en Manuel de Solà-Morales.

33 Braudel, 1987. The Annales School takes its name from the research method practiced there in which annals, yearbooks recording day-to-day life, figure prominently.

34 Maurits de Hoog, *Archipel 1*, Villa Nova, Rotterdam 1987

35 Fortier, 1989

36 See Rein Geurtsen, Jan Heeling and Ed Taverne in *Forum* 34, 7/1990 for some idea of the diversity of stances in the Dutch discourse on the city.

37 Kostof, 1991

38 See also Chapter 6.4, the cultivated landscape

39 Gemeente Amsterdam, *Ons Amsterdam, de historische ontwikkeling van Amsterdam*, Stadsdrukkerij, Amsterdam 1949

40 Van der Hoeven and Louwe, 1985

41 Maas and Berger, 1990

42 See Chapter 2.2 (Miletus)

43 Kostof, 1992

44 See Chapter 2.2, the basic instruments of classical architecture

45 See also Chapter 5.2, the development of "type"

46 This section was prepared using analyses and drawings from Van der Hoeven and Louwe, 1985

47 Daniel Speckle is also referred to in the literature as Daniel Specklin.

48 In its combination of neutral form (uniform square blocks) and specific potential (differentiation through canals and markets), Stevin's diagram is eminently serviceable as a model. His general principles were applied frequently from the seventeenth century on when planning, fortifying and extending cities.

49 The islands of Uilenburg, Marken/Valkenburg, Rapenburg and Vlooyenburg.

50 "Städtebau ist Landschaftssteigerung," a quote from Ernst May in *Amt für industrielle Formgestaltung, Neues Bauen, Neues Gestalten; Das neue Frankfurt/Die neue Stadt; eine Zeitschrift zwischen 1926 und 1933*, Elefanten Press, Berlin 1984

51 Henk Engel and Endry van Velzen, *Architectuur van de stadsrand, Frankfurt am Main, 1925–1930*, DUP, Delft 1987

52 See for instance the ideas of Willem Jan Neutelings and his "carpet metropolis" (or patchwork metropolis) in Paul Vermeulen, *Willem Jan Neutelings, architect*, 010 Publishers, Rotterdam 1991

53 Rafael Moneo, "The Logroño Town Hall," *Lotus* no. 33

54 "Moneo, stadhuis Logroño," *Archis* 4/1986

55 The brief stipulated space for public services and city administration and a large auditorium, plus minor facilities such as a café and an exhibition area.

56 Broadbent, 1990

57 Bacon, 1967

58 The Hôtel de Craon informs all components of the scheme. Having said that, the fine-tuned ensemble of Place Royale, Place de la Carrière and Hémicycle is by no means the work of one brilliant designer; see Lavedan, 1982

59 Aspects of the scheme irrelevant to the relationship between context and design (procedures, organization of Euralille, etc.) are regarded as being beyond the scope of this book.

60 The reduced travelling distance has given Lille a central position between the Randstad, Paris, London and the Ruhr.

61 For an explication of the traffic problems in the station area and the means used to resolve them see OMA and Rem Koolhaas, *Lille*, Institut Français d'Architecture, Paris 1990

62 Besides the new TGV station and a metro line, the Euralille project comprises among other things an international business center, a congress and exhibition complex, a media center and a comprehensive shopping center, together occupying some 120 hectares.

Selected Reading

1 Design and analysis

Leonardo Benevolo, *Storia dell'architettura moderna*, Laterza, Bari 1960. Translated as *History of Modern Architecture*, Routledge & Kegan Paul, Cambridge (Mass.) 1971

Leonardo Benevolo, *Storia della città*, Laterza, Bari 1975. Translated as *The History of the City*, Scolar Press, London 1980

Jean Castex, *Renaissance, Baroque et Classicisme*, Ed. Hazan, Paris 1990

Francis D.K. Ching, *Architecture: Form, Space & Order*, Van Nostrand Reinhold, New York 1979

Giovanni Fanelli, *Architettura Moderna in Olanda 1900–1940*, Florence 1968

Kenneth Frampton, *Modern Architecture: A Critical History*, Thames and Hudson, London 1980/1985

S. Giedion, *Space, Time and Architecture*, Harvard University Press, Cambridge (Mass.) 1941

Emil Kaufmann, *Architecture in the Age of Reason*, Harvard University Press, Cambridge (Mass.) 1955; reprint Dover Publications, New York 1968

Rem Koolhaas, *Delirious New York*, Oxford University Press, New York 1978

Spiro Kostof, *The City Shaped: Urban Patterns and Meanings through History*, Thames and Hudson, London 1991

Spiro Kostof, *The City Assembled. The Elements of Urban Form through History*, Thames and Hudson, London 1992

W. Kuyper, *Dutch Classicist Architecture*, DUP, Delft 1980

A.M. Lambert, *The Making of the Dutch Landscape*, Seminar Press, London 1971

Kevin Lynch, *The Image of the City*, MIT Press, Cambridge (Mass.) 1960

Pierre von Meiss, *De la Forme au Lieu*, Presses Polytechniques Romandes, Lausanne 1986. Translated as *Elements of Architecture. From Form to Place*, Chapman & Hall, London 1990

Lewis Mumford, *The City in History*, Penguin Books, London/Harmondsworth 1966

Peter Murray, *The Architecture of the Italian Renaissance*, Batsford, London 1963

C. Norberg-Schulz, *Intentions in Architecture*, MIT Press, Cambridge (Mass.) 1965

Andrea Palladio, *I Quattro libri dell'architettura*, Venice 1570. Translated as *The Four Books of Architecture*, Dover Publications, New York 1965

Nikolaus Pevsner, *An Outline of European Architecture*, Penguin Books, Harmondsworth 1943

Steen E. Rasmussen, *Towns and Buildings*, The University Press of Liverpool, Liverpool 1951

W. Reh and C.M. Steenbergen, *Architecture and Landscape*, Thoth, 1996 Bussum

John Summerson, *The Classical Language of Architecture*, The Cresset Press, London/Hertford 1949

Aldo Rossi, *L'architettura della città*, Padua 1966. Translated as *The Architecture of the City*, MIT Press, Cambridge (Mass.) 1982

Manfredo Tafuri and Francesco Dal Co, *Modern Architecture*, Academy Editions, London 1980

Robert Venturi, *Complexity end Contradiction in Architecture*, MOMA, New York 1966

F.A.J. Vermeulen, *Handboek tot de geschiedenis der Nederlandsche bouwkunst*, 3 vols. Martinus Nijhoff, The Hague 1928

Vitruvius, *De architectura libri decem*. Translated by Morris H. Morgan as *Vitruvius. The Ten Books on Architecture*, Dover Publications, New York 1960

2 Order and composition

L. van Duin and H. Engel (eds.), *Architectuurfragmenten. Typologie, Stijl en Ontwerpmethoden*, Publikatieburo Bouwkunde, Delft 1991

W. Kandinsky, *Punkt und Linie zu Fläche*, Verlag Albert Langen, Munich 1926

Bernard Leupen, *IJ-plein. Een speurtocht naar nieuwe compositorische middelen*, 010 Publishers, Rotterdam 1989

William J. Mitchell, *The Logic of Architecture*, MIT Press, Cambridge (Mass.)/London 1990

Max Risselada (ed.), *Raumplan versus Plan Libre*, Rizzoli, New York 1988

Colin Rowe, *The Mathematics of the Ideal Villa and Other Essays*, MIT Press, Cambridge (Mass.)/London 1976

Clemens M. Steenbergen, *De stap over de horizon*, Doctoral dissertation TU Delft, Publikatieburo Bouwkunde, Delft 1990

Alexander Tzonis, *Towards a Non-Oppressive Environment*, George Braziller, New York 1972.

Rudolf Wittkower, *Architectural Principles in the Age of Humanism*, Academy Editions, London 1988

3 Design and use

C. Alexander, *Notes on a synthesis of form*, Harvard University Press, Cambridge (Mass.) 1964

Reyner Banham, *Theory and Design in the First Machine Age*, Architectural Press, London 1969

Reyner Banham, *The Architecture of the Well-tempered Environment*, Architectural Press, London 1969

R. Bentmann and M. Müller, *Die Villa als Herrschaftsarchitektur*, Syndikat, Frankfurt 1981

R. Evans, "Figures, Doors and Passages," AD, April 1987, pp. 267–278

D.I. Grinberg, *Housing in the Netherlands 1900–1940*, DUP, Delft 1977

Stefan Muthesius, *The English Terraced House*, Yale University Press, New Haven (Conn.) 1972

C. Mohr and M. Müller, *Funktionalität und Moderne*, Edition Fricke, Frankfurt 1984

Ernst Neufert, *Bauentwurfslehre*, Ullstein, Berlin 1936; 33rd revised edition, Vieweg, Braunschweig 1992. Translated as *Architects"*

Data, Crosby, Lockwood, Staples, London 1970

Martin Steinmann (ed.), CIAM-*Internationale Kongresse für Neues Bauen, Dokumente 1928–1939*, Birkhäuser, Basel 1979

4 Design and structure

Edward R. Ford, *The Details of Modern Architecture*, MIT Press, Cambridge (Mass.) 1990

Le Corbusier, *Vers une architecture*, Editions Arthaud, Paris 1923. Translated as *Towards a new architecture*, Dover Publications, New York 1986

Pier Luigi Nervi, *Structures*, Dodge, New York 1956

Eugene Emmanuel Viollet-le-Duc, *Entretiens sur l'architecture*, Pierre Mardaga, Paris 1978. English translation: *Lectures on Architecture*, two vols., Dover, New York 1987

5 Design and typology

G.C. Argan, "Sul concetto di tipologia architettonica," *Progetto e destino*. Il Saggiatore, Milan 1965

C. Aymonino and A. Rossi, *La formazione del concetto di tipologia edilizia*, Istituto Universitario di Architettura di Venezia, Venice 1965

C. Aymonino and A. Rossi, *La città di Padova*, Rome 1970

J.F. Geist, *Passagen, ein Bautypus des 19. Jahrhunderts*, Prestel, Munich 1979. Translated as *Arcades. The history of a building type*, MIT Press, Cambridge (Mass.) 1983

Giorgio Grassi, *La costruzione logica dell'architettura*, Maersilio, Venice 1967

S. Muratori, *Studi per une operante Storia urbana di Venezia*, Istituto Poligrafico dello Stato, Rome 1959

Philippe Panerai, "Typologies," *Les Cahiers de la recherche architecturale*, no. 4 12/1979

N. Pevsner, *A History of Building Types*, Princeton University Press, Princeton 1976

Quatremère de Quincy, "Architecture," in *Encyclopedie methodique*, vol. III, Paris 1788–1825

Roger Sherwood, *Modern housing prototypes*, Harvard University Press, Cambridge (Mass.) 1978

A. Vidler, "The Third Typology," *Oppositions* 7/1976

6 Design and context

Amt für industrielle Formgestaltung, Neues Bauen, Neues Gestalten, Das neue Frankfurt/ die neue stadt; eine zeitschrift zwischen 1926 und 1933, Elefanten Press, Berlin 1984

Edmund N. Bacon, *Design of Cities*, Thames and Hudson, London 1967

Fernand Braudel, *Civilisation materielle, Economie et capitalisme* XVe–XVIIIe siècle, Paris

Geoffrey Broadbent, *Emerging Concepts in Urban Space Design*, Van Nostrand Reinhold, London 1990

Henk Engel and Endry van Velzen (eds.), *Architectuur van de stadsrand, Frankfurt am Main, 1925–1930*, DUP, Delft 1987

Bruno Fortier, *La Metropole Imaginaire—Un Atlas de Paris*, Pierre Mardaga, Paris 1989

Casper van der Hoeven and Jos Louwe, *Amsterdam als stedelijk bouwwerk, een morfologiese analyse*, SUN, Nijmegen 1985

Ebenezer Howard, *Garden Cities of Tomorrow*, Faber and Faber, London 1946. First published in 1898 as *Tomorrow: A Peaceful Path to Real Reform*.

J.D. Hunt and E. de Jong, *De gouden eeuw van de Hollandse tuinkunst*, Thoth, Amsterdam 1989

W. Kuyper, *Dutch Classicist Architecture*, DUP, Delft 1980

Pierre Lavedan *et al.*, *L'Urbanisme à l'époque moderne*, XVIe–XVIIIe *siècles*, Droz, Geneva 1982

Michael Maass and Klaus Berger (eds.), *Klar und lichtvoll wie eine Regel, Planstädte der Neuzeit vom 16. bis zum 18. Jahrhundert*, G. Braun, Karlsruhe 1990

W. Reh, G. Smienk and C.M. Steenbergen, *Nederlandse landschapsarchitectuur tussen traditie en experiment*, Thoth, Amsterdam 1993

C.M. Steenbergen, *De stap over de horizon, Een ontleding van het formele ontwerp in de landschapsarchitectuur*, Publikatiebureau Bouwkunde, Delft 1990

De bodem van Nederland, Stichting voor bodemkartering, Wageningen 1965

Ed Taverne, *In 't land van belofte, in de nieue stadt. Ideaal en werkelijkheid van de stadsuitleg in de Republiek 1580–1680*, Gary Schwartz, Maarssen 1978

A. Verhulst, *Het natuurlandschap*, AGN 1981

H.A. Visscher, *Het Nederlandse landschap*, Het Spectrum, Antwerp 1972

M.H. Wilderom, *Tussen afsluitdammen en deltadijken*, Vlissingen 1968

Index

Key terms

Credits

Original drawings
Arie Mashiah, Solita Stücken, Petrouschka
Thumann, Jan Verbeek and Arno de Vries

Drawing techniques (text)
Jan Verbeek

Translation into English
John Kirkpatrick

Graphic design
Jan Erik Fokke, Quadraat, Arnhem
Cover design by Mike Suh, VNR

Printed by
Veenman printers, Wageningen,
The Netherlands

Photo acknowledgments
Faculty of Architecture Photographic
 Department, TU Delft: pp. 48, 52, 53, 60,
 74, 94, 110, 111, 114, 122, 126
Hans Werlemann: pp. 64, 130
Bernard Vincent: p. 127

Drawing acknowledgments
Faculty of Architecture, TU Delft: pp. 22, 28,
 32–35, 37, 38, 40, 41, 55, 58, 59, 66, 72, 80,
 92, 97, 110, 111, 114, 115, 129, 148, 152,
 158, 159, 161, 163, 168, 169–171, 174–178,
 184, 187, 192–196, 199, 210
Gemeente Amsterdam: pp. 86, 182, 188
Van der Hoeven, Louwe; pp. 188, 190
Institut Français d'Architecture: pp. 201, 202
Orton: pp. 127, 128
Palmboom: p. 156
Schodek: p. 142

About the authors

Bernard Leupen works at the Faculty of Architecture at Delft University of Technology (Architecture division). He has written the book *IJ-plein, een speurtocht naar nieuwe compositorische middelen* (*IJ-plein, a quest for new compositional means*) 010 Publishers, Rotterdam, 1989, and organized the symposia *Whether Europe* and *Hoe modern is de Nederlandse architectuur*. He is co-editor of the book *Hoe modern is de Nederlandse architectuur?* (*How modern is Dutch architecture?*) 010 Publishers, Rotterdam, 1990.

Christoph Grafe is an architect practicing in Amsterdam and attached to the Faculty of Architecture at Delft University of Technology (Architecture division). He organized the symposium *Hoe modern is de Nederlandse architectuur?* and co-edited a book of the same name.

Nicola Körnig works as an urban designer in Rotterdam. She co-wrote the book *Locatie Zuidpoort Delft* (*Location Zuidpoort Delft*).

Marc Lampe is an architect practicing in Rotterdam. He has published *De grootste kracht is de aantrekkingskracht* (*The greatest power is the power of attraction*), Faculty of Architecture Publications, Delft 1992.

Peter de Zeeuw worked at the Faculty of Architecture at Delft University of Technology (Urban Design division). He was also a practicing landscape architect in Amsterdam. He co-wrote the book *Het montagelandschap* (*Montage Landscape*), Faculty of Architecture Publications, Delft, 1991. He died in 1996.